Overcoming
RACISM
and
Achieving
Success

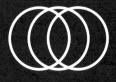 James Battle, Ph.D.

James Battle and Associates
#708 Guardian Building
Edmonton AB
T5N 3W6

International Standard Book Number: 0-9695950-8-5

Canadian Cataloguing in Publication Data

Battle, James
Overcoming Racism and Achieving Success

Includes index.
ISBN 0-9695950-8-5

1. Prejudice and Racism   2. Institutional Racism
3. Success Strategies

I. James Battle and Associates   II. Title
BF637.S8B382 1997 158'.2   C96-910865-6

TABLE OF CONTENTS

PART I
BACKGROUND INFORMATION

PART II
DEVELOPMENT OF PREJUDICE AND RACISM

PART III
RELATIONSHIPS AND RACISM

Part IV

Institutional Racism

PART V
STRATEGIES FOR ACHIEVING SUCCESS

PART VI
GLOSSARY OF TERMS, REFERENCES AND INDICES:

PART VII
BOOKS & RESOURCE MATERIALS

ACKNOWLEDGEMENTS

THE WRITER GRATEFULLY ACKNOWLEDGES the assistance and support of the individuals who contributed to the development and publication of this book. First, I wish to recognize and thank the students and community residents who participated in the research studies summarized. Second, I recognize and thank the many students and clients who participated in the courses, seminars, workshops and therapy sessions I have conducted over the years which provided me the opportunities to develop the strategies described in this book that have proven to be effective in promoting success. Third, I wish to recognize and thank my son Jamie who provided me the insights that made me aware of the problem of racism in our contemporary society and the effects that it has on victims. Fourth, I thank my daughter Christina, son Jamie and secretary Maria Smith for the long hours they put in typing the book. Fifth, I thank Edie Brewster for the excellent job she did in typesetting the manuscript. Sixth, I thank Charlie Turner for his design and development of the cover of the book. Seventh, I thank my wife Dorothy, and mother-in-law Edith Cary for reading the book and making editorial suggestions. Eighth, I thank my family, Dorothy, Christina and Jamie for the assistance, cooperation and support they provided me during the term of this project and over the years. Ninth, I recognize and gratefully acknowledge Nicholas Ameyaw and the Alberta Multiculturalism Commission for the support and sponsorship of the project entitled "Strengthening Black Families: Overcoming Racism and Achieving Success in Mainstream Society". Finally, I dedicate this book to all individuals who strive to promote peace and harmony and make our world a better place for all.

PREFACE

THIS BOOK IS UNIQUE in a number of ways. For one, it provides a comprehensive overview of the problems of negative racial prejudice and racism. Also, in this book, we provide practical strategies that individuals can use to overcome the negative effects of racism and achieve success. In addition, in the book we describe a theory of prejudice and provide quantitative data to support the assumptions incorporated in the theory. As well, a practical program intervention which has demonstrated success in assisting both parents and their children in achieving success is described.

Throughout the book both historical and contemporary perspectives are presented and integrated systematically to facilitate continuity and clarity between the past and present. The book is written in a fashion and with vocabulary that can be readily understood by individuals engaged in a wide variety of roles with diverse needs, goals and desires.

This book is organized into seven parts.

PART I provides background information and an overview of the constructs of race and racism. In this part we show how beliefs and perceptions influence one's actions and delineate the role that both play in the emission of racist acts. Also in this part we provide readers the opportunity to rate themselves and determine the degree of racism they possess.

PART II offers a stage theory of the development of prejudice and racism and describe the steps incorporated at each level. Also in this part we describe the cognitive styles of ethnocentric individuals who emit racist acts and list characteristics of individuals who display negative racial prejudice and racist behavior. In this part we list common stereotypes and delineate the role that they play in the process of racism. In addition, in this part we describe the authoritarian personality and review the controversial issues of intelligence and race, describe theories of prejudice and racism and offer a profile of a racist.

PART III provides an overview of Black-White relationships and delineates the important role that sex plays in these relationships. Also, in this part we show how racism affects victims' self-esteem and provide actual interviews of American black and white males and females.

PART IV provides an overview of the roles institutions play in the process of racism. In this part we show how the process of racism influences the actions and decisions made in the important societal institutions of police services, jails and prisons, criminal courts and the military. Also, in this part we show how teachers' expectations influence racist behavior and the role that schools play in the process of racism. In addition, in this part we provide an overview of black education and history and describe the problem of racism in sports.

PART V provides strategies that individuals can use to overcome racism and achieve success in their lives. In this part we describe practical strategies that work and show individuals how to achieve success in spite of racism. Also, in this part readers are provided the opportunity to rate their success potential and level of encouragement.

PART VI provides a glossary of terms, lists of references and subject matter and author indices to the book.

PART VII provides an annotated list of resource materials.

INTRODUCTION

Racism is a persistent problem that has affected the lives of millions of individuals in the United States, Canada and many locations throughout the world. It (racism) is a problem with a long history that continues to exert its harmful effects in our contemporary society. The effects of racism are observed in the almost daily reports of incidents from many countries including Bosnia, Rowanda, the United States and Canada. Thirty-two years after the landmark civil rights legislation in the United States race is still a very divisive issue in American society.

In the United States the recent, highly publicized cases of Rodney King who was beaten by white police officers in Los Angeles and O.J. Simpson who was accused of murdering his former wife Nicole Brown and her friend Ron Goldman provide vivid, powerful illustrations of the problem of racism in contemporary society.

In Canada, the recent report entitled "Report of The Commission on Systemic Racism in the Ontario Criminal Justice System" provides powerful evidence regarding the incidence and practice of racism in a variety of contemporary institutions including schools, jails, prisons, police services and criminal justice courts. Also in Canada, the incidence in which members of the Canadian Airborne who were conducting peace-keeping duties in Somalia referred to residents as "niggers", tortured and killed a sixteen year old youngster named Shidane Arone and, the rash of bombings of predominately black churches in the United States provide vivid illustrations supporting the position which holds that racism continues to be a persistent problem in North America. Additional support for the tenet that racism continues to exist in America was provided by Cole (1993, p.54) when she said; "Racism is alive and well in America"; by Crenshaw (1988, p.1131) when she said; "Racism is the central ideological underpinning of American Society"; and by Wilkins (1992, p. A1) when he said "This is a racist society, and it will be for a long time to come."

Although some writers (e.g. Fuller, 1969) propose that the concept of race has little biological validation, and that the word black or white provides little information regarding any one or any group; and that of the approximately 100,000 genes that determine human make up only one to six regulate skin color (Amby Burfoot, p. 94) and on this evidence, we can assume almost nothing about anyone based on skin color, the practice of racism continues.

Historical records (e.g. black slavery; maltreatment of aboriginal residents and broken treaties; quotas severely limited for immigrants from Asia; forced internment of Japanese residents during World War II, Attitude surveys (e.g. in 1942 only about 30 percent of white Americans favored integrated schools; in 1968, Gallup poll findings indicated that 54 percent of white Americans reported that they felt that blacks were more to blame for the conditions they were in than whites were) and discrimination (e.g. denial of opportunities for colored people to purchase houses in certain areas) provide strong evidence indicating that racism is an age-old problem that probably will continue to exist well into the twenty-first century.

Available evidence clearly indicates that racism in the United States and Canada is a longstanding problem that has persisted and resulted in the denial of basic civil and political rights of colored residents including exclusion from jobs and schools and limited opportunities to acquire property.

I am of the opinion that racism is not limited to North America, whereas other writers, including the following, propose that it (racism) is universal and has been practiced throughout history:

- Gossett (1963) proposed that racism existed in the ancient civilizations of Egypt, Greece, China and India.
- Gould (1981) proposed that racism is as old as history.
- Todorov (1993) proposed that racism is an ancient form of behavior that is world wide.

The views of a leading western philosopher regarding racism are presented as follows: Hume (1748) said:

> *I am apt to suspect the Negroes, and in general all the other species of men, to be naturally inferior to the whites. There never was any civilized nation of any other complexion than white, nor even any individual eminent in action or speculation. No ingenious manufacturers among them, no arts, no sciences. Such a uniform and constant difference could not happen, in so many countries and ages, if nature had not made an original distinction betwixt these breeds of men...*

Although racism persists and presents a significant problem for both victims and society in general, most North American whites, like their colored counterparts possess the values and principles (e.g. fairness; equality and justice for all residents) that are promoted by our democratic society. However, a significant portion of North American whites find it difficult to employ these values and principles in their interactions with individuals they view as being different. When this incongruence between the democratic values and principles and actual thinking and behaving become evident, the racist individual experiences anxiety which they attempt to fend against by employing defense mechanisms and creating faulty belief systems to justify their negative views and actions towards outgroups.

Racism, in my view, is a symptom of emotional disturbance which is due to the irrational fear of the individual or group that the racist thoughts and actions are directed towards. Support for the position which purports that negative racial and ethnic prejudice is due to emotional disturbance was provided by the French philosopher Jean-Paul Sarte (1948) when he said:

> ...*A man may be a good father and a good husband, a conscientious citizen, highly cultivated, philanthropic, and in addition an anti-Semite. He may like fishing and the pleasures of love, may be tolerant in matters of religion, full of generous notions on the conditions of the natives in Central Africa, and in addition detest the Jews (p. 9)? To Sartre, the answer to this is a resounding "No!" A man who is anti-Semitic is likely to be many other things also; he is a man who is afraid of himself, according to Sartre. It is not the Jews who frighten him, but his own consciousness, his fear of responsibility and of change in himself and the world around him. Hatred of Jews (or of any other minority group) is, to Sartre, a symptom of "fear of the human condition" (p. 54)...*

The problem of racism in North America (i.e: The United States and Canada) is a significant one that should not be tolerated. In this book, we address the issues of negative racial prejudice and racism and offer insights and strategies that can be beneficial to both victims and perpetrators. This book represents my efforts to contribute to the wellbeing of all persons residing in our world community and to promote harmony, cooperation, mutual respect and peaceful interactions among members of our human group.

PART I

BACKGROUND
INFORMATION

CHAPTER 1
RACE: AN OVERVIEW

IN THIS CHAPTER we question the concept of race and provide an overview of the issue of race and racism, ask the question "are you a racist?" and describe the relationship between beliefs and racism and perceptions and racism.

RACE: A QUESTIONABLE CONCEPT

Although race is a commonly used construct, a significant number of scientists are convinced that the concept of race has no legitimate place in either social or biological sciences. Those who support this position include Barricot (1969), Bruce (1969), Klienberg (1954), Livingstone (1962), Ashley and Montagu (1969) and Penrose (1952) who argue that the concept of race only misleads, confuses and serves no legitimate scientific purpose. Regarding the concept of race, Ashley and Montagu (1969) said that race is the most retardative term in social science and that the concept has outlived its usefulness. Support for this position was provided by Allport (1954) when he said that less than one-fourth of American blacks are unmixed and that differences between blacks and whites are not due to racial or biological factors, but rather to cultural factors. Additional support for the position which assumes that race is a questionable concept is provided by Williamson (1980, p. xii) who said: "scientific scholars generally agree that there is actually no such thing as race," by Zack (1994, pp.3-4) who said "the concept of race does not have an adequate scientific foundation", by Todorov (1993, p.370) who said: "whereas racism is a well-tested phenomenon, race itself does not exist," by Gates (1986, p.4) who said: "race as a meaningful criterion has long been recognized to be fiction," and by Shanklin (p.1, p.18) who said: "race is a concept that exists in our minds, not in our bodies. There is no such thing as race."

Biologists, geneticists and anthropologists generally agree that race is not a valid method for dividing individuals into different groups. These experts take this position because the evidence they have accumulated indicates that race does not represent distinct biological categories that are created by differences in the genes that individuals inherit from their parents. These scientists recognize that genes vary, but assert that they do not result in the differentiation of black, white, yellow, red or brown races. These scientists rather assert that race is a social, cultural and political concept based largely on superficial appearances.

Regarding race, Yale University biologist Johnathan Marks said, "the human species simply does not come packaged that way", University of Michigan anthropologist Loring Brace stated that "races are not the product of human genes and that there is no such thing as race" and Yale geneticist Kenneth Kidd asserted that findings derived from DNA research provides evidence which substantiates the point of view which assume that "there is no such thing biologically as race". (Boyd, 1996, p.E8)

Regarding the issue of race, Stanford University geneticist Luigi Cavalli-Sforza said:

> *... The characteristics that we see with the naked eye that helps us distinguish individuals from different continents are, in reality, skin deep. Whenever we look under the veneer, we find that differences that seem so conspicuous to us are really trivial .... (Boyd, 1996, p. E8)*

A significant number of both biological and social scientists purpose that there is no definite, correct number of races of mankind. For instance, Darwin (1871), in his manuscript entitled "Decent of Man" proposed the following thirteen races listed in figure 1:1:

FIGURE 1:1 PROPOSED NUMBER OF RACE	
Author..................Number of Races	Author..........................Number of Races
Virey......................2	Pickering 11
Jacquinot.........................3	Bory St. Vincent...................15
Kant...............................4	Desmoulins..........................16
Blumenbach 5	Morton. 22
Buffon..............................6	Crawford 60
Hunter............................7	Burke 63
Agassiz 8	
Source: Darwin, 1871. Descent of Man.	

Folkmar and Folkmar (1911) proposed in their document entitled "Dictionary of Races and Peoples" that there are 562 races of humankind and Garn (1971) proposed the following nine region geographical races of mankind:

1. Amerindian   4. Melansian-Papuan   7. Indian
2. Polynesian   5. Australian   8. European
3. Micronesian   6. Asiatic   9. African

RACE AND RACISM

To emphasize race, in my view, is counterproductive and generally impedes positive relationships among the peoples of planet earth. However, if distinctions must be made, I am of the opinion that it would be most appropriate to differentiate two groups; the white group and the colored group. In my way of thinking, the white group would be comprised of those individuals whose bodies do not produce melanin (a biochemical substance that produces skin color) whereas the colored group would be comprised of those individuals whose bodies can produce melanin.

I am of the opinion that most individuals (approximately 70 percent) who comprise the "so called" races residing in Canada and the United States tend to display commonly held values such as fairness and equality that our democratic societies consider to be desirable. In spite of this however, racism does exist. For instance, the internment of Japanese American and Japanese Canadian citizens during World War II provides clear evidence of the presence of racism. This is obviously apparent when one notes that German Americans and German Canadians were not placed in internment camps in spite of the fact that the Allies were at war with Germany.

Controversy exists regarding definitions of the concept of racism at both conceptual and operational levels. However, most definitions identify racism very clearly with attitudes, actions or institutional structures that perpetuate white privilege and the subordination of people of color. Gary T. Marx (1967) states that a strict definition of racism suggests that it (racism) involves subordination and even genocide based on biological inferiority (p.101). More recently the term racism has been broadened to encompass the constructs of prejudice, hostility, discrimination, segregation and other negative actions expressed towards ethnic groups, whether or not assumptions about hereditary characteristics are involved (Marx, 1968).

Fredrickson (1981, p. xii) defines racism in the following fashion:

...Racism is a mode of thought that offers a particular explanation for the fact that population groups that can be distinguished by ancestry are likely to differ in culture, status and power. Racists make the claim that such differences are due mainly to immutable genetic factors and not to environmental or historical circumstances...

Jaynes and Williams (1989, p.566) propose that:

...Racism refers to patterns of belief and related actions that overtly embrace the notion of genetic or biological differences between human groups...

Berkhofer, R. (1978, p.55) defines racism in the following fashion:

...Racism rests upon two basic assumptions: (1) the moral qualities of a human group are positively correlated with their physical characteristics, and (2) all humankind is divisible into superior and inferior stocks upon the basis of the first assumption...

Snyder (1962, p.10) proposes that:

...Racism assumes inherent racial superiority or the purity and superiority of certain races; also, it denotes any doctrine or program of racial domination based on such an assumption...

Van DenBerghe's (1967, p.11-13) review of the construct of racism revealed findings which indicate that most writers consider a racist to be a person who views members of another race to be inherently or genetically inferior. Van DenBerghe (1978, p.11) defines racism as follows:

...racism is any set of beliefs that organic, genetically transmitted differences (whether real or imagined) between human groups are intrinsically associated with the presence or the absence of certain socially relevant abilities, hence that such differences are a legitimate basis of invidious distinctions between groups socially defined as races...

Cohen (1980, p.95) proposes that:

> ... *Racism in its simplest and most obvious form is defined as the belief that groups of human beings differ in their values and social accomplishments solely as a result of the impact of biological heredity...*

My definition of the concept of racism is as follows:

> ...*racism is a concept which refers to the emission of negative racial prejudice or racist acts towards an individual or individuals of another identifiable racial group...*

In addition to the definitions listed above, writers have reported various forms of racism including:

1. Intentional: which is a deliberate form of racism
2. Unintentional: which is an unconscious form of racism
3. Dominative: a direct form of racism such as that practiced in the southern states of America
4. Aversive: a non-direct form of racism such as that practiced in the northern states of America
5. Meta: a form of racism generated by modern technology
6. Process: a form of racism that is manifested by non-verbal means

Many writers propose that racism can be both individual and institutional. In the case of individual racism the person possesses racist beliefs and displays racist acts, whereas with institutional racism the structures of society promote and perpetuate racism. Pettigrew (1982, p.4-5) defines institutional racism in the following fashion:

> ... *Institutional racism refers to the complex of institutional arrangements and choices that restrict the life chances and choices of a socially defined racial group in comparison with those of the dominant group.*

Institutional racism was described by Carmichael and Hamilton (1967) in the following fashion:

> ...*Institutional racism relies on the active and pervasive operation of anti-black attitudes and practices. A sense of superior group position prevails: whites are "better" than blacks; therefore blacks should be subordinated to whites. This is a racist attitude and it permeates the society, both covertly and overtly (p.5)...*

Wellman (1977, p.xviii;235) offers the following definition of institutional racism:

> *...Racism can mean culturally sanctioned beliefs which, regardless of the intentions involved...justify policies and instructional priorities that perpetuate racial inequality...*

Jones (1972, p.31) defines institutional racism in the following fashion:

> *...Institutional racism can be defined as those established laws, customs and practices which systematically reflect and produce racial inequalities in American society...*

Carmichael and Hamilton (1967, p.4) offer the following to illustrate the difference between individual and institutional racism:

> *...When white terrorists bomb a black church and kill five black children, that is an act of individual racism, widely deplored by most segments of the society. But when in that city — Birmingham, Alabama — five hundred black babies die each year because of lack of proper food, shelter and medical facilities, and thousands more are destroyed and maimed physically, emotionally and intellectually because of conditions of poverty and discrimination in the black community, that is a function of institutional racism. When a black family moves into a home in a white neighborhood and is stoned, burned or routed out, they are victims of an overt act of individual racism which many people will condemn — at least in words. But it is institutional racism that keeps black people locked in dilapidated slum tenements, subject to the daily prey of exploitative slumlords, merchants, loan sharks and discriminatory real estate agents...*

Although experts offer different definitions of both individual and institutional racism, most agree that the practice of racism typically results in negative consequences for victims. Regarding the negative effects that the problem of racism exerts, Martin Luther King Jr. said; "racism can distort the personality and scar the soul". Other observations of the consequences of racism include data which indicate that:

- approximately one half of American black children live in poverty
- more American black males are in prison than in university

- homicide is the leading cause of death for American black males aged 15 through 34 years
- two-thirds of all black American males are arrested at some point between the ages of 18 and 30 years
- black males are twice as likely as white males to be victims of robbery and aggravated assault
- black males are seven (7) times more likely to be victims of murder than white males
- in the United States, victimization rates for blacks is higher than any other racial group for almost all crimes including murder, rape, robbery, aggravated assault and larceny
- in 1993, the unemployment rate for black Americans was 13.8 percent, whereas the value for all workers was 6.8 percent
- in 1992, blacks made up 12.4 percent of the American population, and 30.3 percent of arrests; 44.1 percent of jail inmates and 49 percent of murder victims
- American blacks make up 13 percent of regular drug users in the United States and 35 percent of narcotic arrests; 55 percent of drug convictions and 74 percent of those sentenced

Also on average, blacks in the United States earn significantly less than their white counterparts. For instance in 1992, the median income for American black households was $18,660.00, whereas the value for all households was $30,786.00.

In Canada the economic trend is similar to that of the United States with disparities favoring whites. For instance, findings derived from a series of studies in Canada indicate that south Asians, blacks and Chinese earn less than whites. Recently (1996) Ravi Pendakur (a sociologist) and his brother Krishna (an economist) conducted a study in which they analyzed the salaries of colored Canadians who were born and raised in Canada and found that their colored group earned less than their white counterparts. Pendakur and Pendakur (1996) summarized their impressions regarding the findings of their study in the following fashion:

> *... we did find a gap and it's much more difficult to justify and much more difficult to understand why it would be there for some reason other than discrimination ....* (SOURCE: Edmonton Journal, Sunday, January 19, 1997, p.A3)

Findings of another recent study conducted by the Canadian Black Communities Demographic Project at McGill University (1997) indicates that the average income for all Canadians is $24,001.00 whereas the value for blacks is $20,617.00 – 15% lower than that of non-black residents; this disparity exists although blacks in Canada are as well educated as their non-black counterparts. (SOURCE: Edmonton Journal, "Canada's Black Population Tops 500,000– Edmonton, Sunday February 9, 1997, p.A7.)

Additional support for the position which hold that colored people in Canada are exposed to racist practices that impede their ability to earn salaries comparable to whites was revealed recently (February 1997) after employees who work for Health Canada complained that they were denied promotions to managerial positions because they were not white. These individuals persisted in their efforts and as a consequence were able to obtain the right to have their allegations heard by a human rights tribunal which ruled that Health Canada practiced systemic racial discrimination and ordered the department to award nearly one-fifth of all executive and management jobs to colored people for the next five years. The authors of the report continued by saying:

> ... There are a number of staffing practices at Health Canada that have a disproportionately negative effect on visible minorities in Health Canada which the tribunal finds to be discriminatory...

The tribunal's report contains a damning list of indictments including the following:

- a senior manager told an East Indian doctor that "colonials" didn't interact well with others and that brainy guys had to come from the United Kingdom.
- an employee from Trinidad was greeted with "hello darkness, my old friend" and "blackie"
- an employee complained that a manager said a graduate student "worked like a nigger"; the manager who received the complaint said the term wasn't that offensive and added that his family once had a dog named nigger.

SOURCE: Edmonton Journal. Thursday March 20, 1997, p. A.3

Most writers report that a negative effect that institutional racism generally exerts on victims is that it (institutional racism) typically limits power-based employment opportunities. The following personal experience is provided to serve as an illustration:

> ... over the years I made numerous applications for employment in the department at the University of Alberta where I completed my Ph.D.. However, I have never been able to acquire a teaching position in this department although I have relevant experience and have written sixteen books, developed a variety of assessment instruments, and produced one video and two audio cassette tapes...

Because of the racist practice of black slavery in the United States some writers feel that the American Government should pay reparations to the ancestors of slaves. Some proposals suggest that:

- American blacks should be paid 17 billion dollars for work without receipt of income that their ancestors provided,
- American blacks should be paid 4.7 trillion dollars for work without receipt of income that their ancestors provided,
- Each American black family should receive $198,149.00 plus a fair rate of interest accrued for the period 1865 to the present

SOURCE: (Disouza, 1995, p.69.)

A racist, in my view, is an individual who possesses the belief that his or her race is genetically superior to another identifiable race. The genetic traits which racists believe that their group is superior when compared to other racial groups, generally include physical and mental capabilities. It is important for the reader to note that simply because a person possesses racist beliefs, it doesn't mean that he or she will display negative racial prejudice or racist acts. However, if an individual possesses the belief that his or her race is genetically superior to another identifiable racial group, the probability that this individual will display negative racial prejudice and racist acts towards individuals he considers to be members of other racial groups is greater. Conversely, if the individual does not possess the belief that his or her race is genetically superior to another identifiable racial group, the probability that this individual will display negative racial prejudice towards individuals he or she considers to be members of other racial groups is less.

Some writers consider racism to be a factor in the following letter written by Benjamin Franklin (1754):

...It would be a strange thing *if six nations of ignorant savages should be capable of forming a scheme for such a union, and be able to execute it in such a manner as that it has subsisted for ages and appears indissoluble, and yet that a like union should be impracticable for ten or a dozen English colonies, to whom it is more necessary and must be more advantageous, and who cannot be supposed to want an equal understanding of their interests...* Source: (Bellah, 1975).

The following statement by Gumpers, president of the American Federation of Labor, in my view is blatantly racist:

...Sixty years contact with the Chinese, twenty-five years experience with the Japanese, and two or three years of acquaintance with the Hindus should be sufficient to convince an ordinarily intelligent person that they have no standards by which a Caucasian may judge them... Source: (Takaki, 1993).

The process of racism also appears to be apparent in the following letter written by President Woodrow Wilson in 1901 in which he said:

... An extraordinary and very perilous state of affairs had been created in the South by the sudden and absolute emancipation of the Negroes, and it was not strange that the Southern legislatures should deem it necessary to take extraordinary steps to guard against the manifest and pressing dangers which it entailed. Here was a vast "laboring, landless, homeless class," once slaves; now free; unpracticed in liberty, unschooled in self-control; never sobered by the discipline of self-support; never established in any habit of prudence; excited by a freedom they did not understand, exalted by false hopes, bewildered and without leaders and yet insolent and aggressive; sick of work, covetous of pleasure - a host of dusky children untimely put out of school...
Source: (Atlantic Monthly January, 1901)

The following two statements taken from literature reviews and delivered by Battle (1974) in a series of lectures which addressed the issues of prejudice and discrimination vividly illustrate the process of racism:

...In the matter of Chinese and Japanese Coolie immigration, I stand for the national policy of exclusion. The whole question is one of assimilation of diverse races. We cannot make a homogeneous population out of people who

do not blend with the Caucasian race. Democracy rests on the equality of the citizens. Oriental Coolieism will give us another race problem to solve, and surely we have had our lessons...

...I suppose I should be ashamed to say that I take the Western view of the Indian. I don't go so far as to say the only good Indians are dead Indians, but I do believe that nine out of every ten are, and I shouldn't inquire too closely into the case of the tenth. The most vicious cowboy has more moral principle than the average Indian...

ARE YOU A RACIST?

Have you ever asked yourself the question "Am I a racist?" If you truly feel that "we are all of equal worth", chances are you are not a racist. If you truly feel and believe that you are just as worthy as anyone else and conversely that others are just as worthy as you are, chances are you are not a racist. If you generally feel comfortable in your interactions with members of other identifiable racial groups, chances are you are not a racist. However, if you truly feel and believe that you and members of your racial group are better than others and if you generally feel uneasy in your interactions with members of other identifiable racial groups, chances are you are a racist.

If you say that blacks are better basketball players than whites because they possess genetically determined qualities that promote success in the sport of basketball at the professional level that are superior to those of whites, your statement is racist. However, if you say that a higher than expected percentage per capita based on population size of blacks than whites perform better in the professional sport of basketball, your statement is not racist because it merely represents observable, objective data.

If you say that the average black American child earns scores that are lower than their white chronological age mates on commonly used standardized tests of intelligence such as the Wechsler Intelligence Scale for Children and the Stanford-Binet Intelligence scale, your statement is not racist because it merely represents observable, objective data. However, if you say that black American children on the average earn lower scores on standardized intelligence tests than their white counterparts because whites possess genetically determined qualities that promote success on intelligence tests that are superior to those of blacks, your statement is racist.

If you say that the average Asian American child earn scores that are higher than their white counterparts on standardized tests of arithmetic achievement your statement is not racist because it merely represents observable data. However, if you say that white American children on average earn lower scores on standardized arithmetic achievement tests than their Asian counterparts because Asians possess genetically determined qualities that promote success on arithmetic tests that are superior to those of whites your statement is racist.

It is apparent that racism exists. However, if you ask white and colored Americans and Canadians if they are racist, their typical reply will be "no". Complete the following inventory in your efforts to gain insights about your views regarding racial relationships.

RACE RELATIONS INVENTORY

James Battle, Ph.D.

Directions: Please check each question in the following way. For each of the questions there are five options: 5, 4, 3, 2 and 1. Put a check (✓) mark in the option that describes your caring relationship. When choosing an option for each question at least two friends must be identified in order to check a score of 2 or higher. This is not a test and there are no "right" or "wrong" answers.

1. If you had the opportunity to associate with 10 or more individuals of Anglo ancestry (e.g.: Caucasian; white) at school, work or in the community, how many of these do you feel you would consider to be friends and truly care about?
   ☐ 5+   ☐ 4   ☐ 3   ☐ 2   ☐ 1-

2. If you had the opportunity to associate with 10 or more individuals of African ancestry (e.g. Black) at school, work or in the community, how many of these do you feel you would consider to be friends and truly care about?
   ☐ 5+   ☐ 4   ☐ 3   ☐ 2   ☐ 1-

3. If you had the opportunity to associate with 10 or more individuals of Aboriginal ancestry (e.g.: Indian; Eskimo; Inuit) at school, work or in the community, how many of these do you feel you would consider to be friends and truly care about?
   ☐ 5+   ☐ 4   ☐ 3   ☐ 2   ☐ 1-

4. If you had the opportunity to associate with 10 or more individuals of Asian ancestry (e.g.: Chinese; Japanese) at school, work or in the community, how many of these do you feel you would consider to be friends and truly care about?

☐ 5+   ☐ 4   ☐ 3   ☐ 2   ☐ 1-

5. If you had the opportunity to associate with 10 or more individuals of Hispanic ancestry (e.g.: Chicano) at school, work or in the community, how many of these do you feel you would consider to be friends and truly care about?

☐ 5+   ☐ 4   ☐ 3   ☐ 2   ☐ 1-

6. If you had the opportunity to associate with 10 or more individuals of East Indian ancestry (e.g.: Pakistani) at school, work or in the community, how many of these do you feel you would consider to be friends and truly care about?

☐ 5+   ☐ 4   ☐ 3   ☐ 2   ☐ 1-

7. If you had the opportunity to associate with 10 or more individuals of Polynesian ancestry (e.g.: Hawaiian) at school, work or in the community, how many of these do you feel you would consider to be friends and truly care about?

☐ 5+   ☐ 4   ☐ 3   ☐ 2   ☐ 1-

8. If you had the opportunity to associate with 10 or more individuals of Middle East ancestry (e.g: Lebanese) at school, work or in the community, how many of these do you feel you would consider to be friends and truly care about?

☐ 5+   ☐ 4   ☐ 3   ☐ 2   ☐ 1-

9. If you had the opportunity to associate with 10 or more individuals of Latin American ancestry (e.g: Puerto Ricans; Latinos; Cubans) at school, work or in the community, how many of these do you feel you would consider to be friends and truly care about?

☐ 5+   ☐ 4   ☐ 3   ☐ 2   ☐ 1-

10. If you had the opportunity to associate with 10 or more individuals of mixed ancestry (e.g: part white/part colored) at school, work or in the community, how many of these do you feel you would consider to be friends and truly care about?

☐ 5+   ☐ 4   ☐ 3   ☐ 2   ☐ 1-

Score the *Race Relations Inventory* in the following fashion: five yields a score of 5 for each item; four yields a score of 4, three yields a score of 3, two yields a score of 2, whereas the value for one is 1. The highest possible score you can earn on the Race Relations Inventory is 50, whereas the lowest possible score is 10.

Use the Classification of scores listed in table 1:1 to determine your level of race relations:

TABLE 1:1 RACE RELATIONS INVENTORY CLASSIFICATION OF SCORES	
SCORE	**CLASSIFICATION**
42+	Very High
36 - 41	High
24-35	Intermediate
18-23	Low
17-	Very Low
Source: Battle, J. 1996. Race Relations Inventory. Edmonton, James Battle and Associates, Ltd.	

If you earned a score of 42 or better your level of caring and friendliness for other races is very high; a score ranging between 36 and 41 indicates that the values are high; whereas those between 24 and 35 indicate that your feelings of friendliness and caring for individuals who comprise human races are intermediate or average, while a score of 23 or below indicates that your levels of caring and friendliness tend to be low to very low.

The problem of racism in the United States and Canada is a significant one that should not be tolerated. Although the problem of racism is serious, my estimate of the number of racists in North America (i.e: The USA and Canada) is not as high as that of some writers (e.g. Pettigrew proposed that only 20 percent of North American whites were not prejudiced). I am of the opinion that the majority of North American blacks and whites are not racist. However, of those 30 percent of whites and 10 percent of blacks who are racist, the degrees of racism range from very low to very high.

In table 1:2 we list the degrees of racism and percents for each level for white Americans.

TABLE 1:2 DEGREES OF RACISM AMONG AMERICAN WHITES	
DEGREE OF RACISM	PERCENT
Very High	3
High	5
Intermediate	14
Low	5
Very Low	3

Data listed in table 1:2 indicate that 14 percent of whites display an average or intermediate degree of racism in their interactions with colored people; the values for low and very low are 5 and 3 percent respectively, whereas the values for high and very high degrees of racism are 5 and 3 respectively. These data indicate that approximately 8 percent (those experiencing high and very high degrees of racism) possess levels of racial prejudice that are strong enough for them to display racist acts.

Blacks in the United States and Canada typically do not have strong bases of power. Because of this, they generally do not practice or promote the practice of institutional racism. However, I suspect that a small percent of blacks who reside in these countries (approximately 10 percent) experience individual racism and a very small proportion of these (approximately 3 percent) may display racist behavior. I am also of the opinion that of those 10 percent of American blacks who are racist, the degrees of racism ranges from very low to very high. In table 1:3 we list the degrees of racism and percents for each level for black Americans.

TABLE 1:3 DEGREES OF RACISM AMONG AMERICAN BLACKS	
DEGREE OF RACISM	PERCENT
Very High	1
High	2
Intermediate	4
Low	2
Very Low	1

Data listed in table 1:3 indicate that 4 percent of blacks display an average or intermediate degree of racism in their interactions with white people. The values for low and very low are 2 and 1 percent respectively, whereas the values for high and very high degrees of racism are 2 and 1 respectively. These data indicate that approximately 3 percent (those experiencing high and very high degrees of racism) possess levels of racial prejudice that are strong enough for them to display racist acts.

BELIEFS AND RACISM

It is important that we address the issue of beliefs because they are powerful forces that influence an individual's thinking and the behavior that he or she displays. A belief is a disposition that an individual possesses which he or she considers to be true. It is an attitude involving the recognition or acceptance of some things as being true. Beliefs are synonymous with terms such as conviction, feeling, idea, notion, opinion, persuasion, position, sentiment and view.

It is important for the reader to realize that simply because a white person possesses a faulty or distorted belief system regarding blacks and other colored people, it doesn't necessarily mean that the person is a racist. However, in my view, white individuals who possess faulty or distorted belief systems regarding blacks and other colored groups are more susceptible to becoming racists because they tend to be more prone to employing defense mechanisms such as projection (attributing one's own undesirable characteristics to others) and rationalization (providing a socially acceptable reason or excuse for one's own undesirable behavior) in their attempts to reduce the anxiety that they experience because of their belief system.

The beliefs that individuals possess tend to influence their behavior, compel and direct their actions on all occasions. In the following three illustrations, we show how personal belief systems influence behavior.

...A black single parent, who was a client of mine and mother of three young children, told me during a psychotherapy session that her white social worker said: "blacks are hot-blooded people who cannot control their sexual impulses; so you had better keep a close watch on your girls as they grow up because if you don't they will be pregnant by the age of twelve"...

...I recall hearing two well educated, university-trained individuals residing in a mid-western Canadian metropolitan area adamantly insist

that O.J. Simpson was guilty of murder charges, Supreme court nominee, Judge Thomas was guilty of sexual harassment and that Mike Tyson was guilty of sexual abuse. These individuals were adamant in their views, although they possessed limited information regarding what actually occurred in these three cases. These same individuals, however did not offer comments regarding the ruling of "not guilty" for the four Los Angeles police officers who were seen on video tape beating Rodney King...

...During the fall of 1992, I flew to a small community to conduct a series of lectures for the teachers, parents and students of their local elementary, junior high school. I was to be met at the airport by a member of the support staff and driven to the school. Upon arrival at the airport, I picked up my luggage and waited for my driver. After most of the arriving passengers had left the airport, I noticed a white couple sitting near the baggage pick-up area. While leaving this area to go to the bathroom, I overheard the man say in a humorous fashion: "maybe that's Dr. Battle"; his female companion replied "no way". At that point, I knew they were my drivers. Approximately fifteen minutes later the woman paged me on the airport's intercom system; when I approached her she was surprised and appeared to be quite embarrassed. During the trip from the airport to the school, the husband and wife team shared with me many of their strong Christian views and made it clear to me that they were dedicated to doing God's work...

Knowledge regarding the important role that beliefs play in influencing human behavior is crucial for both victims of racism and perpetrators as well, because beliefs exert significant effects in the lives of both groups. For instance, it is important to realize that if criminal court judges possess the belief that blacks are more pre-disposed to committing violent acts they will tend to find more blacks guilty of charges levied against them and award more severe sentences to them, than to their white counterparts who are charged with the same offenses. This disposition tends to prevail even if whites have more extensive criminal records than their black counterparts. Support for this position is provided from data derived from a recent study of Systemic Racism in the Ontario Criminal Justice System (December, 1995) in which 80 percent of respondents who participated in the study reported that they felt that judges treated black defendants worse than their white counterparts. Also, 40 percent of defense counselors and 33 percent of provincial division judges that were appointed in 1989 and subsequent to this date reported that they felt that whites were treated better in the Ontario Criminal Justice System than blacks.

If teachers possess the belief that black students are less intelligent then white students they will tend to assign black pupils lower marks for the same quality of work. Support for this position is provided by the following:

...A thirteen year old black grade eight student with very superior intelligence attending a junior high school in a mid-sized community in northwestern Canada was awarded grades of 79 percent in four classes, whereas her white girlfriends with significantly lower IQ scores who were in the same classes received higher grades. The black girl who was more intelligent and produced better school work received lower grades than her less capable girl friends who produced inferior school work...

...White friends of mine told me that their adopted part black/white daughter was being awarded grades on an average of 50 percent by her white teachers while attending a large high school in midwestern Canada. During parent-teacher interviews they expressed their concerns regarding the "low" grades that their daughter was receiving. The teachers told them to be "content" with their daughter's grades because she was doing the "best" that she could. Rather than be content as recommended by the teachers, my friends spoke with their daughter, told her what the teachers had said and arranged a schedule of reinforcements for academic performance for her. Their daughter's grades improved dramatically, she graduated from high school, completed her Bachelor's degree at an American University and was the first colored student to win the University's most prized academic achievement award. She is currently completing her Ph.D. degree under the supervision of a high profile Afro American professor at a prestigious American university...

...When attending a Canadian university while studying for my Ph.D. degree I was routinely awarded lower grades by white instructors although in many instances I produced better quality work than my classmates who received higher grades...

...While attending an American university during my under-graduate years, I enrolled in a course with an older white woman who most football players considered to be a friend because she was a kind, caring person who provided small loans to athletes who required emergency funds. She was a special friend to me and I was a frequent recipient of

financial assistance on many occasions because I left home at age seventeen and subsequent to my departure did not receive any money from family members. I sat beside my friend while in this class in which the professor gave examinations on Fridays of each week. Commencing with the return of the first test to us, my friend and I exchanged marked examinations for viewing and comparisons. On the first test she received an A and I received a C, although my answers to test questions were of better quality than her's. On the next three tests she received two A's and a B, while I was awarded two C's and one B although I provided better answers to questions. After observing this trend I was convinced that the professor possessed the belief that blacks were less intelligent than whites. I also felt quite strongly that he had stereotyped me as being at best a C student and that he would give me a C for the course in spite of the answers I provided to examination questions. Because of this, I stopped studying for the course and simply wrote whatever came to my mind during subsequent examinations. I continued to receive C's on these tests on which I didn't study whereas my friend received A's. My friend's final mark in the course was an A and, of course, I was awarded a C. Thirty-five years later, I subscribed to the Alumnus Magazine of the school after I was honored with the award of "hall of fame" for my athletic contributions to the university. While reading a copy of this magazine I noted that this instructor had been chosen as a "Professor of the Century"...

I am of the opinion that in both of the personal accounts described above, the beliefs that the white professors possessed regarding black's ability to perform academic tasks played an important role in determining the grades that were awarded to me.

Support for the position which purports that some white individuals possess the belief that blacks are less intelligent than whites is provided by the findings of a research study that I conducted (Battle, 1973). For instance, data derived from responses provided by subjects to the item "Negroes are not as intelligent as whites" indicate that:

- 0 percent of black subjects reported that they strongly agreed with the item and the same value (0 percent) of this group said that they agreed with the item.
- 3 percent of white subjects reported that they strongly agreed with the item, while an additional 6 percent of this group said that they agreed with the item.

PERCEPTION AND RACISM

Perception plays a major role in the display of racist behavior. The following statement provided by Bowman (1966) emphasizes the important influence that perception has on behavior:

> ...*It is generally assumed that the way a person thinks of himself determines the general intent and direction of a person's behavior. In other words, persons who think of themselves negatively will behave in self-defeating ways, even though they may choose a variety of behavioral patterns in the process....*

I am of the opinion that perception which operates at a conscious level determines behavior. Because of this I support the position which assumes that if blacks and whites consciously perceive a racially related situation differently, they will tend to behave differently to the same stimulus. Support for the position which propose that perception compels behavior and that blacks and whites tend to perceive race related issues differently is provided by findings from research studies that were conducted during the highly publicized O.J. Simpson murder trial. Results derived from research findings indicate that the majority of white respondents felt that O.J. was guilty, whereas the majority of blacks reported that they felt he was innocent. After the jury reached its ruling of "not guilty" many whites reacted with rage whereas many blacks expressed jubilation. The not guilty ruling by a mostly black jury in Los Angeles was countered by an all white civil court panel in Santa Clara California who found O.J. Simpson guilty and responsible for the deaths of Nicole Brown-Simpson and Ronald Goldman. Again, after this ruling, the majority of whites who were surveyed reported that they felt that O.J. was guilty, whereas the majority of blacks said that they felt he as innocent.

In another well publicized case the jury ruled that the Los Angeles police officers who beat Rodney King were "not guilty". After hearing this decision, some blacks responded with rage and there were riots in the streets of Los Angeles, whereas whites did not respond to the ruling in a similar fashion to that of their black counterparts.

Additional support for the position which assumes that whites tend to perceive blacks in a fashion that is contrary to that of their black counterparts is provided by the findings of a research study I conducted while teaching for the psychology department of a medium sized mid-western university. In the study I asked my students who were enrolled in a course entitled "psychological determinants of prejudice and discrimination" to complete the following instructor evaluation inventory.

INSTRUCTOR EVALUATION INVENTORY

To the student: This is a confidential form. <u>DO NOT</u> sign your name! Please rate your instructor on each of the following items. Check (✓) only <u>one</u> blank for each item.

1. Does your instructor appear to be competent in the subject matter that he/she is teaching?
   ☐ Good ☐ Above Average ☐ Average ☐ Below Average ☐ Poor

2. How does your instructor communicate information to his/her class?
   ☐ Good ☐ Above Average ☐ Average ☐ Below Average ☐ Poor

3. Is your instructor sensitive to the level of student comprehension?
   ☐ Always ☐ Usually ☐ Sometimes ☐ Seldom ☐ Never

4. How is your instructor's evaluation (grading) procedures?
   ☐ Good ☐ Above Average ☐ Average ☐ Below Average ☐ Poor

5. Is your instructor willing to help students who need additional assistance?
   ☐ Always ☐ Usually ☐ Sometimes ☐ Seldom ☐ Never

6. Does your instructor tend to disregard his students opinions concerning class procedures?
   ☐ Always ☐ Usually ☐ Sometimes ☐ Seldom ☐ Never

7. Is your instructor effective in clarifying the purpose, objectives and goals of the course?
   ☐ Good ☐ Above Average ☐ Average ☐ Below Average ☐ Poor

8. How effective is your instructor in providing resource materials for his/her students?
   ☐ Good ☐ Above Average ☐ Average ☐ Below Average ☐ Poor

9. Is your instructor unwilling to share his/her feelings with class members?
   ☐ Always ☐ Usually ☐ Sometimes ☐ Seldom ☐ Never

10.Does your instructor share the values and ideas of the field with his/her students?

☐ Always   ☐ Usually   ☐ Sometimes   ☐ Seldom   ☐ Never

Findings of the study indicate that black students rated my competence as an instructor more positively than their white counterparts on each of the items (Battle, 1974).

Conscious perception which compels behavior is derived from thought. Thoughts are similar to beliefs which were discussed earlier in this chapter. However, they differ in that thought typically operates at an unconscious level, whereas beliefs generally function at a conscious level.

Summary

- Some scientists propose that the concept of race has no legitimate place in either social or biological sciences.

- Some scientists propose that race is the most retardative term in social science.

- The number of human races proposed by experts vary.

- Emphasis on race generally impedes positive relationships among the peoples of planet earth.

- Battle proposes that if racial distinctions are to be made only two groups, whites and colored should be identified.

- Battle proposes that most American whites are not racist.

- Definitions of racism vary.

- Racist attitudes can be measured.

- Battle proposes that there are degrees of racism for American blacks and whites.

- Beliefs are powerful forces that influence racist thoughts and acts.

- Perceptions play a major role in racist thoughts and the subsequent display of racist behavior.

- Research findings indicate that whites and blacks tend to perceive racially related situations differently.

- Black university students tend to rate black professors more positively than their white counterparts.

- Thoughts generally operate at an unconscious level.

- Beliefs generally operate at a conscious level.

PART II

DEVELOPMENT OF PREJUDICE AND RACISM

CHAPTER 2
DEVELOPMENT OF PREJUDICE

IN THIS CHAPTER we list and describe stages and steps that are involved in the development of negative racial prejudice, delineate the role that stereotypes play in the development of prejudice and racism and provide an overview of the authoritarian personality.

DEVELOPMENT

Allport (1958) identifies three distinct chronological stages in the development of prejudice; pregeneralization, total rejection and differentiation. The pregeneralization stage emerges between the ages of five and six, at about the same time that the child's superego begins to stabilize. During this stage the child is incapable of generalizing in an adult fashion. He does not really understand what a black is or what his own attitude toward blacks should be.

The second stage (total rejection) commences as early as age seven or eight and reaches its peak in early puberty. Researchers have found that ten and eleven year old prejudiced white youngsters tend to totally reject blacks. For example, Blake and Dennis (1943) found that their ten year old subjects tended to ascribe all negative traits to blacks.

The individual moves into the final stage in the development of prejudice around the age of sixteen or seventeen. During this stage the adolescent becomes capable of differentiating between black and white traits in a more objective and/or realistic fashion. The individual at this stage of development does not assign all negative traits to blacks and all positive traits to whites. For example Blake and Dennis (1943) found that white adolescents tended to ascribe a few favorable stereotypes to blacks; they considered blacks to be more musical, more easy-going and better dancers.

I propose that the development of negative racial prejudice commences during the early childhood phase (e.g. birth through age five years, Battle 1995) and in time becomes a stable personality disposition. I propose that there are eight steps in the development of negative racial prejudice.

DEVELOPMENTAL STEPS OF PREJUDICE

STEP I: Living with parents or parent surrogates who possess negative racial beliefs.

STEP II: Introjection of negative racial beliefs from parents or parent surrogates.

STEP III: Incorporation of negative racial beliefs into the personality.

STEP IV: Predisposition towards displaying negative racial behavior.

STEP V: Stabilization of negative racial perceptions and stereotypes.

STEP VI: Beliefs and expectations based on negative racial perceptions and stereotypes.

STEP VII: Display of negative racist behavior.

STEP VIII: Employment of defense mechanisms (e.g. rationalization or providing a socially accepted excuse for racist acts) to justify negative racist behavior.

STEREOTYPES AND RACISM

In 1922, Walter Lippman originally coined the term stereotype to refer to the "picture in his head" that the individual develops in his attempts to simplify and codify his perceptions of his complex world. Stereotypes, according to Lippman were rigid, and resistant to logical reasoning and education.

In 1933 Katz and Brady conducted the first empirical study of ethnic "stereotypes." In their study of college students at Princeton University they found the traits that were most commonly assigned to blacks were:

- lazy
- happy-go-lucky
- ignorant
- musical
- ostentatious
- very religious
- stupid

Klineberg (1951) said that stereotypes, unlike other generalizations, are not based on an inductive (from particular to general) collection of data but on hearsay, rumor and anecdotes; that is, evidence which is insignificant to justify the generalization.

A stereotype is an exaggerated belief associated with a category which functions to justify or rationalize by employing the processes of selective perception (attention to only that information that is in agreement with one's belief) and selective forgetting (promptly forgetting or repressing information that is not in agreement with one's belief). An ethnic stereotype is a generalization made about an ethnic group concerning a trait attribution that is not justified or substantiated by factual evidence.

Lipmann (1922) proposes that stereotypes are:
1. Primary images within a category that are invoked by the person to justify either love-prejudice or hate-prejudice.
2. Important in prejudice.
3. Maybe totally unsupported by facts.
4. Factually incorrect, rigid and produced through illogical reasoning.
5. Fixed ideas that accompany a category.
6. Pictures in your mind.

To Lippman (1922), stereotypes act as:
1. A justificatory device for categorical acceptance or rejection of a group.
2. A screening or selective device to maintain simplicity in perception and in thinking.

Brown and Campbell (1958) shared their views regarding the faultiness of stereotypes when they said that stereotypes:
1. Are not well-founded in direct experience.
2. Sometimes serve to rationalize selfish behavior.
3. Often persist in spite of evidence that is contrary to them.
4. Ascribes or attributes to racial inheritance that which may be culturally acquired.
5. Tend to be ethnocentric.
6. Tend to emphasize cultural absolutism.
7. Suggest that ethnic groups have inborn and unalterable psychological characteristics.

Campbell (1964) proposed the following four faulty general characteristics of stereotypes:

1. Phenomenological absolutism of in-group members imagery of the out- group (e.g. whites imagery of blacks)
   (a) in-group members perceive that an out-group member is as the in-group member perceives him or her .

2. Perceived between group difference
   (a) in-group and out-groups perceive each other differently (e.g. blacks perceive whites differently; whites perceive blacks a certain way but blacks perceive blacks differently; e.g. white writers often report that the black family represents a matriarchal type of hierarchy in which the female has most power, whereas blacks tend to perceive the opposite and assume that black families are generally patriarchal with the husband being the most powerful person).

3. Erroneous causal perception
   (a) the stereotype is liable to attribute group differences to racial, rather than environmental causes or factors.

4. Stereotypers tend to believe that it is the undesirable characteristics of the out-group that cause his hostility rather than recognizing his pre-existing hostility.

Gordon Allport (1954), in his classic book entitled "The Nature of Prejudice" provides the following dialogue to illustrate the process involved in stereotypes:

Mr. X: The trouble with Jews is that they take care of their own group.

Mr. Y: But the record of the Community Chest campaign shows that they gave more generously in proportion to their numbers to the general charities of the community, than do non-Jews.

Mr. X: That shows they are always trying to buy favors and intrude into Christian affairs. They think of nothing but money, that is why there are so many Jewish bankers.

Mr. Y: But a recent study shows that the percentage of Jews in the banking business is negligible, far smaller than the percentage of non-Jews.

Mr. X: That's just it; they don't go in for respectable business; they are only in the movie business or run night clubs.

Elliot Aronson (1976), in his book entitled: "The Social Animal" summarizes the dialogue between Mr. X and Mr. Y in the following fashion:

> *This dialogue illustrates the insidious nature of prejudice far better than a mountain of definitions. In effect, the prejudiced Mr. X is saying "Don't trouble me with facts, my mind is made up." He makes no attempt to dispute the data as presented by Mr. Y. He either proceeds to distort the facts in order to make them support his hatred of Jews, or he bounces off them, undaunted, to a new area of attack. A deeply prejudiced person is virtually immune to information. It is reasonably safe to assume that all of us are prejudiced - whether it is against an ethnic, national, or racial group, against specific geographical areas as places to live, or against certain kinds of food. Let's take food as an example: In this culture, we tend not to eat insects. Suppose someone (like Mr. Y) were to tell you that caterpillars, grasshoppers, or ants were a great source of protein and, when carefully prepared, were extremely tasty. Would that convince you to eat them? Probably not. Like Mr. X, you'd probably find some other reason for your prejudice, such as the fact that insects are ugly. After all, in this culture, we eat only aesthetically beautiful creatures— like lobsters!* (P.179)

S.I. Hayakawa offers the following example regarding stereotypes which he considers to be irrational and negative dispositions:

> *Mr. Miller is a Jew. If Mr. Miller succeeds in business that proves that Jews are smart; if he fails in business it is alleged that he still has money salted away somewhere. If Mr. Miller has different customs than ours, that proves that Jews don't assimilate. If he is indistinguishable from other Americans he is trying to pass himself off as one of us. If Mr. Miller fails to give to charity, that is because Jews are tight; if he gives generously, he is trying to buy his way into society. If he lives in the Jewish section of town, that is because Jews are clannish; if he moves to a locality where there are no Jews, that is because they try to horn in everywhere. In other words, in general Mr. Miller is automatically condemned, no matter who he is or what he does.*

Support for the position which purports that some individuals possess stereotypes towards others is provided by the findings of a research study that I conducted. For instance, data derived from responses provided by subjects to the stereotype "Jews are striving, intelligent and dishonest" indicate that:

- 0 percent of black subjects reported that they strongly agreed with the stereotype, while 10 percent of this group said that they agreed with the stereotype.
- 1 percent of white subjects reported that they strongly agreed with the stereotype, while an additional 3 percent of this group said that they agreed with the stereotype.

In this same study, data derived from responses provided by subjects to the stereotype "Negroes tend to be happy-go-lucky, lazy and over-sexed" indicate that:

- 0 percent of black subjects reported that they strongly agreed with the stereotype and the same value (0 percent) of this group said that they agreed with the stereotype.
- 1 percent of white subjects reported that they strongly agreed with the stereotype, while an additional 9 percent of this group said that they agreed with the stereotype.
SOURCE: Battle, 1973.

Janowitz and Bettelheim (1964) state that the majority of prejudiced people have to fight against the sins within their nature. For instance, they feel that the sins of prejudiced people are personified in their stereotypes of blacks who they say are lazy and happy-go-lucky and of Jews who they say are deceitful and cannot be trusted.

Unfortunately, victims of stereotyping often adapt similar stereotypes about themselves. For instance, Bayton (1941) found that black students at Virginia State College tended to stereotype other blacks as being musical, superstitious, very religious, lazy and happy-go-lucky. Dewey and Humber (1966) found that Jewish high school students tended to accept prevailing stereotypes (e.g. ambitious, shrewd) of Jews.

McAlister and Hamer (1956) studied black and white subjects and found that stereotypes varied more as a function of class than race, and reported that upper class blacks and whites tended to be stereotyped as being intelligent, ambitious, neat and progressive, whereas their lower class counterparts were seen as being ignorant, lazy, loud and dirty. McAlister and Hamer (1956) concluded that people tend to rate blacks more negatively because they assume that most blacks are lower class, and rate whites more positively because they assume that whites are mostly middle and upper class.

The following personal account is provided to illustrate how stereotypes operate:

While performing as an athlete at an American University I was, in my view, the only senior who deserved the honor of Captain of the football team. On the occasion when players voted for Captain, the head football coach viewed each vote and gave the ballots to an assistant coach who recorded them. The final result was that an individual who played the same position that I did, who possessed, in my view, less football talent, fewer leadership qualities and lower grades was elected Captain. I was very upset because of this result and was convinced that I was not elected Captain because I was black. Because of this I wrote an article in which I expressed my views regarding why I felt I was not elected Captain of the football team. After viewing this article five talented black athletes at the college signed it. After receiving their signatures, I gave it to a white student who wrote articles for the University and asked him to consider publishing it in the student newspaper. He however, without my knowledge, wired the article to the Associated Press in Chicago and as a result we received national attention. After viewing the article, local readers were convinced that none of the athletes who signed their names were capable of writing the letter that was published. They generally reported that they felt that the only black athlete at the college who was capable of writing the article did not sign it. However, they were quite surprised when they learned that I wrote the article. Those individuals who assumed that none of the athletes who signed the letter were capable of writing the article were, in my view, employing negative stereotypes.

THE AUTHORITARIAN PERSONALITY AND RACISM

Adorno, Frenkel-Brunswik, Levinson and Sanford (1950) developed the concept of the authoritarian personality, which they propose is characterized by:

- generalized loyalty to the in-group and rejection of out-groups
- rigidity
- rationalization (providing socially acceptable excuses for behavior the individual knows is wrong)

Adorno and his colleagues, and other experts in the field generally agree that racists tend to score high on measures of authoritarianism.

These scholars propose that authoritarian individuals tend to:

- emphasize the importance of conventional behavior
- support authoritarian aggression
- support submission to authority
- display preoccupation with power and "toughness"
- display anti-intraception (impatience with subjective or "tender mindedness")
- employ superstition and stereotypy
- possess a destructive and cynical outlook (general hostility)
- employ projectivity (a preoccupation with evil forces in the world)
- possess over-concern with sexual "goings on" of others.

SOURCE: (Adorno, Frenkel-Brunswik, Levinson and Sanford, 1950)

Support for the point-of-view which proposes that racists tend to be more authoritarian than their non-racist counterparts is provided by findings derived from a research study of 181 blacks and whites enrolled in an introductory psychology course at a mid-western American University, which indicate that both blacks and whites who possess authoritarian views tend to agree with the following items:

1. Important household decisions should not be made by women.
   - 17 percent of black subjects and 7 percent of white subjects reported that they strongly agreed with the item, while 33 percent of black subjects and 21 percent of white subjects said that they agreed with the item. A total of 50 percent of black subjects reported that they support the position that "Important household decisions should not be made by women"; the value for white subjects was 28 percent.

2. Obedience and respect are the most important virtues children should learn.
   - 17 percent of black subjects and 11 percent of white subjects reported that they strongly agreed with the item, whereas 40 percent of black subjects and 31 percent of white subjects said they agreed with the item. A total of 57 percent of black subjects reported that they support the position that "Obedience and respect are the most important virtues children should learn"; the value for white subjects was 42 percent.

3. The average man is squeezed between the rich and the poor.
   - 7 percent of black subjects and 10 percent of white subjects reported that they strongly agreed with the item, while 43 percent of black subjects and 58 percent of white subjects said that they agreed with the item. A total of 50 percent of black subjects reported that they support the position that "The average man is squeezed between the rich and the poor"; the value for white subjects was 68 percent.

4. Voting is the only way I can have a say in governmental matters.
   - 7 percent of black subjects and 7 percent of white subjects reported that they strongly agreed with the item, while 33 percent of black subjects and 21 percent of white subjects said that they agreed with the item. A total of 40 percent of black subjects reported that they support the position that "Voting is the only way I can have a say in governmental matters"; the value for white subjects was 28 percent.

5. Getting ahead depends on who you know.
   - 17 percent of black subjects and 16 percent of white subjects reported that they strongly agreed with the item, while 50 percent of black subjects and 38 percent of white subjects said that they agreed with the item. A total of 67 percent of black subjects reported that they support the position that "Getting ahead depends on who you know"; the value for white subjects was 54 percent.

6. Stricter gun laws are needed.
   - 3 percent of black subjects and 13 percent of white subjects reported that they strongly agreed with the item, while 13 percent of black subjects and 27 percent of white subjects said that they agreed with the item. A total of 16 percent of black subjects reported that they support the position that "Stricter gun laws are needed"; the value for white subjects was 40 percent.

7. Negroes should not push themselves where they are not wanted.
   - 7 percent of black subjects and 3 percent of white subjects reported that they strongly agreed with the item, while 13 percent of black subjects and 21 percent of white subjects said that they agreed with the item. A total of 20 percent of black subjects reported that they support the position that "Negroes should not push themselves where they are not wanted"; the value for white subjects was 24 percent.

8. Negroes and whites can never live comfortably together.
   - 17 percent of black subjects and 1 percent of white subjects reported that they strongly agreed with the item, while 33 percent of black subjects and 7 percent of white subjects said that they agreed with the item. A total of 50 percent of black subjects reported that they support the position that "Negroes and whites can never live comfortably together"; the value for white subjects was 8 percent.

9. The government doesn't attend to the problems of the average man.
   - 7 percent of black subjects and 5 percent of white subjects reported that they strongly agreed with the item, while 23 percent of black subjects and 30 percent of white subjects said that they agreed with the item. A total of 30 percent of black subjects reported that they support the position that "The government doesn't attend to the problems of the average man"; the value for white subjects was 35 percent.

10. Hard working people like me are not doing as well as most Negroes.
    - 0 percent of black subjects and 2 percent of white subjects reported that they strongly agreed with the item, while 10 percent of black subjects and 7 percent of white subjects said that they agreed with the item. A total of 10 percent of black subjects reported that they support the position that "Hardworking people like me are not doing as well as most Negroes"; the value for white subjects was 9 percent.

11. Busing elementary students harms their education.
    - 1 percent of black subjects and 23 percent of white subjects reported that they strongly agreed with the item, while 13 percent of black subjects and 26 percent of white subjects said that they agreed with the item. A total of 14 percent of black subjects reported that they support the position that "Busing elementary students harms their education"; the value for white subjects was 49 percent.

12. It is wrong to enroll students who do not meet the necessary standards.
    - 3 percent of black subjects and 8 percent of white subjects reported that they strongly agreed with the item, while 0 percent of black subjects and 13 percent of white subjects said that they agreed with the item. A total of 3 percent of black subjects reported that they support the position that "It is wrong to enroll students who do not meet the necessary standards"; the value for white subjects was 21 percent.

13. Poverty programs promote laziness.
    - 7 percent of black subjects and 7 percent of white subjects reported that they strongly agreed with the item, while 23 percent of black subjects and 26 percent of white subjects said that they agreed with the item. A total of 30 percent of black subjects reported that they support the position that "Poverty programs promote laziness." The value for white subjects was 33 percent.

SOURCE: (Battle, 1973)

I encourage you to use the information in this section to assist you in overcoming racism and achieving success.

SUMMARY

- Experts propose distinct stages in the development of prejudice.

- Battle proposes eight steps in the development of negative racial prejudice.

- Walter Lippman coined the term stereotype.

- Many writers consider stereotypes to be irrational, negative dispositions.

- Individuals who possess authoritarian personalities tend to display preoccupation with power.

- Racists tend to be more authoritarian than their non-racist counterparts.

- Research findings derived from studies conducted by Battle indicate that authoritarian personalities generally feel that obedience and respect are the most important virtues children should learn .

CHAPTER 3
INTELLIGENCE AND RACE

HISTORICALLY RACISTS have proposed that blacks are inferior to whites because they (blacks) are innately less intelligent than whites. This position is supported by Kent (1764, p. 11-13) when he said:

> *The Negroes of Africa have received from nature no intelligence that rises above the foolish. The difference between the two races is thus a substantial one: it appears to be just as great in respect of the faculties of the mind as in color....*

Racists who consider blacks to be less intelligent than whites use assumptions made by some researchers as proof for their position. For instance, twenty-six years ago racists referred to the writing of Jensen (1972) who proposed that blacks are intellectually inferior to whites and that this intellectual inferiority is due to genetic factors. Jensen also proposed that the intelligence of blacks is less abstract than that of whites and that blacks score lower on intelligence tests because they possess less or lower intellectual potential. However, psychologists generally disagree with Jensen and suggest that black's lower performance on standardized intelligence tests occur as a result of culturally specific tests that are biased toward blacks and other minority members. For instance, Merger (1972) in her study of 664 American children in Riverside California found that 300 percent more Mexican Americans and 50 percent more black Americans were classified as being retarded than one would expect from their population proportion in Riverside. Whites on the other hand were under represented in the retarded category. For example, she discovered that there were only 60 percent as many whites as one would expect from their population proportion in Riverside. Merger concluded from her comprehensive study that:

1. Ethnic groups, particularly those of low socio-economic status are more likely to be penalized by current intelligence tests and are more likely to be labeled retarded.
2. Intelligence tests are Anglocentric; they measure the extent to which an individual's background matches the average cultural pattern of American Society.
3. Minority children whose families are least like the average Anglo family tend to score lower on current intelligence tests (IQ mean score=82.7).
4. Minority children whose families matched the Anglo pattern best, have test scores equal to the national norm (IQ mean score=99.5).

The black-white IQ controversy continues. For instance, recently Herrnstein and Murray (1994) in their book entitled "The Bell Curve: Intelligence and Class Structure in American Life" propose that blacks as a group are intellectually inferior to whites and that this inferiority is due to genetic rather than environmental factors. These authors also propose that social pathologies such as poverty, welfare dependency, illegitimacy and crime are strongly related to IQ.

In response to Herrnstein and Murray's book, the American Anthropological Association adopted the following statement in which they declared that:

> ... differentiating species into biologically defined "races" has proven meaningless and unscientific as a way of explaining variation, whether in intelligence or other traits ... (October, 1996)

The IQ issue has persisted for generations and a historical review of the developments of this controversy revealed that in:

- 1575, Spanish physician Juan Huarte defined intelligence as being the ability to learn, be imaginative and exercise judgement.
- In 1839, American physician Samuel George Morton coined the term "Craniometry" to refer to the measurement of skull and brain size to determine the intelligence of different races.
- In 1859, Charles Darwin published his manuscript entitled "Origin of Species" in which he argued that, in part, intelligence is inheritable.

- In 1904, British psychologist Charles Spearman reported findings which indicated that people who do well on one type of intelligence test do well on others, a trait he called general intelligence and used the symbol g to represent this factor.
- In 1905, French psychologist Alfred Binet developed the first intelligence test which incorporated tasks involving analogies, patterns and reasoning skills.
- In 1912, German psychologist Wistern proposed what he called the intelligence quotient which he derived by dividing mental age by chronological age.
- In 1912, Henry H. Goddard, who coined the word moron administered intelligence tests to immigrants at Ellis Island.
- In 1917, the United States Army started administering intelligence tests to large groups of recruits.
- In 1936, developmental psychologist Jean Piaget proposed that intelligence arises from both environmental and biological factors.
- In 1966, William Shockley advocated the sterilization of individuals with low IQ's and proposed a sperm bank for geniuses.
- In 1969, Educational psychologist Arthur Jensen proposed that programs like Head Start fail because many of the participants have fixed IQ's.
- In 1971, American psychologist, Richard Herrnstein asserted that social and economic status are tied to heritable differences in IQ.
- In 1971, United States Supreme Court outlawed the practice of using intelligence tests as a hiring tool in most cases.
- In 1981, American biologist Stephen Jay Gould published the manuscript "The Mismeasure of Man" in which he blasted past and present intelligence testing as being unscientific.
- In 1990, findings derived from the Minnesota study of twins which indicate that genetic factors account for approximately 70 percent of the variation in IQ were reported.

SOURCE: Cowley G. Newsweek, October 24, 1994, p.57.

Most psychologists, however continue to disagree with those who propose that there exists significant differences in intelligence among races due to innate factors. Among the earlier writers to take this stance were Loehlin, Lindzey and Spuhler (1975) who made it very clear in their book entitled "Race and Intelligence" that:

...Intelligence is clearly not innate, it is developed....

Kamin (1973) provided support for the position that assumes that intelligence is not inherited when he said:

...A critical review of the literature produces no evidence which would convince a reasonably prudent man to reject the hypothesis that intelligence test scores have zero heritability...

Another expert, Brace contended that intelligence is the only human trait that does not seem to vary from one population to another. Rather basic intellectual capacity, according to Brace, is distributed equally among all peoples regardless of their skin color. Brace continues by stating that differences in performance on intelligence tests are due to social, environmental and cultural factors, but not to biological inheritance. SOURCE: Edmonton Journal, 1996, p.8.

In a classic study of race and intelligence Eyberth compared the IQ scores of children of black American soldiers and white German women with those of white American soldiers with white German women. In the study Eyberth and her colleagues administered the German version of the Wechsler Intelligence Scale for children to 264 children born in Germany from these biological unions during the years 1945 to 1963 and found that:

1. For boys, the average IQ was significantly higher for the sons of white fathers (mean IQ for white father's offspring = 101; the value for black fathers offspring = 97).
2. For girls, the average IQ was significantly higher for the daughters of black fathers (mean IQ for black father's offspring = 96; the value for white father's offspring = 93).
3. Over all, for both boys and girls, there were no significant differences in the IQ scores of children whose fathers were black and of those whose fathers were white.

The findings of Eyberth and her colleagues are significant when we realize that during this period, black soldiers on average scored about one standard deviation below their white counterparts on the Army General Classification Test, indicating that the mixture of black males and white females exerted a stronger positive effect on the IQ of their offspring than the white male, white female union. Support for this position is provided by my observations while working as a school psychologist for more than 20 years in a large school district in mid-western Canada. During this period I administered the Wechsler Intelligence Scales to more than 5000 children enrolled in grades kindergarten through twelve. Of these, I have tested a significant number of children whose fathers were black and mothers white and have not found one to possess lower than average intelligence as measured by the Wechsler Scales.

This data however, in my view, does not provide evidence to indicate that intelligence is due to heredity. Actually, there is evidence which indicates that a significant portion of black Americans are products of mixed ancestry. For instance, Reed (1969) estimated that 22 percent of American blacks had white ancestry. Terskovitsc (1930) found that approximately 15 percent of his United States sample reported genealogies that contained more white than black ancestry.

I am of the opinion that intelligence is generally influenced most strongly by environmental factors. The classic research of Heber and his colleagues (1970) provides strong evidence in support of this point-of-view. In the study Heber and his associates worked with mothers of limited intelligence who resided in a slum area of Milwaukee, Wisconsin. Heber employed 20 of the children of these mothers to function as experimental subjects and another 20 to serve as controls. Commencing in early infancy, the children in the experimental group were provided with an intensive program of educational intervention. Heber described the program of intervention of the children in his experimental group in the following fashion:

> ...At the Infant Education Center, the infants receive a customized, precisely structured program of stimulation. The infants are picked up in their homes early each morning by their teachers and are transported to the Center where they remain until late afternoon. Infant stimulation teachers follow an intensive program which has been prescribed in detail. Essentially, it includes every aspect of sensory and

language stimulation which we believe may have relevance for the development of intellectual abilities. Its major emphases are efforts designed to facilitate achievement motivation, problem-solving skills and language development....

Findings of the study provide strong evidence indicating that the intervention which experimental subjects were exposed to had a dramatic positive effect on their intelligence. Both control and experimental subjects were tested at 3 to 6 month intervals between the ages of two and five and a half years. The control group (those children who did not receive any intervention) averaged an IQ score of approximately 95, whereas the experimental group (those children who received the intervention) averaged an IQ score of approximately 125, roughly 30 IQ points higher than their control counterparts (Heber and Garber, 1970).

Additional support for the position that intelligence is influenced more strongly by environment is provided by Karnes, Hodgins and Teska (1968) who employed 27 nursery school aged children who functioned as experimental subjects and a comparable group of 28 who comprised the control group. Both groups were administered the Stanford-Binet Intelligence Scale prior to the commencement of the intervention strategy. During this pre-test period, when the children were approximately 4 years of age, the mean IQ score for the experimental group (those who were provided educational intervention) was 96.0, whereas the mean IQ score for the control group (those who received traditional nursery school instruction) was 94.5. When the study ended one year later both groups earned higher mean IQ scores but those of the experimental group were significantly higher. The mean IQ score during post tests for the experimental group was 110.3, whereas the value for the control group was 102.6.

Blacks are not the only group that "experts" have said possessed lower levels of intelligence. For instance, Kamin (1973) reported that earlier intelligence tests produced results which indicated that more than 75 percent of Jews, Russians, Hungarians and Italians were "feeble minded" (p.91).

After reviewing available data, the enlightened observer may wonder; "Why is there an IQ controversy?" For instance, research findings indicate that the correlation between intelligence (IQ) and academic achievement is only about 0.3, which suggests that knowing a student's IQ score will only enable one to predict 9 percent of the total variance in the scores on academic achievement measures.

Some writers propose that self-esteem is a better predictor of academic success than measured intelligence. Support for this position is provided by Morse (1963) who stated that self-concept is a better predictor of classroom achievement than intelligence. Wattenberg and Clifford (1964) found that measures of self-concept at the beginning of kindergarten proved to be more predictive of reading achievement two-and-a-half years later than IQ. Additional support for the position that assumes that self-esteem is a better predictor of academic success than measured intelligence is provided by Smith (1969), who found that the correlation between self-esteem and achievement was higher than the correlation between intelligence and achievement, and Jones and Grieneekz, (1970) who propose that self-concept is the most effective and consistent predictor of academic achievement, even better than test scores.

Yaniw (1983) administered the Culture-Free Self-Esteem Inventory, For Children, Form A, to 716 junior high boys and girls and found a linear correlation between self-esteem and actual grades. That is, he found that students who earned the lowest grades earned lower self-esteem scores, whereas those who earned the highest grades earned the highest self-esteem scores. Findings of his study of five academic level groups in Mathematics, Language Arts, Social Studies and Science are presented in Tables 3:1 through 3:4.

TABLE 3:1: SELF-ESTEEM MEANS FOR
FIVE ACHIEVEMENT LEVEL GROUPS
IN MATHEMATICS

Pos. Score		80-100	65-79	50-64	40-49	<40
TOTAL	50	38.98	37.62	34.13	33.46	31.03
GENERAL	20	15.87	15.81	14.67	14.77	14.24
SOCIAL	10	7.38	7.38	7.01	7.18	7.07
ACADEMIC	10	7.72	6.63	5.26	4.35	3.36
PARENTAL	10	7.94	7.66	7.18	7.15	6.23
	n=	161	187	200	93	75

Table 3:2: Self-esteem Means for Five Achievement Level Groups in Language Arts

	Pos. Score	80-100	65-79	50-64	40-49	<40
Total	50	39.73	37.79	34.86	30.95	29.09
General	20	15.76	15.89	15.07	13.96	13.00
Social	10	7.52	7.33	7.23	6.73	6.82
Academic	10	8.35	6.74	5.16	3.83	3.41
Parental	10	7.97	7.76	7.32	6.44	5.85
	n=	89	248	256	89	34

Table 3:3: Self-esteem Means for Five Achievement Level Groups in Social Studies

	Pos. Score	80-100	65-79	50-64	40-49	<40
Total	50	40.00	38.03	35.05	31.38	31.45
General	20	15.86	15.94	15.18	13.85	14.33
Social	10	7.47	7.34	7.07	7.13	7.08
Academic	10	8.20	7.03	5.26	4.03	3.48
Parental	10	8.35	7.59	7.50	6.38	6.52
	n=	104	215	212	125	60

Table 3:4: Self-esteem Means for Five Achievement Level Groups in Science

	Pos. Score	80-100	65-79	50-64	40-49	<40
Total	50	39.94	37.98	34.92	32.21	30.23
General	20	15.99	15.92	15.09	13.97	14.08
Social	10	7.37	7.37	7.04	7.22	7.26
Academic	10	8.22	6.80	5.39	4.16	3.24
Parental	10	8.24	7.69	7.34	6.84	5.64
	n=	110	187	261	105	53

Recently, Wechsler (1991) found the correlation between the full scale IQ on the Weschler Intelligence Scale for Children-Revised-3 and grade point average to be .47 and the values for verbal IQ and performance IQ with grade point average to be .42 and .39 respectively.

Yaniw (1983) found the correlation between actual grades and the academic self-esteem facet of the Culture-Free Self-Esteem Inventory For Children, Form A, to be .57 for Math .59 for Language Arts .60 for Science and .61 for Social Studies; all higher than the correlations between WISC-R-3 IQ's and grade point average. The findings of these studies are presented in Table 3:5.

TABLE 3:5: GRADE POINT AVERAGE, SELF-ESTEEM AND IQ

	VARIABLE	GRADE POINT AVERAGE
WISCR-3-IQ	verbal	.42
	performance	.39
	full scale	.47
CFSEI-2	ACADEMIC SELF-ESTEEM	
	1) Social Studies	.61
	2) Science	.60
	3) Language Arts	.59
	4) Math	.57

Yaniw's (1983) findings which delineated the relationships between the academic facet of self-esteem and academic achievement are summarized in Table 3:6:

TABLE 3:6: ACADEMIC SELF-ESTEEM AND ACADEMIC ACHIEVEMENT (N = 716)				
	YEAR END FINAL GRADES			
	MATH	LANGUAGE ARTS	SOCIAL STUDIES	SCIENCE
ACADEMIC	.57xxx	.59xxx	.61xxx	.60xxx

xxx p< .001
SOURCE: (Battle, 1995, p. 74-77)

The data listed above clearly indicate that self-esteem is a better predictor of academic success than measured intelligence. It is very important for the reader to note that only 2,200 children aged 6 through 16 years participated in the most recent revision (1991) of the very popular Wechsler Intelligence Scale for Children. The 2,200 subjects who participated in the standardization of the WISC-R-3 make up only a very small proportion of children residing in the United States of America.

The question continues, "Why is there a black/white IQ controversy?" I encourage the reader to develop his or her own personal hypothesis regarding why the problem of black/white intelligence exists and continues to persist.

SUMMARY

- Racists propose that blacks are inferior to whites because they are innately less intelligent

- Loehin, Lindzey and Spuhler state that intelligence clearly is not innate

- Kamin proposes that intelligence test scores have zero heritability

- Battle reports that the children he has tested from mixed ancestry generally earn average to above average IQ scores

- Terskovitsc found that 15 percent of his American sample reported genealogies that contained more white than black ancestry

- Battle proposes that intelligence is most strongly influenced by environmental factors

- In his classic study, Heber provided young children with an intensive program of education intervention which resulted in them earning IQ scores that were significantly higher than those of the standardization population

- Karnes, Hodgins and Teska were able to employ educational intervention strategies to enhance the IQ scores of the young children who participated in their study

CHAPTER 4
PREJUDICE AND RACISM: THEORIES AND CAUSES

In THIS CHAPTER we commence with an overview of theories that address the issues of prejudice and racism and end by providing a profile of a racist. A number of theories have been postulated to explain psychological dynamics that are basic to the development and maintenance of racial prejudice. Among the most popular ones are theories that emphasize historical factors, socio-cultural factors, situational factors, psychodynamics, phenomenological properties and those that emphasize earned reputations as causes of prejudice.

Many theories of racial prejudice emphasize historical determinants of prejudice, that is, they postulate that anti-black prejudice in the United States had its genesis in slavery and has emerged as a result of carpetbagging and the failure of reconstruction in the Southern states following the Civil War. Historically oriented theories of prejudice suggest that current anti-black prejudice in the United States is due to the basic assumptions of white Americans which were developed during the initial stages of black-white interactions. Basic to anti-black prejudice in the United States was the assumption that blacks were inherently inferior to whites and because of this, were not capable of interacting as equals to the superior whites.

Although historically oriented theories of prejudice differ, they, as a group generally tend to stress the importance of economics in the development and maintenance of prejudice toward out-groups. For instance, the exploitation theory of prejudice formulated by Marxists suggest that racial prejudice is a social attitude projected among the people by an exploiting class for the purpose of stigmatizing some group as being inferior so that the exploitation of either the group itself, or its resources may both be justified (Cox 1948, p. 393). Proponents of the exploitation theory of prejudice suggest that racial prejudice and subsequent segregation and discrimination toward out-groups are developed as a device or mechanism for preventing sympathy and sentiments of equality. Although the exploitation theory provides some insights into the development of prejudice, it does not adequately explain the basic determinants of prejudice. For example, it fails to explain why there is not equal prejudice toward all exploited out-groups.

Closely related to historically oriented theories of prejudice are the socio-cultural theories. Socio-cultural theories emphasize the role of urbanization in the development of prejudiced attitudes toward out-groups. Theories of urbanization suggest that the plasticity of highly mechanized societies foster the development of prejudice towards members of out groups. Urbanization theories further suggest that the highly complex and mechanistic metropolitan cities are representative of what is inhuman, impersonal and threatening and as a result, facilitates loneliness, insecurity and a type of free floating paranoia which makes those who are visually and/or philosophically different, a threat to the city dweller. Color obviously, is the most vivid readily identifiable aspect of differences and because of this, it represents the greatest degree of threat to the insecure, highly threatened city dweller. The city, with its mechanical way of life, tends to de-emphasize humanness and at the same time reward materialism; that is, it tends to enhance those who possess materialistic goods and demean the poor and have-nots. Because of these tendencies, blacks and other groups (who make up the major portion of the city's poor), become highly available, all-duty scape goats. The city dweller then tends to hate the mechanical inhuman atmosphere of the city and tend to think adversely of highly identifiable city dwellers. For instance, a number of whites have suggested that intense prejudice toward Jews occurs as a result of them being identified with urban life. For example, Rose (1948) writes "The Jew is hated today basically because he serves as a symbol of city life."

Situational theories of prejudice, (which tend to be between or intermediate to historical and socio-cultural theories of prejudice), places greater emphasis on current forces within the environment which fosters the emergence of prejudice between groups. For example, factors such as employment, social change, heterogeneity of the culture and the opportunity for upward mobility of out-group members have an effect on the development, maintenance and intensity of prejudice toward these members.

The frustration theory of prejudice (which emphasizes psycho-dynamic determinants of prejudice), state that frustration plays a major role in the intensification of prejudice. The frustration theory holds that frustrations facilitate the emergence of hostilities and subsequent tendencies to aggression. These hostilities, often time are displaced upon colored (scape-goating) individuals who are viewed as being less powerful and less threatening than members of the dominant group who were responsible for the emergence of the hostile feelings.

The character structure theory of prejudice (which also empha-sizes psychodynamic determinants of prejudice) holds that certain types of individuals are more susceptible towards developing pre-judice than others. For example, the character structure theory of prejudice suggests that individuals who possess authoritarian type personalities tend to more readily incorporate prejudice as a mode of existence as compared to individuals who possess democratic type personalities.

Phenomenological theories of prejudice state that the major determinant of prejudice is perception. Phenomenological theories state that if an individual (stimulus object) is perceived as being a member of an out-group which represents a threat to the perceiving individual's in-group, he will be reacted to in a hostile fashion. For example, whites attack blacks because they are perceived as being threatening and dangerous.

Earned reputation theories of prejudice stress the stimulus object and state that individuals and/or groups of individuals become victims of prejudice because they possess negative, menacing traits and as a result, themselves (the victims), have earned or deserve the hostilities that they, as victims of prejudice receive.

In my efforts to provide theoretical conceptualizations of preju-dice, I offer the following theory of prejudice, based upon ancestral guilt which is passed on from one generation to another.

ANCESTRAL GUILT THEORY OF PREJUDICE

Historical, socio-cultural, situational, psychodynamics, pheno-menological and earned reputation theories of prejudice have made major contributions toward the development of a more thorough understanding of psychological determinants which are basic to the development and maintenance of racial prejudice. These theories nevertheless, do not provide us with a complete picture of processes involved in the syndrome of prejudice. These theories do not singly or collectively, provide means by which we may completely understand the problem of prejudice. Prejudicial attitudes (that are so basic to the "White American Personality") have been so well interwoven into the personalities of white Americans for so many generations that they cannot be, or should not be interpreted as being due merely to situational factors. Prejudice is much deeper than the superficially of the situation and as a result, only an in depth theoretical orientation can provide clues to its genesis and maintenance.

Ancestral guilt as postulated by this writer is not an innate or hereditary phenomenon which is automatically passed from parents to offspring. On the contrary, ancestral guilt is a learned socially conditioned response. Ancestral guilt however, is so persuasive and encompassing that it is inherently communicated to children by their parents. Prejudice then, is a highly infectious disease which is overtly or covertly transmitted from one generation to another.

In order to understand white prejudice toward blacks in the United States it is necessary that we review the institution of slavery, because the American black slave system and the subsequent anti-black prejudice which followed were unique in the western hemisphere. For example, American anti-black prejudice has continued to be traditionally and currently more intense than anti-black prejudice in other North American British colonies. The American slave system was the most harsh, inhumane system implemented in America. The South American slave system on the other hand was much more humane. For instance, slavery in South America was regarded as being a misfortune which could happen to anyone and carried little, if any taint of inferiority. The South American system was an open system (not based on black inferiority) which permitted the black slave, once he gained his freedom to be assimilated into the dominant society in a relatively easy fashion. In contrast, the American slave system was based on the assumption that blacks were inferior, and as a result were incapable of being free. The following ruling ("a negro has no rights which a white man may respect"), by Chief Justice Taney in 1857 expressed white Americans sentiments toward black slaves. The American slave system (in contrast to the South American slave system), was a closed one which did not permit assimilation of blacks into the dominate white society.

The American white personality, because of the many indignities which they (whites), have imposed upon blacks, traditionally and currently has resulted in an intense degree of guilt. This profoundly intensified guilt is due primarily to the inhumanness, and recency of slavery, as well as the extent of exploitation, oppression and genocidal practices that have been directed toward black Americans by white Americans.

The institution of slavery then, in conjunction with past atrocities towards blacks have left a residue of guilt in white Americans which continue to persist even today. Freud suggested that feelings of guilt may be handled in a number of ways. For instance, the individual may repress his guilt feelings or deny that they exist. Both methods however, are indicative of defensive functioning which invariably result in feelings of anxiety. The guilt experienced by white Americans is a symptom which occurs because of conflict which arises as a result of perceived discrepancy within the individual between the "American Ideal" and actual behavioral experiences. That is, white Americans simultaneously are deeply committed to the American constitutional principles of freedom, equality and the right to pursue happiness for all Americans, and, at the same time tend to exhibit behavioral patterns which oppress, inhibit, and deny, a large portion of Americans the opportunity to realize the "American Ideal". This incongruence which white Americans almost inherently experience, inevitably results in feelings of guilt.

The aspirations of the American ego-ideal is rarely achieved. The democratic principles of equality, freedom, and liberty for all, which the American superego insists upon is rarely achieved. Americans, as a result of not achieving the demands of their superego develop guilt feelings. This anxiety, arousing guilt feelings are usually handled by the defensive mechanism of repression. If the defense is successful in repressing these feelings of guilt the individual will function fairly adequately. If repression is not chronically successful, and previously unconscious guilt feelings demand conscious expression, pathological sympathology will occur. Ancestral guilt is transmitted from one generation to another through the process of introjection. That is, the white American child takes in or introjects those feelings of guilt from significant adult stimulus objects (usually his parents), and incorporates them into his personality as if they were his own.

Earlier in this section, I reviewed Allport's stages in the development of prejudice. His final stage of differentiation parallels my second stage in which the individual for the first time becomes aware of the incongruence between the ego-ideal and his overt and covert behavioral patterns. It is at this particular stage that the prejudiced individual develops a sense of guilt, and experiences anxiety which is associated with these guilt feelings and engages the assistance of defense mechanisms in an attempt to remove or reduce his feelings of guilt and anxiety.

In the Ancestral guilt theory of prejudice, I propose that the development of racial prejudice occurs in the following four stages illustrated in Figure 4:1:

FIGURE 4:1: DEVELOPMENTAL STAGES OF RACIAL PREJUDICE

STAGE ONE

I.   Superego Development
   • based on democratic principles (e.g. equality; equal opportunity for all persons)
   • in Freudian theory the superego is comprised of two parts, the conscience and the ego-ideal
   a) the conscience represents our views regarding what we consider to be right or wrong
   b) the ego-ideal represents what we feel we "ought" to do or be

STAGE TWO

II. Awareness of Incongruence
   • between the ego-ideal and organismic reality
   a) incongruence between what we feel we ought to do and what we actually do

STAGE THREE

III. Guilt Feelings

STAGE FOUR

IV. Employment of Defense Mechanisms
   • to protect the individual from feelings of guilt
   Freud (1927) proposed the following regarding psychological defenses:
   1. Operate at an unconscious level.
      • The individual employing defenses does not know that she is utilizing them.
   2. Protect from anxiety and guilt.
      • The individual uses defenses to reduce threat.

3. The use of defenses indicate varying degrees of psychopathology or emotional disturbance.
   - More frequent use of certain defenses indicate more serious degrees of adjustment problems.
4. All individuals use defense mechanisms.
   - Perfection does not exist in personality.

The six defenses that racist individuals commonly employ are; repression, reaction-formation, projection, displacement, rationalization and denial.

REPRESSION

Repression is the first defense mechanism that the racist white person employs in his or her efforts to diminish feelings of guilt. Repression is a protective device because for the racist white person to consciously admit to himself that he is prejudiced against colored people would be to accuse oneself of being both irrational and unethical. The same of course, is true for the racist colored person.

Repression is a defense in which anxiety-arousing thoughts are pushed (repressed) into the unconscious. Repression is motivated forgetting in which anxiety-arousing stimuli are removed from consciousness and placed in the unconscious. For example, a prejudiced white person cannot remember the first time he felt sexually inadequate to his black counterpart, but possesses the belief that blacks are more potent sexually and feels uncomfortable when showering in the presence of blacks.

REACTION-FORMATION

Reaction-formation is the second defense mechanism that the racist white person employs in his or her efforts to diminish feelings of guilt. The individual employing the defense of reaction-formation feels compelled to behave in a fashion that is exactly opposite to how he truly feels. That is, reaction-formation involves the creation of a pattern of behavior which is directly opposite of that which is appropriate for the arousal of instinctual impulse. The utilization of the defense of reaction-formation enables the individual to emit behavior that is more socially acceptable, which in turn, reduces threat by reassuring him that he is not thinking undesirable thoughts or desiring to gratify unacceptable impulses. Hence, reaction-formation is due to containment, rather than expression. The defense of reaction-formation enables the racist white person to discredit and despite what he envies most (e.g. color). Thus, rather than say that he prefers color the racist white individual feels compelled to say that he hates color. The same, of course, is true for the racist colored person who employs the defense of reaction-formation.

PROJECTION

Projection is the third defense mechanism that the racist white person employs in his or her efforts to diminish feelings of guilt. Projection is a defense in which the individual rids him or herself of threatening drives, impulses and needs by attributing them to others. Thus, the projecting individual attributes his own characteristics or impulses (usually always undesirable ones) to others. Employing the defense of projection enables the racist white person to attribute his own negative characteristics to blacks. For example, rather than admit that he is lazy, the racist white person states that blacks and Indians are lazy. The defense of projection permits the racist white individual to justify his negative actions toward people of color. The same, of course, is true for the racist colored person.

DISPLACEMENT

Displacement is the fourth defense mechanism that the racist white person employs in his or her efforts to diminish feelings of guilt. In the defense of displacement, psychic energy is rechannelled or redirected from one object, person or situation to another. The individual employing the defense of displacement chooses a substitute object on which to direct his feelings, that are usually always hostile ones, because he perceives the original source of his frustration to be too threatening to attack directly. This form of displacement is called "scapegoating" and is characterized by the tendency to transfer or displace feelings towards a powerful person to someone or something else which is considered to be less threatening. For example, the racist white employee becomes angry with his white boss, but rather than confront him he displaces his hostility (scapegoating) onto his black colleague who he views as being weak. The same, of course, is true for the racist colored person.

RATIONALIZATION

Rationalization is the fifth defense mechanism that the racist white person employs in his or her efforts to diminish feelings of guilt. Rationalization is a defense in which the individual provides a socially acceptable reason for his undesirable behavior. It provides the individual with an excuse which enables him to reduce threat by justifying his socially unacceptable actions to himself and others. Sour grapes is a form of rationalization in which the rationalizing individual, after trying many ways of obtaining a given goal, finally gives up and states "I really didn't want it anyway." Sour grapes is vividly depicted in Aesop's fable, "The Fox and the Grapes." The fox in this fable was very fond of grapes and attempted on numerous occasions to get some from a vine, but was unable to obtain them. After many attempts, he finally gave up and proclaimed "they were probably sour grapes anyway; who wants sour grapes? Certainly not I!" With the defense of rationalization, the racist white person who cannot produce color because of the inability of his body to make melanin, employs sour grapes in his efforts to convince others that he really doesn't like color.

Another type of rationalization is compartmentalization. Compartmentalization is a process in which the racist individual forms logic-tight compartments in which he psychologically walls off his attitudes so that they do not interfere with one another. For instance, with compartmentalization the white racist person will maintain the position which assumes that blacks are genetically inferior to whites in spite of evidence that is contrary to this stance. Allport (1958) calls compartmentalization refencing. With refencing the racist white person admits an exception to his position regarding the inferiority of blacks when compared to whites when contrary evidence is presented to him (e.g. blacks are just as good as whites) but shortly afterwards promptly forgets that this exception ever existed. For example, a white racist will readily accept invalid evidence which indicates that blacks are innately less intelligent than whites; however, when this individual meets an intelligent black person, he promptly represses this experience because it does not fit into his system. The same, of course, is true for the racist colored person.

DENIAL

Denial is the sixth defense mechanism that the racist white person employs in his or her efforts to diminish feelings of guilt. Denial is a defense in which individuals refuse to admit realities that are anxiety producing. The white racist who employs the defense of denial attempts to keep from conscious awareness that colored people are just as good as he is. The same, of course, is true for the racist colored person.

Support for the aspect of the Ancestral Guilt Theory which proposes that prejudiced individuals employ defense mechanisms is provided by Robert Blauner (1972) when he said:

...The tendency of the West to view people they oppress as animals or children must somehow be related to European culture's psychological denial and repression of both the animality of the human species and the universal presence of the child and his traces in the makeup of the adult. This is what makes people of color such convenient targets for the psychic projection of those character tendencies and desires that Western man has suppressed in himself, in part due to the powerful dualism of the Protestant world view, which sees good-evil, life-death, child-adult, animal-human, heaven-hell, and so on, as polar opposites rather than as interpenetrating realities... (pp.41-42).

In an attempt to provide empirical data to support this theory, I conducted a comprehensive survey in a test of my hypotheses. In the study I employed 225 white males and females residing in a university community in Southwestern Michigan. Table 4:1 presents the composition of the group which participated in the study.

TABLE 4:1 COMPOSITION OF PARTICIPATING SUBJECTS

Group	Male	Female	North	South	Foreign	Protestant	Catholic	Jewish	Other
Freshmen	43	57	89	4	7	35	40	10	15
Seniors	66	34	86	6	8	35	12	6	16
Outsiders	69	31	80	11	9	69	22	7	11

SOURCE: Battle, J. 1973, A cross group analysis of white perceptions and attitudes toward blacks.

Finding from the survey presents empirical data which supports the proposed ancestral guilt theory of prejudice. For instance, 38 percent of the freshmen, 42 percent of the seniors and 31 percent of the outsiders (subjects that were not currently enrolled in university courses) reported that they felt guilty because of the way blacks are currently being treated in the United States. Similarly, 70 percent of the freshmen, 50 percent of the seniors and 61 percent of the outsiders reported that they felt guilty because of the way blacks were treated in the past in the United States.

Results of the above mentioned study strongly indicate that whites experience a considerable amount of guilt as a result of the incongruence between their ego-ideal (which stresses equality, freedom and the pursuit of happiness for all) and organismic reality (actual real-life experiences). Furthermore, if one assumes that the defense of repression is currently being employed by some of the subjects and they presently are not consciously aware of their guilt feelings, he would expect that even a greater percentage of the subjects (more than those who are consciously aware of their guilt feelings) are experiencing guilt feelings, but are not consciously aware of these feelings. Further support for a theory of prejudice based on ancestral guilt is provided by Adorno (1950) in his studies of the authoritarian personality. Adorno (1950) suggests that authoritarianism which is highly correlated with prejudice, tend to be most abundant in older southern born Americans who have less education, and who tend to experience a greater degree of anxiety and insecurity. These findings support the author's position which assumes that prejudice will be greatest among individuals whose ancestors have been most oppressive (Southerners toward blacks) to out-groups and subsequently have experienced a greater degree of guilt, and as a result have transmitted a greater degree of guilt to their children.

Further support for an ancestral theory of guilt is provided by Pettigrew (1971) in his extensive study of Wallace supporters during the 1968 presidential campaign. Pettigrew found Wallace supporters to be mostly southern working class males who did not feel that blacks were as intelligent as whites, who were against protest marches and favored the use of force in solving urban unrest; they blatantly exhibited more anti-negro prejudice (more willing to discriminate against blacks in school, education, etc.) and were more resistant to racial change in all facets of society.

Additional support for the position which assumes that individuals who possess negative racial prejudice towards others experience guilt and conflict, was provided by Gordon Allport (1954) when he said most prejudiced people possess feelings of guilt and conflict, and Gunmar Myrdal when he said white Americans experience guilt and inner conflict because their actions and practices do not conform with the American creed of freedom and equality for all.

In sum, the ancestral guilt theory of prejudice postulates that white Americans experience guilt as a result of perceived incongruence between their ego-ideal and their actual behaviors.

THE CRESS THEORY OF
COLOR-CONFRONTATION AND RACISM

In her theory of color confrontation, Welsing (1972) proposes that whites display racism and neurotically strive for superiority and domination of colored people because of perceived inadequacies due to:

1. Numerical Inferiority
   - most people on earth are colored
   - whites are a minority on earth
   - whites make up 14 percent of the world population

2. Genetic Inadequacy
   - whiteness, according to Welsing, is a genetic deficiency state that is due to the lack of ability to produce melanin. Melanin is a biochemical substance located in cells called melanocytes that produce skin color
   - the inability to produce color is abnormal because most people on earth can create varying degrees of color.

Dr. Welsing hypothesizes that because of the inadequacies listed above (i.e. numerical inferiority; genetic deficiency) whites neurotically strive for superiority in their attempts to dominate all people of color. She continues by stating that whites strive hardest to dominate blacks because blacks possess the greatest color potential. Dr. Frances Cress Welsing, states that:

...Whites have a fear of white genetic annihilation because of the genetic recessive characteristic of skin whiteness (which is an albinism variant), so that their evolved system of behavior (which is operative in all areas of people activity), is consciously and subconsciously designed to ensure white genetic survival and prevent white genetic annihilation on planet Earth....(1996, p.1)

Dr. Welsing proposed, in her theory of Color-Confrontation and Racism, that white behavioral scientists assist the white collective in becoming comfortable with their color and their numerical minority on earth. She continues by stating that:

...Whites attempt to compensate for their feelings of genetic and numerical vulnerability by projecting that they are genetically superior to people with skin coloration and that it is the non-white global majority that is of minority status on planet earth....(1996, p.2)

The alienation that whites experienced initially, according to Dr. Welsing, M.D. was towards the self, but evolved into alienation towards others, especially towards colored people. Dr. Welsing continues by stating that white hostility and aggression towards non-whites is due to inner hate, hostility and rejection of self.

Dr. Welsing proposes that the following are ways that whites attempt to compensate for their feelings of numerical inferiority and genetic inadequacy:

1. Drive towards materialism
2. Drive towards a technical society
3. Drive towards power
4. Acquisition and accumulation of materialistic goods.

In addition, she proposes that whites in their efforts to diminish feelings of inadequacy, employ the defenses of repression, reaction-formation and projection.

ROKEACH'S THEORY

Rokeach (1967), in his theory of Belief Similarity and Dissimilarity versus Race as Determinants of Prejudice proposed that:

1. Prejudice is more directly a function of belief dissimilarity than of ethnic or racial membership.

2. Whites display negative prejudice towards blacks because of their belief that blacks are different from them.

3. Belief effects are generally larger or more important than ethnic or race effects.

4. When whites interact with blacks they believe are more similar to them they tend to perceive them in a more positive fashion and display less prejudice towards them. For example, an American white Christian who is a football player and college student would, according to Rokeach, tend to perceive an American black Christian who is a football player and college student in a more positive fashion than he would a black who did not play football and was not a college student.

5. White Americans rejection of black Americans is motivated more strongly by assumed belief and value differences than racism. Thus, according to Rokeach, it is the beliefs and perceptions that whites possess which lead them to assume that blacks possess dissimilar beliefs; it is not race per se that results in whites rejecting blacks.

Research findings (e.g. Rokeach, et al, 1960; Rokeach and Mezei, 1966; Smith et al, 1967; Stein, 1966; Stein et al, 1965 and Triandis and Davis, 1965) which indicate that whites tend to prefer to interact with blacks who possess beliefs that are similar to their views over their white counterparts who possess dissimilar views provide support for Rokeach's theory.

PROFILE OF A RACIST

In the following psychological profile, we list common characteristics and behaviors often displayed by racist individuals.

PERSONA

The persona is the mask which individuals present to others. Racist individuals tend to display a persona of toughness, whereas in reality they are frightened. These individuals try to induce anxiety in others to mask their fear so that others cannot observe it. Racist individuals often talk tough and verbalize their distaste for members of out-groups. However, when confronted face-to-face with members of the out-group, these individuals tend to experience intense anxiety.

PSEUDO SELF-ESTEEM

Self-Esteem is a powerful force which exerts a strong effect on all humans (Branden, 1969; Battle, 1982, 1987, 1990, 1995). Branden (1969) states that self-esteem is a need that cannot be avoided; and that those who fail to achieve self-esteem or who fail to a significant degree in their search for self-esteem, strive to fake it. Because they fail to ascertain self-esteem, they attempt to hide behind a facade and display pseudo self-esteem. Pseudo self-esteem, according to Branden, is an irrational pretense of self-value. It is a non-rational self-protective device designed to reduce anxiety and enhance a sense of security. It (pseudo self-esteem), is maintained by the use of defense mechanisms (e.g. rationalization or false but acceptable excuses created for one's unacceptable behavior; denial or refusal to admit realities; projection or attributing one's own behavior or character-istics to others).

The racist tends to display pseudo self-esteem in his efforts to dis-guise his authentic self, reduce anxieties and maintain a sense of security.

DEFENSE MECHANISMS

Defense mechanisms are unconscious processes that individuals employ in their attempts to protect themselves from feelings of anxiety and guilt. The six defenses that racist individuals commonly employ are:

1. REPRESSION
   - Repression is a defense in which anxiety-arousing thoughts are pushed into the unconscious.

2. REACTION-FORMATION
   - Reaction formation is a defense in which the individual feels compelled to behave in a fashion that is exactly opposite to how he feels.

3. PROJECTION
   - Projection is a defense in which the individual rids him or herself of threatening drives, impulses and needs by attributing them to others.

4. DISPLACEMENT
   - Displacement is a defense in which psychic energy is rechannelled or redirected from one object, person or situation to another.

5. RATIONALIZATION
   - Rationalization is a defense in which the individual provides a socially acceptable reason for his undesirable behavior.

6. DENIAL
   - Denial is a defense in which the individual refuses to admit realities that are anxiety producing. (see pages 59 through 62 for more detailed definitions of the six defenses listed above)

Authoritarian Personality

The racist individual tends to possess what Adorno, Frenkel-Brunswik, Levinson and Sanford (1950) call the authoritarian personality. Individuals who possess authoritarian personalities tend to be:

- anti-Semitic
- anti-homosexual
- anti-foreigners
- ethnocentric
- conservative in political views
- conservative in economic views
- supportive of institutions
- rigid in their beliefs
- prone to using stereotypes in their political perceptions and judgements
- supportive of using violence against individuals and groups they perceive as being enemies
- supportive of making sharp distinctions between their in-group and out-groups
- prone to viewing out-groups as being threats to their security
- compelled to present an exaggerated assertion of strength and toughness
- cynical and preoccupied with destructiveness
- overly concerned with sexual going ons
- submissive to powerful individuals
- prone to responding in disrespectful and demeaning fashions toward individuals they view as being powerless.

Summary

- Theories that emphasize historical factors propose that anti-black prejudice had its genesis during slavery.

- Historically oriented theories of prejudice stress the importance of economics in the development and maintenance of racial prejudice.

- Socio-cultural theories emphasize the role of urbanization in the development of prejudice towards out-groups.

- Situational theories of prejudice place emphasis on forces within the environment that fosters the emergence of prejudice.

- The frustration theory of prejudice emphasizes psychodynamics and proposes that frustration plays a major role in prejudice.

- The character structure theory of prejudice emphasizes psychodynamics and proposes that certain types of individuals are more susceptible towards developing prejudice than others.

- Phenomenological theories of prejudice propose that perception is the major determinant of prejudice.

- Earned reputation theories of prejudice propose that victims of prejudice deserve what they receive.

- Battle proposes an ancestral guilt theory of prejudice.

- The American slave system was harsh and inhumane.

- A chief justice ruled that a negro has no rights which a white man may respect.

- Battle proposes four stages in his ancestral guilt theory of prejudice.

- Racists employ defense mechanisms in their attempts to reduce anxiety and guilt feelings.

- Research findings derived from studies that Battle conducted provide evidence which indicate that whites experience guilt because of the way blacks are treated.

- Dr. Welsing purposes that whites display racial prejudice towards colored people because of perceived inadequacies.

- Whites make up only about 14 percent of the world population.

- Rokeach proposes that prejudice is more directly a function of belief dissimilarity than of ethnic or racial membership.

- Racists tend to display a persona or mask in efforts to conceal their fear.

- Battle provides a profile of a racist.

- Racists tend to possess authoritarian personalities.

PART III

RELATIONSHIPS AND RACISM

CHAPTER 5
BLACK-WHITE RELATIONSHIPS:
PAST AND PRESENT

In THIS CHAPTER we provide an overview of past and present black-white relationships, show how concerns regarding black-white sex have influenced the practice of racism and identify some perceptions and attitudes of white Americans towards blacks.

From the beginning the relationships between black and whites in the United States have always been one in which whites have dominated and maintained the base of power. Although slavery legally ended in the United States in 1865, many white Americans subsequent to this date found it difficult to allot blacks full human status and as a result have traditionally viewed blacks as being inferior. Concerning human status for blacks, the supreme court of the United States in 1857 declared that blacks were not citizens and that they had always been considered as having no rights which the white man was bound to respect (Negro Digest 1947). Viewing blacks as sub-human then, was not only a popular position adopted by the masses, but it was a prominent conviction of the highest court of the land. Senator Vardamis, in a speech concerning the voting rights of blacks further illustrates this above mentioned position when he stated:

> ...It matters not what his (The Negro's) advertised mental and moral qualifications may be. I am just as much opposed to Booker Washington as a voter, with all his Anglo-Saxon reinforcements, as I am to the coconut- headed, chocolate covered, typical little coon, Andy Dotson, who blackens my shoes every morning. Neither is fit to perform the supreme function of citizenship.... (Source Lewinson 1932 pp.84-85)

Further support for this position is illustrated by Sir Harry Johnston (1913) when he wrote:

> ...He is possessed of great physical strength, docility, cheerfulness of disposition, a short memory for sorrows and cruelties, and an easily aroused gratitude for kindness and first dealing. He does not suffer from homesickness to the over bearing extent that affects other people torn from their homes, and provided he is well fed, he is easily made happy. Above all, he can toil hard under the hot sun and in the unhealthy climates of the torrid zone. He has little or no race fellowship, that is to say, he has no sympathy for other negroes, he recognizes, follows and imitates his master independently of any affinities and, as he is usually a strong man and a good fighter, he has come into conquest not only as a laborer but also as a soldier....

To Johnston and to many whites the black man was seen as a biological sub-human to be used and manipulated by the white man as he so desires. Many whites of yesteryears, and some contemporary ones feel that blackness is equated with sin, evil, the devil and that blackness must be punished; to them blackness is the crime of crimes; possibly because it is a threat to whiteness, and white supremacy. Individuals who support this position assume that everything ugly, filthy or, dishonorable is either yellow, brown or black.

According to Thomas (1901) the black man devoid of any sense of responsibility to public opinion, is moved to the commission of criminal acts, by impulse and thoughtless disregard of consequences. Thomas further writes that the primary impulse of the black man to steal is derived from his appetites and as he grows in intelligence and wants, the area of motives which induce theft will enlarge. Thomas, continuing in his evaluation of the black man states that blacks are always creatures of impulse, consequently they laugh and cry, not that the ridiculous excites them to merriment or pity to tenderness, but simply and solely because the vacuity of their minds is such that every passing sensation is likely to move them to hilarity or tears. Thomas' view of the black man is far from positive, in fact it supports this writers position; that is, if Thomas' feelings equated the feelings of white men of his time, they (the white men of his time) tended to view the black man as being sub-human.

Some white men have proposed that the black man is competent only in the biological dimension. These individuals maintain the position that psychologically blacks are dense and grossly incompetent, when compared to their white counterparts. This position is illustrated in the following statement by Dr. H.L. Gordon, attending physician at the Mathalii Mental Hospital in Nairobi, who declared in an article in the East African Medical Journal (1943): "A highly skilled examination of series of one hundred brains of normal natives has found naked eye and microscopic facts indicative of inherent new brain inferiority". "Quantitatively" he added, "the inferiority amounts to 14.8 percent".

Dr. Gordon is suggesting that African natives in Nairobi are not as intelligent as whites because they do not have the brain potential: that is the ratio or discrepancy between brain weight and body weight is greater for the natives than for the whites which suggests that whites inherently possesses more intellectual potential than blacks. It appears that Dr. Gordon's position is an attempt to scientifically establish the position that blacks are sub-human, and grossly inferior to the white man; particularly in the psychological realm.

Concerning intellectual inferiority, Thomas William (1901) states that I'm firmly rooted in the conviction that blacks, as exemplified in the American type, is an attitude of mental density, a kind of spiritual sensuous.

Medical doctors, educators and politicians are not the only professional groups that have responded to blacks negatively. White psychologists, as well as whites from other professional disciplines have viewed blacks negatively. For instance Kardiner and Ovesey (1951) listed the following as being typical characteristics of black personality organization:

1. Superficiality
2. Apathy and resignation
3. Repressed hostility
4. The wish to be white
5. Identification with feces
6. Intragroup aggression
7. White ego-ideal
8. Inclined to gamble
9. Distrustful
10. Disorderly-unsystematic
11. Magical thinking
12. Inclined to alcoholism
13. Unconsciously resentful and anti-social
14. Weak superego development
15. Sexual freedom
16. Reject education
17. Poor discipline in childhood
18. Maternal neglect and rejection
19. Little respect for parents
20. Psychologically crippled
21. Hedonistic
22. Live for the moment

Inspite of the above mentioned statements black Americans, in many cities, have made considerable progress in their battle for equality. However, it has been an up hill fight all the way and there is still many obstacles to overcome. The roughness of the road that blacks have had to travel is indicative in the fact that in 1919 seventy-seven blacks were lynched in the United States of America. Of these seventy-seven, fourteen were publicly burned and eleven were burned alive (Dubois, 1970). Because of the incidents of 1919, and those prior to this period the Dyer anti-lynching bill was introduced in 1924 in an attempt to stop the lynching of black Americans. However, a filibuster resulted in the death of this bill on the floor of the senate. Slavery had terminated fifty-nine years past, but freedom, safety, security and the right to pursue happiness, were out of the grasp of many black Americans.

Social equality has been the most difficult for blacks to obtain. I am not suggesting that blacks have acquired equality in other segments of the American population but I am proposing that progress has been made in other areas; that is, the least progress has been made in the socialization between blacks and whites. In an attempt to impede the socialization process of blacks and whites the chairman of the committee in the state of Missouri legislature, in 1913 developed the Jim Crow Car Bill which proposed the following:

1. Blacks should not object to being separated on the trains by "just a small railing".
2. If they do object to being separated it shows that they are adverse to associating with themselves.
3. If they insist on associating with whites, it shows that they want social equality (Crisis, April 1913).

Abraham Lincoln, the great emancipator, in a speech in 1858 said:

...I will say then that I am not nor ever have been in favor of bringing about in any way the social and political equality of the white and black races. That I am not nor ever have been in favor of making voters or jurors of negroes, nor of qualifying them to hold office, nor to intermarry with white people; and I will say in addition to this that there is a physical difference between the white and black races which I believe will forbid the two races living together in terms of social and political equality and in as much as they cannot so live, while they do remain together, there must be the position of superior and inferior and I as much as any other man am in favor of having the superior position assigned to the white race....(Silberman, pp.92-93)

One, may argue that Lincoln's speech is a political one and that politicians tend to do what they feel is needed to be elected. This line of reasoning, in my view, is a valid one. However, I am of the opinion that Lincoln, like all great American presidents rose above the level of rhetoric and behaved in a fashion that was in concert with the principles of the American Constitution. He ended the practice of black slavery in America and by this he did what was best for the United States of America. Lincoln, in my view, was a positive exception during his era who made very positive contributions for all Americans.

In recent decades however, blacks have acquired a significant proportion of the political power base in the United States and the relationship between black and white Americans have generally been more collegial. Evidence for support of this fairly recently established relationship is provided by statistics which indicate that there were 39 blacks in the 104th congress; of these 38 were in the House, whereas the value for the senate was 1. Also, in the United States a significant portion of blacks have acquired political positions in other levels of government including municipal and state.

BLACK-WHITE SEX AND RACISM

Historically sex between blacks and whites (especially black males and white females) has been a persistent factor influencing the practice of racism in the United States. Thus, the fear of black - white sexual intercourse has played a major role in the emergence of racism in the American society. Many authors have commented on the apparent attractiveness between black and white males and females. The white man in the past has attempted through out the centuries to divorce white women from the black man. Ironically, however, according to Hernton (1965) if a black man and a white woman have intercourse in the South the white woman usually is the aggressor. A number of writers suggest that the so called sexual mythology pre-disposes the white woman to be attracted to the black man for two reasons; sex and striving for equality. According to the myth, the black man is viewed as being an erotic system to the white woman and she feels that he is sexually more powerful than the white man. It is felt that she finds it difficult to return to the white man after she has been loved by the black man.

Davis (1972) suggests that white women perceive black males as being more active (e.g. Hot, excitable, fast and active) and more potent (e.g. strong, hard, heavy, big and masculine) than white males. Davis (1972) concluded from his study of 360 college subjects that:

1. A sexual mythology does exist concerning the black male.

2. The nature of the mythology appears to be that the black male is perceived as being more potent than the white male regardless of whether he is engaged in hard core sex or merely sexually fantasy. He's also perceived as being more active when engaged in sexual fantasy (pp. 84)

As mentioned earlier in this section a major determinate of racial prejudice (Black - White) has been the white man's fear of the consequences which may occur if the black man and white woman engage in sexual intercourse. This point is illustrated by Hernton (1965), who suggests that racism has become sexualized to such a degree that the sexual mythology may be the primary factor fostering current racism in America. However, there is some evidence which suggests that relationships between sex and racism is not as prominent as it was in the past. For instance, Davis (1972) concludes:

1. A white female is responded to no differently when she is having sex with a black male than with a white male.

2. The social taboos against interracial sex appears to have broken down on the college campus.

3. Authoritarianism is not related to reactions toward interracial sex or sexual mythology.

4. Sex experience is not related to reactions toward interracial sex or sexual mythology.

Interracial dating and inter-racial marriages have increased tremendously in the last decade. Although hostilities arising from interracial relationships have lessen, the majority of the American society, however, do not support interracial marriages (particularly between black males and white females). Dubois (1970) states that the crux of the race problem in the United States is interracial marriage. He suggests, that whites who deny blacks equal rights fear that equality will lead to amalgamation. He further states that white men are not moved by hatred of blacks, instead they are moved by the fear of amalgamation. A number of writers suggest that unimpeded social interaction between blacks and whites present a threat to many American white men. The threat being due to the fear that the (white men) may lose what they value highest (white women) to the sexually powerful black. Concerning interracial marriage, Louis T. Archille in his report to the Interracial Conference of 1949 stated:

> *...In so far as truly interracial marriage is concerned, one can legitimately wonder to what extent it may not represent for the colored spouse a kind of subjective consecration to wiping out in himself and his own mind the color prejudice from which he has suffered long. It would be interesting to investigate this in a given number of cases and perhaps to seek in this clouded motivation the underlying reason for certain interracial marriages entered into outside the normal conditions of happy household. Some men or some women, in effect, by choosing partners of another race, marry persons of a class or culture inferior to their own whom they would not have chosen as spouses in their own race and whose chief asset seems to be the assurance that the partner will achieve denaturalization and deracialization. Among certain people of color the fact that they are marrying someone of the white race seems to have overridden every other consideration. In this fact they find access to complete equality with the illustrious, the master of the world, the ruler of the people of color... (Fagan, 1967)*

Black Muslims in contrast to the above statement, denounce inter-racial marriages; it seems that they feel that most of the cruelties inflicted upon black people have occurred as a result of the white man's apparent paranoiac fear of losing his woman. A number of writers have suggested that the black man symbolizes a biological threat to the white man, that he is seen as a physical gladiator, with extraordinary sexual powers, which represents a constant threat. This position is illustrated by Etimible (1950) when he states that racial jealousy produces the crimes of racism. To many white men, the black man is simply that marvellous sword which, once it has transfixed their wives, leaves them forever transfigured. Some white men tend to see the black man as being a "penis symbol". Because of this many lynchings of blacks have occurred as a result of this mythical symbolism. The lyncher is usually not motivated by hatred of hue; as a result when the white man lynches a black man he often times is seeking sexual revenge. Throughout history, groups in power have lynched and murdered minorities, the Romans murdered Christians, the Germans murdered the Jews. However the only race of people that have been castrated and then lynched have been blacks. Killing blacks apparently wasn't enough, revenge was acquired only after castration. Concerning castration, Freud suggests that girls feel castrated because they do not have a penis, or external sexual organs. As a result, she envies the penis of the male. In Freudian theory, the penis symbol is the most powerful sexual symbol which is centrally fixed in the personalities of humans; because of the importance of the symbolic representation of the penis, penis size has attracted a considerable amount of attention. Concerning penis size, Pales states that the average length of black penises in Africa rarely exceeds 120 millimetres (4.646 inches) and Testient, in his Trait "d" Anatoine Humaine quotes the same length for European penises, 4.646 inches (Fanon 1967, pp.170).

Pales, like many writers has stated that there are no differences between the size of black and white penises. It seems ironical, that scientists have found differences in practically all areas of whiteness and blackness, except in this area. The validity of Pale's research at best is questionable, nevertheless, penis size has generated a considerable amount of attention. For example, Cournot (1948) writes:

> ...*The black man's sword is a sword. When he has thrust it into your wife, she has really felt something. It is a revelation. In the chasm that is left, your little toy is lost. Pump away until the room is awash with your sweat, you may just as well be singing. This is goodby...Four negroes with their penises exposed would...fill a cathedral. They would be unable to leave the building until their erections had subsided; And in such close quarters that would not be a simple matter. To be comfortable without problems, they always have the open air. But then they are faced with the constant insul. The palm tree, the bread, fruit tree and so many other proved growths that would not slacken for an empire, erect as they are for all eternity, and piercing heights that are not easily reached at any price .... (pp.13-14)*

Penis size however, according to this writer, is not very relevant to the issue at hand. The important factor is that whites tend to feel that blacks have larger penises and that blacks are more potent sexually. Support for the position which proposes that some individuals possess the perception that the genitals of black males are larger than the genitals of white males is provided by the findings of a research study which I conducted. For instance, when subjects were asked to compare the genitals of black and white males, data derived from the responses they provided indicate that:

- 40 percent of black subjects reported that they felt that the genitals of black males were much larger, while 27 percent of this group said that they felt that black male genitals were larger than white male genitals
- 2 percent of white subjects reported that they felt that the genitals of black males were much larger, while 13 percent of this group said that they felt that black male genitals were larger than white male genitals

In the same study, when subjects were asked to compare the sexual potency of black and white males, data derived from the responses they provided indicate that:

- 60 percent of black subjects reported that they felt that the sexual potency of black males is much stronger, while 17 percent of this group said that they felt that the sexual potency of black males is stronger than the sexual potency of white males
- 4 percent of white subjects reported that they felt that the sexual potency of black males is much stronger, while 9 percent of this group said that they felt that the sexual potency of black males is stronger than the sexual potency of white males

Also in the same study, when subjects were asked to compare the eroticism in black and white females, data derived from responses they provided indicate that:

- 43 percent of black subjects reported that they felt that the eroticism in black females is much stronger, while 30 percent of this group said that they felt that the eroticism in black females is stronger than the eroticism in white females
- 1 percent of white subjects reported that they felt that the eroticism in black females is much stronger, while 8 percent of this group said that they felt that the eroticism in black females is stronger than the eroticism in white females.

SOURCE: Battle, 1973

Over the years, writers have postulated, and it seems reasonable to assume that this relationship, black man - white woman, seems to be the key to much of the racial tension and conflict in the United States of America.

PERCEPTIONS AND ATTITUDES OF AMERICAN WHITES TOWARDS BLACKS

The study of the perceptions and attitudes of white Americans toward black Americans have become extremely popular since the national advisory commission on civil disorders (1968) ruled that "white racism" (i.e. whites attitudes towards blacks) was the major cause of violent civil disorders and black-white conflict in the United States.

The importance of white attitudes toward blacks is further emphasized by Rokeach, Smith and Evans (1960) who state that white reactions toward blacks and other colored group matters are more related to belief similarity or dissimilarity of the groups involved than they are to ethnic or racial membership. Similarity, other writers, Anderson and Cole (1966) Byrne and Wong (1962), Stein, Hardyck and Smith (1965), Triandis, Loh and Lewin (1956) and Wrightman, Baxter and Jackson (1917) have also, concluded that belief effects (similarity or dissimilarity) tend to be more significant than race effects.

In my efforts to obtain quantitative data regarding the perceptions and attitudes that white Americans possess toward their black counterparts, I conducted a study in which I employed 255 white males and females. Of these three groups were identified for participation; university freshmen, university seniors and outsiders (those who were not attending university). Each individual who participated in the study was asked to complete a modified version of the National Research Inventory which included items developed by the National Research Council, Pettigrew and myself. The survey items were divided into three groups; internal, stereotype and authoritarian.

INTERNAL ITEMS

The finding from internal items indicate very strongly that American whites possess varying degrees of guilt, because of the way blacks have traditionally, and currently are being treated in the United States of America. For instance, 38 percent of the freshmen, 42 percent of the Seniors and 31 percent of the outsiders reported that they felt guilty because of the way blacks are currently being treated in the United States. Similarly, 70 percent of the freshmen, 50 percent of the seniors and 61 percent of the outsiders reported that they felt guilty because of the way blacks were treated in the past in the United States. The percentages for the degree of personal guilt was not as high as the percentages for national guilt; For example, only 5 percent of the freshmen, 12 percent of the seniors and none of the outsiders reported that they felt guilty for their past treatment of negroes. Similarly only 3 percent of the freshmen, 8 percent of the seniors and none of the outsiders reported that they felt guilty because of their current treatment of blacks. An important finding, one that many contemporary Americans would not expect, was that 80 percent of the freshmen, 76 percent of the seniors and 76 percent of the outsiders reported that they liked blacks at least as much as they did whites.

The findings listed above regarding feelings of guilt by white Americans because of the treatment of black Americans provide strong support for my Ancestral Guilt Theory of Prejudice (see pp.55 through 63).

STEREOTYPE ITEMS

Data derived from the findings of the study indicate that some American whites still support negative black stereotypes; For instance, 10 percent of the freshmen, 2 percent of the seniors and 12 percent of the outsiders reported that they felt negroes were happy-go-lucky, lazy and oversexed. Similarly, nine percent of the freshmen, 1 percent of the seniors and 11 percent of the outsiders reported that they felt that negroes were not as intelligent as whites.

Also, data derived from the responses that participants provided to items intended to assess stereotypes indicates that whites tend to view blacks as being more potent and powerful sexually then whites. For instance, 15 percent of the freshmen group, 4 percent of seniors and 15 percent of the outsiders reported that they felt that black male genitals were larger than white male genitals, none of the freshmen and seniors, and only 2 percent of the outsiders reported that they felt black male genitals were smaller than white male genitals. Similarly, 13 percent of the freshmen, 9 percent of the outsiders and none of the seniors reported that they felt negro males were sexually more potent than white males, as compared to only 1 percent of the freshmen, none of the seniors and 2 percent of the outsiders who reported that they felt that black males, were less potent sexually than white males. Findings for females were similar to those for the males;

for example, 9 percent of the freshmen, 6 percent of the seniors and 11 percent of the outsiders reported they felt that black females were more erotic than white females. Only 3 percent of the freshmen, 4 percent of the seniors and 2 percent of the outsiders reported that they felt that black females were less erotic than white females.

It is interesting to note that subjects recorded the largest number of no responses on sexual stereotype items. This high degree of no response to sexual items suggest that Americans still view sex as being a threatening topic, not to be discussed openly. For example, 27 percent of freshmen, 18 percent of seniors and 29 percent of outsiders refused to respond to item 8 (comparison of the size of black and white males genitals). On item 9 (a comparison of black and white male sexual potency) 19 percent of the freshmen, 12 percent of the seniors and 35 percent of the outsiders refused to respond. On the final sexual statement, item 10 (a comparison of the eroticism of black and white females) 18 percent of the freshmen, 12 percent of the seniors and 33 percent of the outsiders did not respond. Although the responses to sexual items were low, it appears to be apparent that the so called sexual myth continues to exist.

AUTHORITARIAN ITEMS

Data derived from participant responses to authoritarian items indicate that 8 percent of the freshmen, 6 percent of seniors and 19 percent of outsiders reported that they felt that negroes and whites could never really be comfortable with one another even if they were close friends, as compared to 83 percent of the freshmen, 84 percent of the seniors and 72 percent of the outsiders who felt that negroes and whites could live comfortably together. A fair proportion of the subjects (24 percent of the freshmen, 8 percent of the seniors and 44 percent of the outsiders) felt that blacks should not push themselves where they are not wanted. A large majority of subjects in all three groups reported that they felt that busing elementary students to schools in other parts of the city harms their education. For example, 49 percent of the freshmen, 22 percent of the seniors and 67 percent of the outsiders reported that they felt busing was detrimental to elementary students education. Similarly, 33 percent of the freshmen, 22 percent of the seniors and 56 percent of the outsiders reported that they felt that poverty programs promoted laziness.

Although there have been significant progress in black / white relationships in North America, considerable conflict between the groups continues to exist and unfortunately too many people do not recognize the magnitude of this problem. The following letter to the editor of a local newspaper in Edmonton, Alberta Canada entitled "Racism Issues must be confronted" provide support for the tenet which holds that racism continues to be a problem confronting North American residents.

RACISM ISSUES MUST BE CONFRONTED

Ten years ago I was a concerned parent of minority children attending Harry Ainlay high school; there were confrontations between ethnic groups and the response from the principal was, "No problem here—you are over- reacting".

The first time I heard the word "nigger" used on a playground was here in Edmonton. Having both children of color and white children I was acutely aware of the subtle and overt forms of racism in our community. We do not fight these ignorant responses and fears by pretending they do not exist. They are every bit as strong as in the U.S. or South Africa, expressed less openly.

I do not blame the schools for doing nothing. They simply reflect parents' wishes. When communities speak up and say we will no longer tolerate confrontations along racial lines and do something constructive, then perhaps teachers and administrators in co-operation with communities will first inform themselves so they can in turn fight the values and intolerance that ignorance and apathy breed. Then perhaps teachers will feel free to speak out and sign their names. (Edmonton Journal, July 1996, pp. A7).

Summary

- The relationship between blacks and whites in the United States has always been one in which whites have dominated and maintained power

- The United States Supreme Court ruled in 1857 that blacks had no rights which the white man was bound to respect

- Some writers believe that the black man is competent only in the biological dimension

- In 1919 seventy-seven blacks were lynched in the United States

- Sex between black males and white females have been a persistent factor influencing the practice of racism in the United States

- Davis proposed that white women perceive black males as being more active and more potent than white males

- Dubois stated that the crux of the race problem in the United States is interracial marriages

- Dubois stated that white men are moved by fear of amalgamation

- some whites tend to see the black man as being a "penis symbol"

- In Freudian Theory, the penis symbol is the most powerful sexual symbol which is centrally fixed in the personalities of humans

- Pales proposed that there are no differences between the size of black and white penises

- Battle found that 40 percent of his black subjects reported that they felt that the genitals of black males were much larger than the genitals of white males

- Battle found that 2 percent of his white subjects reported that they felt that the genitals of black males were much larger than the genitals of white males

- Battle found that 60 percent of his black subjects reported that they felt that the sexual potency of black males is much stronger than the sexual potency of white males

- Battle found that 4 percent of white subjects reported that they felt that the sexual potency of black males is much stronger than the sexual potency of white males
- Battle found that white Americans feel guilty because of the way black Americans are treated
- Battle reported findings which indicate that some American whites still support negative black stereotypes
- Battle found that 15 percent of his freshmen group, 4 percent of his seniors and 15 percent of his outsiders reported that they felt that black male genitals were larger than white male genitals
- Battle found that none of his freshmen and senior groups and only 2 percent of his outsiders felt black male genitals were smaller than white male genitals
- Battle found that 9 percent of his freshmen group, 6 percent of his seniors and 11 percent of his outsiders reported that they felt that black females were more erotic than white females
- Battle found that only 3 percent of his freshmen group, 4 percent of his seniors and 2 percent of his outsiders reported that they felt that black females were less erotic than white females

CHAPTER 6
RACISM AND VICTIM'S SELF-ESTEEM

IN THIS CHAPTER we provide a brief overview of the construct of self-esteem and show how racist behavior affects victim's perceptions of self-worth.

I consider self-esteem to be a fundamental need and one of the most important variables affecting the lives of all groups of humans. I am of the opinion that self-esteem affects one's:

- accomplishments
- interactions with others
- achievement patterns
- levels of mental health
- state of well being.

(Battle, 1992, pp. 22; 1993, pp. 19; 1995, pp. 21)

Support for this position is provided by Dorothy Briggs when she said:

...A person's judgement of self influences the kinds of friends he chooses, how he gets along with others, the kind of person he marries, and how productive he will be. It affects his creativity, integrity, stability, and even whether he will be a leader or a follower. His feelings of self-worth form the core of his personality and determine the use he makes of his aptitudes and abilities. His attitude toward himself has a direct bearing on how he lives all parts of his life. In fact, self-esteem is the mainspring that slates each of us for success or failure as a human being....

Self-Esteem is a construct which:

...Refers to the perception the individual possesses of his/her own worth. An individual's perception of self develops gradually and becomes more differentiated as he/she matures and interacts with significant others. Perception of self-worth, once established, tends to be fairly stable and resistant to change.... (Battle, 1995).

To understand what self-esteem is, one must visit briefly with Freud's psychoanalytic theory. Freud proposed that the personality is comprised of three components or subsystems, the id, ego and superego. The id is the original part of the personality that contains all instincts. The id is the most powerful aspect of personality that contains the psychic energy or libido which is the major driving force of the personality. The id is the reservoir of man's innate primitive, biological drives (e.g. sex, thirst, hunger, aggression). Freud proposed that the id operates in accordance with the pleasure principle. Thus, its major concern is to reduce tension and obtain immediate gratification. The id at all times attempts to avoid pain and increase pleasurable experiences. The id, according to psychoanalytic theorists, represents the primitive purely selfish portion of personality which is not concerned with reality or moral factors. The id utilizes what Freud calls primary-process thinking, a primitive or infantile level of thinking which makes no allowances for reality.

The ego, unlike the id, is capable of reasoning and utilizing intellectual resources to provide gratification for the id and deal with the demands of reality simultaneously. The ego is the rational segment of the personality which utilizes properties such as judgement, perception, recognition and memory to permit the id to obtain tension reduction in an acceptable fashion. Thus, the ego utilizes what Freud calls secondary process thought (intellectual resources), in its efforts to permit id gratification. The ego is the mediator and controller of the personality which operates in accordance with environmental demands. Therefore, it has the delicate and often conflicting task of delaying id gratification and permitting its expression only when environmental demands are receptive to such expression.

The ego is an efficient system, but it is limited because it does not consider moral aspects of functioning. Therefore, Freud developed a third component of personality which he called the superego. The superego is comprised of the conscience and ego- ideal. The conscience represents our views regarding what we consider to be right or wrong, whereas the ego-ideal represents what we feel we "ought" to do or be. Hence self- esteem emerges from the ego-ideal which is a consequence of early interactions between parents or parent surrogates and the child. Thus, self-esteem is a subjective construct which is strongly tied to personality, namely the ego-ideal portion of Freud's superego.

Although early interactions between parents or parent surrogates and the child influence the youngster's self-esteem most strongly initially, as he develops other individuals (e.g. teachers, caregivers, authority figures) can exert either positive or negative effects on his perception of self-worth. Because of this, the behavior that racists direct towards victims can exert a significant effect on the recipient's self-esteem.

Among all of the colored groups in North America, racism has had the greatest negative effect on the self-esteem of aboriginal residents. Support for this position is provided by findings which indicate that:

- approximately 70 to 80 percent of aboriginal students drop put of school and do not obtain their high school diplomas
- violent deaths of aboriginals residing in Canada are more than three times greater than that of non-aboriginal Canadian residents
- the suicide rate for aboriginals residing in Canada is at least three times greater than that of non-aboriginals
- the suicide rate of aboriginal youth aged 15 to 25 years is approximately five times greater than that of their non-aboriginal counterparts
- the unemployment rate for aboriginals residing in Canada is significantly greater than that of their non-aboriginal counterparts
- the incidence of alcohol abuse for natives residing in Canada is significantly greater than that of their non-native counterparts.

In a study sponsored by Employment and Immigration Canada and Correction Services Canada, Battle, Saulnier and Christian (1990) interviewed recently released federal offenders in the Edmonton Metropolitan area and found that:

- twice as many natives than non-natives reported that they drank alcohol very often
- only 4.9 percent of natives reported that they had completed grade 12, whereas the value for non-natives was 33.7 percent
- natives comprised 35.9 percent of subjects who participated in the study, although they make up only 2 percent of the total Canadian population

- the self-esteem of natives was significantly lower (native mean total self-esteem score = 19.44; non-natives mean total self-esteem score = 22.33) than that of their non-native counterparts
- both aboriginals and non-aboriginals reported that low self-esteem was the main reason why they ended up being incarcerated.

Data derived from research findings (e.g. Wandzura, 1992; Battle, Saulnier, and Christian, 1990) generally indicate that aboriginal groups experience lower levels of self- esteem than their non-aboriginal counterparts. For instance, John Wandzura, principal of the Joe Duquette High School for aboriginal students in Saskatoon, Saskatchewan, administered the Culture-Free Self-Esteem Inventory for Adults to students attending his school and found that they earned self-esteem scores that were significantly lower than that of the standardization population (standardization total score mean = 23.08; Joe Duquette students total score mean = 20.57). The results earned by the students at the Joe Duquette school was also lower than those earned by students attending six high schools in the Province of Alberta. The mean total self-esteem scores for the Alberta schools were 24.66, 23.92, 23.10, 23.59, 23.43 and 23.76, whereas the value for the Joe Duquette school was 20.57.

Another group of colored residents living in the United States that have been vulnerable to the negative effects of racist behavior are Vietnamese Amerasians. Vietnamese Amerasians are the offspring of American servicemen and Vietnamese women who immigrated to the United States under the terms of the Amerasian Homecoming Act of 1989. Support for this position is provided by findings of a study conducted by Julie Hung. Hung (1993) translated the Culture-Free Self-Esteem Inventory For Adults into Vietnamese and had it administered to fifty-nine participants by directors of Amerasian programs in Minnesota, New Jersey, Connecticut and North Carolina. Results derived from the findings of the study indicate that the self-esteem scores of her subjects were significantly lower than that of the standardization population (standardization total score mean = 23.08; Amerasian participants total score mean = 16.53). Also, Amerasian participants earned scores that were significantly lower than that of the standardization population for each facet of self-esteem. The mean scores for the standardization population on the general, social and personal facets were 11.78, 6.62 and 4.68 respectively, whereas the values for the Amerasians who participated in the study were 8.03, 5.08 and 3.42 respectively.

Victims of negative prejudice and racist acts typically experience hostility which they generally cannot express or direct toward perpetrators who exploit them. Because of this victims tend to employ the defense of repression in their attempts to deal with this hostility and generally direct this anger toward themselves. Hostility which is directed toward the self typically results in depression and low levels of self-esteem. In their efforts to deal with these pathological conditions, victims often resort to excessive intake of substances such as alcohol or illegal drugs. This form of behavior however, is self-defeating and often results in a form of suicide that I call suffering hero type. The person who experiences this pathological condition cannot express intense hostility that he or she has towards perpetrators. Rather, they direct it toward themselves and reason in a very irrational fashion that "I cannot tell you how much I hate you, so I'll kill myself and you will be sorry forever." This form of behavior however, tends to have little effect on perpetrators because they tend to use the process of denial (deny that things exist) and the defense of rationalization (excuses for behavior to justify their actions).

Victims of negative prejudice employ the defense of displacement, a process in which they direct the hostility which results from negative prejudice and racist acts toward family members and individuals in their own ethnic group. Support for the position which assumes that victims of negative prejudice and racist acts tend to direct hostility towards the self is provided by research findings which indicate that aboriginals in North America tend to experience suicide rates that are three to five times higher than those of their non-aboriginal counterparts. Support for the position which assumes that victims of negative prejudice and racist acts tend to displace hostility towards family members and individuals in their own ethnic group is provided by overwhelming evidence which indicates that the greatest amount of violence occurs within families and among acquaintances.

Both quantitative data presented in this section and qualitative observations indicate that the behavior displayed by racists generally tends to exert a negative effect on the victim's self-esteem and well-being.

Summary

- self-esteem is a fundamental need that affects the lives of all groups of humans
- Briggs proposed that self-esteem is the mainspring that slates each of us for success or failure as a human being
- self-esteem is the perception that the individual possesses of his or her own worth
- Freud proposed that the id is the reservoir of a human's innate, primitive, biological drives
- Freud proposed that the ego is the rational segment of the personality
- Freud proposed that the superego is the moral segment of the personality
- Freud proposed that the conscience is the aspect of the superego that represents the individual's views regarding what he considers to be right or wrong
- Freud proposed that the ego-ideal is the aspect of the superego that represents the individual's views regarding what he feels he "ought" to do or be
- the behavior that racists direct towards victims can exert a significant effect on the recipient's self-esteem
- approximately 70 to 80 percent of aboriginal students drop out of school and do not obtain their high school diplomas
- the suicide rate of aboriginal youth aged 15 to 25 years is approximately five times greater than that of their non-aboriginal counterparts
- Battle, Saulnier and Christian report findings which indicate that the self-esteem of natives is significantly lower than that of their non-native counterparts
- Hung report findings which indicate that Vietnamese Amerasians on average earn self-esteem scores that are significantly lower than that of the standardization population
- victims of negative prejudice and racist acts typically experience hostility which they generally cannot express or direct towards perpetrators who exploit them

CHAPTER 7
BLACK-WHITE INTERVIEWS

INFORMATION IN THIS CHAPTER is taken from interviews with four Americans, two black, two white. It is important for the reader to note that the information incorporated in this section represents the views of only four Americans, not a substantial cross section of black and white Americans.

BLACKMAN

QUESTION: How do you see the black man?
ANSWER: The black man's biological system makes it difficult for him to acquire self- determination. He needs a revolution to facilitate the acquisition of self- determination. The black man is in a human predicament which because of limitations, brings about alienation (socially, politically, and economically). The black man needs to pursue and obtain particularly economic self-determination and of course self-determination in other aspects of the American society.

QUESTION: How do you see the black woman?
ANSWER: The American black woman is beautiful and is closer to becoming self actualized than the black man. The black woman is accepted more easily by the white community because she is less of a competitor with the white man. The white man and black woman currently rule America. However, this is changing and eventually we will conversely witness the black man and white woman controlling America. As a result of this developing trend the black woman must reorder her priorities because when the positions shift she will move from second position to fourth. Black women have in the past, dominated the social aspects of the black man, however this is shifting and currently the black man is accepting more responsibilities and is becoming more dominate in the control of the black family.

QUESTION: What does black religion mean to you?
ANSWER: Some black religions say that God is black, and that there is no available reliable literature that suggests that he is white. They say Jesus is black and came to relieve the black man of his oppression. Black religion is a cohesive, unifying force designed to unite blacks together.

QUESTIONS: How do you see black Muslims?
ANSWER: The black Muslims started in Chicago by Fart who said he was the messenger of Allah. Fart approached Elijah Mohammed who later became the leader of the black Muslim movement. The purpose of black Muslims is to unite blacks and develop a separate nation of blacks. Black Muslims are striving for self determination (educationally, politically and socially) in a society dominated by blacks. Personally I feel that is beneficial to some people for it develops dignity and proves to the black man that he can become self-sustained in American society. Most Muslims are from lower social economic status and Muslim doctrines provide them some hope. Today Muslimism is too constricting and does not give an individual an opportunity to develop total human potentialities. Black Muslims feels that the white man has in the past and currently is, exploiting the black man.

QUESTION: What are your views concerning black education?
ANSWER: Education should teach black children to realize their position in life and to be aware of what society will allow them to encounter because they are black. They should at all times know where they are in black society and white society as well. Black study departments on college campuses should not be separate, because knowledge is universal, not black or white or otherwise. Besides a black man does not need to go to university to learn how to be black. Black schools in black communities should be dominated by blacks.

QUESTION: How do you see the black man - white woman relationship?
ANSWER: This is indeed a strange relationship which however varies from individual to individual. The white woman is curious toward the black man because the white man has constantly put the black man down. The white man states that blacks are superior physically but nil mentally, as a result the white woman associates with the black man to get back at the white man. Few black-white

relationships stem from intellectual equality, they usually occur because of the white woman's curiosity toward the black man.

QUESTION: Please comment on the black riots in the U.S.A.
ANSWER: Riots are the result of extreme oppression of the black population. Blacks, because of their progress, felt the pain of oppression at this point more severely and as a result exploded. The white man holds the power position and the keys to rewards. Because of the white man's control of these, and of his denial to share them with the black man, he becomes even more frustrated and as a result riots erupt. Riots were good for the black psyche and spirit because they brought about more economical, social and political change than the non-violent movement. However, currently whites are, as in the past, attempting to buy blacks. Blacks who refuse to be bought are being oppressed.

QUESTION: What do you think of black athletes?
ANSWER: Because of various circumstances the black athlete represents the old notion of the entertainer. He is symbolic of old days in the south when blacks were chosen to sing, dance, show their teeth etc. for the enjoyment of the white man. The black entertainer who entertains for pay is better than most blacks financially and he generates more prestige and better social position than the average black; however he is still controlled by the white man. His success in sports is determined by the white man. Many athletes possess false impressions of their true abilities and because of their financial position they tend to develop superior attitudes. Black athletes can help other blacks by organizing more and developing more programs in the black community. Many blacks have made enormous sums of money but, through poor management, have lost all of their finances. Black athletes, regardless of ability, must display certain attitudes that the white man feels are desirable if they are to be successful as an athlete.

QUESTION: How do you see the black artist?
ANSWER: Black artists are basic to the black culture because they bring feelings to the consciences of the people. They have done a tremendous job because they brought out good things in black people; they are a sign of progress for minorities in general, from them lies the hope for the future. Black artists will continue to motivate and sustain black movements; furthermore black artists will eventually bring the white man out of his mental ghetto.

QUESTION: What are your views concerning the black soldier?

ANSWER: Shit! No black man in his right mind should fight in a war to assist the white man's interests. Black Americans are in a constant war with the white man because of the boundaries and barriers that he develops to inhibit the blackman. His fight is in the United States of America and if he should go to war he should fight here and kill as many whites as possible.

QUESTION: What is the major issue in the black-white dichotomy?

ANSWER: The black man has built this country and has been denied systematically and institutionally, those things that are necessary to accomplish self- actualization. The major problem is that whites have developed a rationale which makes blacks inferior and they have consistently maintained this rationale. He has used the teaching of the bible to maintain this rationale; he has used an evolutionary theory which suggests that blacks through evolution, have developed a smaller brain than whites and as a result are inferior intellectually. He has used genetic theories which suggest that blacks are inferior because their genetic strains are different from whites. The white man uses theories to justify his superiority over the black man and he uses the legislature and law enforcement systems to enforce these myths. Blacks must confront whites and bring about direct confrontations to prove, not to himself but to the white man that he can meet the challenge and throw the same shit back in the white man's face. Black men with self- awareness are more self-actualized than any white man can ever become because they are more down to earth.

QUESTION: Are there any solutions?

ANSWER: A solution is that the black man establish an economic base that will provide possibilities and opportunities to become self-actualized. The white man should provide this economic base for slave labor that blacks still haven't collected.

WHITE WOMAN

QUESTION: How do you see the black man?
ANSWER: I see a black man just as any other man. The important thing is the man and the race makes no difference to me. Black people, because of historical and genetical heritage are different, and this difference should be seen as something beautiful, not inferior. The problem is when we make comparisons and identify differences, we either assign labels of superiority or inferiority; differences should be recognized and enjoyed for what they are, not as a focus for comparisons. I feel guilty because I am white.

QUESTION: How do you see the black woman?
ANSWER: The only difference is in her appearance, Otherwise there is no difference. Black and white women are members of a minority with similar problems.

QUESTION: What does black religion mean to you?
ANSWER: Black religion is bible belt and lower class religion. Religious black people have made one achievement I cannot understand. Black people have been punished for hundreds of years, and still have not reacted to the white community with bitterness. This is remarkable, black people and black religion have made a tremendous contribution toward world peace and understanding. It is almost inconceivable that blacks can react positively in the American society after so many years of torture.

QUESTION: How do you see the black Muslim movement?
ANSWER: Muslims represent a backlash toward respectability and toward constructing a respectable self. Black Muslimism is an attempt by blacks to obtain middle class status. However, this type of striving will not produce positive results. The black Muslim movement will not last. The Muslims are not great any more.

QUESTION: What are your views concerning black education?
ANSWER: Schooling is of no prime need for either black or white; however meaningful education is desirable. All education should be an integrated process regardless of intelligence, age, etc. We don't need any more failure channels. Education is a device for passing old achievement ways to our children. People need education to become aware of their cultural heritage. There is little need for technical education. To be treated at a lower level

gives you a lower self-image, the experience of being a kid is the experience of being a "nigger" - you don't matter.

QUESTION: How do you as a white woman see the black man?
ANSWER: Opposite color has always been an attraction, especially during adolescence when youths have a crush on individuals of different races. White women are a symbol of liberation for black men, as a result black men seek white women. However human blackness is just one interesting aspect.

QUESTION: How do you feel black men see white men? Conversely, how do white men see black men?
ANSWER: Black and white men are competitors of sex, because of the myth of the black man being sexually superior to the white man. This myth is unfortunate for the woman also because she is the object involved in this competition. Both black men and white women are placed in a difficult position because they are both viewed as sex symbols by the white man; as a result black men and white women have a lot in common.

QUESTION: Please comment on the black rioting in American cities.
ANSWER: If you deny individuals middle class benefits and goods they will take it, as mere justice. Black demands for economic adequacy have been denied for hundreds of years; because of this denial riots were inevitable. The white population deserves more than the riots; riots were a mild response. Blacks should have burned the country, not just a few ghettos.

QUESTION: What do you think of the black athlete?
ANSWER: Physiologically blacks are somewhat different from whites, their pelvis is different and their Achilles tendon is more forward than whites, which gives them an advantage in running. Blacks found in sports, one of the few areas where they could obtain economic justice, to make money. Black inheritance, historically and genetically has facilitated them in athletics.

QUESTION: Please comment on the black artist.
ANSWER: Every culture has its own artists and African rhythmic patterns are as sophisticated as any. Black art, painting, sculpture, is the result of black historical and genetic foundations.

QUESTION: What are you views concerning the black soldier?
ANSWER: Black military men are on an achievement trip, some are brain-washed; in fact some feel grateful to be able to fight for the United States. I can't see why any black man would wear a United States military uniform. Black casualties during wars are very high, because they are poor, blacks suffer more.

QUESTION: What is the major issue in the black-white dichotomy?
ANSWER: The major problem is that people are still embedded with social cultural matricide that inhibits them and keeps them from viewing people as real humans. There are differences between blacks and whites but people refuse to talk about them because in our society, differences denote positions, either superiority or inferiority. People should be honest about these differences and treat them for what they really are, interesting but nothing more; and differences do not rate labelling. When we label people we tend to see them in a stereotyped way as objects, not people.

QUESTION: What solutions do you have concerning the black-white issue?
ANSWER: There are no group solutions but there are individual ones. The solution as I see it is to be human and to treat other individuals as humans with no reference to sex or color.

WHITE MAN

QUESTION: Describe a black man.
ANSWER: A black man is a man with black skin, who because of the contemporary world design is forced to learn early in his life about the role of skin color in social affairs. What a black man is in today's world is largely a function of the culture in which he is raised. Because certain cultures conspire against people with black skin it is sometimes made more difficult. What a black man is economically and socially is basically a function of whether his society is prejudiced in favor or against his skin color.

QUESTION: Describe a black woman.
ANSWER: A woman must adjust to the culture her man lives in no matter what the color of skin, therefore the fundamental disadvantages of being a black man directly influence a black woman. This is likewise true with the social and economic situation.

QUESTION: How do blacks see religion? Are they religious?
ANSWER: It seems to me that blacks have more emotion, passion and physical involvement in their religious worship than do whites, at least in the North American culture. Whether this is due to cultural heritage I do not know. Perhaps it is more related to their socio-ecomonic status where you commonly find them more passionately involved in religion among the lower income groupings. This holds true for Catholics and certain denominations of protestants as well. Social factors being constant though, I doubt if blacks are any more religious than anyone else.

QUESTION: What are black Muslims?
ANSWER: I'm not too sure, I think black Muslims are a sect or some type of religious denomination that stresses black identity, black culture and black history, and probably black separatism. As I understand it is kind of a puritan type movement that stresses clean living, the avoidance of things which poison the body (alcohol, drugs, etc.). I think it is essentially a non-violent organization which also stresses strong self-defense (which makes them different from the traditional Jewish form of non-violence).

QUESTION: How are blacks educationally?
ANSWER: Well, as is common knowledge, blacks are discriminated against probably even more so than their socio-ecomonic class would justify in a capitalist society. I suppose the evidence is convincing enough that people are educationally what they have been given the opportunity to be. Whether a people who have been deprived of an opportunity for a long period of time can recuperate or rebound rapidly when an opportunity is provided is hard to say. I suppose it is very possible that a group of people deprived of the opportunity to learn for a long time could develop cultural habits and mechanisms which in fact prevent them from learning effectively. But whether these are susceptible to change or not is hard to say.

QUESTION: How do white women see black men? And black men see white women?
ANSWER: This is hard to say, I suppose white women have a rather glamorous view of black men because of the high proportion of black men who are in athletics and entertainment (occupations which have a glamorous image regardless of race). Stereotypes about black men usually involve their sexual powers,

athletic powers and rhythmic abilities. The extent to which these stereotypes are accurate stereotypes is hard to say. My guess is that white women probably at either a conscious or unconscious level, have a glamorous image of black men because of the things that I mentioned.

QUESTION: How do white men see black women?
ANSWER: I don't know how to answer. I don't think the glamorous stereotype exists as much. I don't think black women are considered to be especially attractive; nor to be especially erotic or anything like that. I don't think there really is a consistent theme of how white men view black women.

QUESTION: What do you think about black riots?
ANSWER: I am ambivalent about this because on the one hand I have some kind of understanding of the things at a socio-economic and political level that go into making up conditions which cause people to riot. On the other hand I also see many factors at work in the causes of riots which are really of a non-justifiable nature. Black riots essentially come from frustration. I cannot personally understand the frustration because I am not a black man and have never been in a socio-economic condition that is basically closed, i.e. when upper mobility is virtually out of the question.

QUESTION: What do you think about black artists?
ANSWER: I don't think much about it. I am not knowledgable of anything that can be understood as black art, and am not knowledgeable of any black artist per se, excepting a few in the literary field, such as James Baldwin.

QUESTION: What kind of soldiers do blacks make?
ANSWER: They must be pretty good because they do most of the fighting as I understand. I have never been a soldier so really would not know. I do know that during World War II some of the Texas Black Infantry were considered to be some of the outstanding military foot soldiers in the United States Army. I suppose there would be a problem as far as from a military point of view with black soldiers who were subservient to white commanders who showed a lot of racism. And I suppose the converse would be true too. Whether this influences actual combat activity, I don't know.

QUESTION: What's the major difficulty with the black-white racial issue?

ANSWER: The major difficulty is that the blacks and whites don't get along. The cause of the difficulty is probable rooted in the American history of white supremacy which the black man cannot escape at any level of social existence. I am of the opinion that North America, especially the U.S.A.'s preoccupation with white supremacy is definitely less intense than it used to be but whether this makes any difference in the comparative problems of being a black man in a white man's society is hard to say. If all of the white supremacy sentiment immediately ceased in the U.S.A. society there would probably be still quite a bit of black-white conflict just because of the institutions which racism itself has created as well as psychological frames of mind in the black as well as white population. Most whites consider blacks to be partially inferior. This of course, at a basic level of understanding is true. The basic question is whether the inferior position of the black man is due to the fact that he has been forced into it by a racist society or basically was forced into it because of his inability to compete equally with whites who were by nature more superior. I suppose there has been a time when even many blacks accepted the concept of white supremacy but this certainly is becoming an obsolete idea - but still a functional subconscious trait.

QUESTION: What are the solutions?

ANSWER: I do not even fully understand the problem so I have a great deal of difficulty with solutions. There can be no solution until White America comes to recognize that America is a racially mixed country. And at the same time Black America comes to the realization that much of the present day milieu is the by-product of the cultural heritage which the white man today is no more responsible for than the black man. This is not a plea to escape responsibility but merely a piece of information to appease hatred and hostility.

BLACK WOMAN

QUESTION: Describe a black man.

ANSWER: Black men are beautiful; black men make me feel, in a special way, a way that I can't feel with a white man. Young black men are different from older ones, they have different ideas; black young men express themselves more openly. Young blacks are very strong in their beliefs and are willing to die for them. Black men are more sexually potent than white men. People say black superiority sexually is a myth, I don't feel it is a myth, black men are definitely superior sexually. Black men are distinctly different from all other men. White women who marry black men soon learn that black men have moods that are different from whites. Black men are superior sexually, musically and athletically.

QUESTION: Describe a black woman.

ANSWER: More black men marry white girls than black girls marry white men. It always seems to be the black man and the white girl. Black women are different from white women, they are more moody and they can be extremely evil. Black women are very aggressive; they have always been the dominant one in the black family because the black man rarely is around. Young black women are looking for security in marriage and less mobile husbands. There is real beauty in the old black woman who would perform subservient duties for whites, however young black women are different, they are more career oriented. Many black women have to take jobs outside the home to give their children many things that they couldn't have on just the husband's salary. I am often annoyed with white men who feel that black women are sexually potent and an easy fuck. Black women are good sexually because they can relax more, they are less inhibited than white women, they are extremely emotional individuals and they are not afraid to show their feelings.

QUESTION: What are your views about black religion?

ANSWER: I was born in Harlem and everyone in my district was Catholic, however I think black religion is beautiful, the singing, the spiritualism etc. When I was in university my husband and I would go to mass real early then later go over to the black church and sing and shout, we loved every bit of it. I love gospel music.

QUESTION: How do you see black Muslims?

ANSWER: I met some black Muslims and I wanted to go to their meeting but they refused to let me because I wasn't a member of their sect. I am somewhat confused about their objectives and where they are going. I thought Malcolm X was a great leader, for he lifted up the dignity of the black man. He taught blacks to stand up and fight for their rights. I believe in some things that Muslims propose but many things they support I cannot agree with.

QUESTION: How do you see the black man?

ANSWER: I get annoyed sometimes when I see a black man with a white woman; in fact sometimes I feel jealous because he prefers her to a black woman. It makes me upset when the only relationship the black man and white woman have is sexually. However, if they are really in love it is fine. My daughter is married to a white man and we love him very much, it never enters our minds that he is white. I would like to see my sons marry black women, but if they marry white girls, I would not put them down, I would accept their wives. My two brothers married white women, they had bad experiences with black women and as a result feel safer with white women.

QUESTION: How do you see the black man-white man relationship?

ANSWER: Black and white men are powerful competitors, the white man is constantly competing with the black man; he feels he has to be better than the black man. The white man is threatened by the black man, economically, intellectually and especially sexually.

QUESTION: What are your views on black education?

ANSWER: Many universities are offering black study programs, I feel that these programs are desirable, but should be seen as enrichment subjects. In fact I would like to see whites take more of these courses, then they may discover that we all are not musicians or athletes. We need more psychological testing that is geared for ghetto dwellers because current literature is not facilitating realistic growth for black children. Many blacks do not know other blacks. Southern blacks and northern blacks are different, most blacks don't know their national anthem. Blacks need more black literature, written by black writers.

QUESTION: Please comment on the black riots.

ANSWER: I am against rioting without a cause; however many real issues have inspired riots and if I was in the district where the rioting was occurring I would have participated. Blacks don't get anything by marching and singing, however this is how whitey likes it; when blacks start burning he says that they are ungrateful.

QUESTION: How do you see the black athlete?

ANSWER: There are distinct differences between blacks and whites, biologically and physiologically differences; these differences usually assist the blacks in sports. The black man has always been good in sports but some sports haven't been as open to him (e.g. hockey, swimming). The black athlete is definitely superior to the white athlete.

QUESTION: How do you view the black artist?

ANSWER: Nothing turns me on more than black entertainers. I can appreciate some white entertainers, but they just don't have soul. When I was talking to Louis Armstong a reporter asked him to define soul music, Louie said "If you have to describe soul music to someone he will never know what it is." Soul is emotional and you just can't verbalize it.

QUESTION: What do you think of the black soldier?

ANSWER: War is awful for it destroys the cream of the society, the youth. It also seems that the ratio of black deaths is higher than white deaths. When working in a hospital in New York I also noticed that most of the wounded were black.

QUESTION: What is the major difficulty in the black-white relationship?

ANSWER: The major problem with the black-white relationship is the matter of acceptance; not equality, but acceptance. This means that the black man wants the white man to accept him as an individual and to forget that he is black.

QUESTION: Do you have any solutions?

ANSWER: The solution to the racial issue is war, there must be a war. I can't see any other way out. Blacks need a stronger representation in Washington they need better leaders, who are a combination of Martin Luther King, Malcolm X, Rev. Jesse Jackson and Julius Bond.

SUMMARY

- black and white Americans tend to see the black man differently

- the black American man who was interviewed by Battle reported that he feels that the black man's biological system makes it difficult for him to acquire self- determination

- the black American man who was interviewed by Battle states that he feels the black man needs a revolution to facilitate the acquisition of self-determination

- the black American man who was interviewed by Battle, stated that he considers the American black woman to be beautiful and closer to becoming self-actualized than the black man

- the black American man who was interviewed by Battle said that he was of the opinion that the black woman is accepted more easily by the white community because she is less of a competitor with the white man

- the black American man who was interviewed by Battle said that eventually the black man and white woman will control America

- the black American man who was interviewed by Battle stated that black religion is a cohesive, unifying force designed to unite blacks together

- the black American man who was interviewed by Battle stated that the purpose of the black Muslim movement is to unite blacks and develop a separate nation of blacks

- the black American man who was interviewed by Battle said that most Muslims are from lower social economic status and that Muslim doctrines provide them some hope

- the black American man who was interviewed by Battle states that black schools in black communities should be dominated by blacks

- the black American man who was interviewed by Battle reported that he is of the opinion that black-white relationships occur because of the white woman's curiosity toward the black man

- the black American man who was interviewed by Battle said that black riots were good for the black psyche and spirit because they brought about more economical, social and political change than non-violent movements
- the black man who was interviewed by Battle said that black athletes can help other blacks by organizing more and developing more programs in the black community
- the black man who was interviewed by Battle stated that the black artist is basic to the black culture because he brings feelings to the consciences of the people
- the black man who was interviewed by Battle said that he feels that the black artist will eventually bring the white man out of his mental ghetto
- the black man who was interviewed by Battle stated that he feels very strongly that no black man in his right mind should fight in a war to assist the white man's interests
- the black man who was interviewed by Battle states that the white man uses theories to justify his superiority over the black man and uses the legislature and law enforcement systems to enforce these myths
- the black man and white man who were interviewed by Battle possess views regarding black-white relationships that differ significantly
- the white woman who was interviewed by Battle said that she felt guilty because she is white
- the white woman who was interviewed by Battle said that she cannot understand why black people have not reacted toward the white community with bitterness
- the white woman who was interviewed by Battle said that black people and black religion have made a tremendous contribution toward world peace and understanding
- the white woman who was interviewed by Battle said that it is almost inconceivable that blacks can react positively in the American society after so many years of torture

- the white woman who was interviewed by Battle said that white women are a symbol of liberation for black men and because of this black men seek white women
- the white woman who was interviewed by Battle said that black men and white women have a lot in common because they are both viewed as being sex symbols by white men
- the white woman who was interviewed by Battle said that blacks should have burned the whole country, not just a few ghettos
- the white woman who was interviewed by Battle said she couldn't understand why any black would wear a United States military uniform
- the white woman who was interviewed by Battle said that the solution to the black-white issue is to treat other individuals as humans with no reference to sex or color
- the white man who was interviewed by Battle said that a woman must adjust to the culture her man lives in
- the white man who was interviewed by Battle said that people deprived of the opportunity to learn for a long period of time can develop cultural habits and mechanisms which prevent them from learning effectively
- the white man who was interviewed by Battle said that white women probably at either a conscious or unconscious level have a glamorous image of black men
- the white man who was interviewed by Battle said; "I don't think black women are considered to be especially attractive or especially erotic"
- the white man who was interviewed by Battle said that he was not knowledgeable of anything that could be understood as black art
- the white man who was interviewed by Battle said that most whites consider blacks to be partially inferior
- the black women who was interviewed by Battle said that black men are more sexually potent than white men
- the black women who was interviewed by Battle said that black men are superior sexually, musically and athletically

- the black woman who was interviewed by Battle said that the black woman has always been the dominant one in the black family because the black man is rarely around
- the black woman who was interviewed by Battle said that black women are superior sexually because they can relax more, are less inhibited and more emotional
- the black woman who was interviewed by Battle said: "sometimes I feel jealous because a black man prefers a white woman over a black woman"
- the black woman who was interviewed by Battle said: "the white man is threatened by the black man economically, intellectually and especially sexually"
- the black woman who was interviewed by Battle said that the black athlete is definitely superior to the white athlete
- the black woman who was interviewed by Battle said that she was of the opinion that the major problem with the black-white relationship is acceptance, not equality
- the black woman who was interviewed by Battle stated that she was of the opinion that the solution to the racial issue is war
- the black woman who was interviewed by Battle said that blacks need a leader who is a combination of Martin Luther King Jr., Malcolm X, Jesse Jackson and Julius Bond

PART IV

INSTITUTIONAL RACISM

CHAPTER 8
INSTITUTIONS AND RACISM

MOST WRITERS PROPOSE two types of racism, individual and institutional. Individual racism involves overt acts by racist individuals that harm victims, whereas with institutional racism societies systematically oppress individuals and groups.

In this chapter we address the insidious issue of institutional racism and focus our emphasis on this aspect because it (institutional racism) is, in my view, a powerful force that can exert devastating effects on the lives of victims. Because of the pervasive negative effects that institutional racism can exert on the lives of colored residents, it is important for readers to understand the role that some institutions play in the facilitation of racist acts. Actually, institutions do not cause individuals to display racist acts, but they provide the power base in which racist individuals feel safe to discriminate against individuals they consider to be members of hated out-groups. Because of this perception of security and power, racist individuals often seek employment at certain institutions. Institutional areas of employment in which writers have reported that the practice of racism is a significant factor include police services, jails and prisons, the criminal courts and the military. Although there are other institutional systems that attract racists, the ones listed above are mentioned frequently.

RACISM AND POLICE SERVICES

Historically blacks in the United States and Canada have been the victims of racist acts and police brutality. Support for this position is provided by the data incorporated in many reports regarding the role that police brutality played in black riots. Riots are not a recent development within the American Society, but are almost as old as the country itself. In the United States there were black riots in 1712 and 1741. During the riots of 1741 a white judicial tribunal in New York city slaughtered an average of two blacks a week. In 1900 an average of two blacks were lynched in the United States by whites each week (one hanged, one burned). In 1919 seventy-seven blacks were lynched and of these fourteen were publicly burned and eleven burned alive. In 1909 Ida Wells Burnett stated that 3,284 men were murdered by mobs in the United States (Dubois, 1970). Additional riots in the United States of America included the Stampout riot of 1765, the Doctor's riot of 1788, the Spring Election riots of 1834, the Abolition riots of 1834 and 1835, the Flour riot of 1837, the Astor Place riots of 1849, the Police, Dead-rabbits and Bread riot of 1857 the Draft riots of 1863, the Orange riots of 1870-71 and the Railroad riot (Treat, 1877). The United States also experienced the Springfield, Ohio riot of 1906, the Springfield Illinois riot of 1908, the East Saint Louis riot of 1917, the Washington D.C. riot of 1919 and the Chicago riot of 1919.

In addition to those listed above the United States of America experienced many other riots including the following:

- Cincinnati, Ohio 1862
- New York, 1900
- Greensburg, Indiana 1917
- Chester, Pennsylvania 1917
- Philadelphia, Pennsylvania 1917
- Omaha, Nebraska 1919
- Charleston, 1919
- Longview, Texas 1919
- Knoxville, Tennesse 1919
- Tulsa, Oklahoma 1919
- Detroit, Michigan 1943
- Harlem, New York 1943

SOURCE: Report of the National Advisory Commission on Civil Disorders, 1968.

Literature reviews indicate that throughout the years blacks have been victims of police brutality. For instance, General Sheridan made the following comments regarding the brutality of police officers towards blacks in New Orleans:

...At least nine-tenths of the casualties were perpetuated by the police and citizens by stabbing and smashing in the heads of many who had already been wounded or killed by police; it was not just a riot, but an absolute massacre by the police ; a murder which the mayor and police perpetuated without the shadow of necessity....

SOURCE: Report of the National Advisory Commission on Civil Disorders, 1968, p.213.

Charges of police brutality on blacks occurred in practically every major city in the United States. For example, during the period 1965-1967 police maltreatment of blacks was isolated as being a major factor in the development of riots in New York City, Los Angeles, Detroit, Cleveland and Chicago. The National Advisory Commission on Civil Disorders (1968) suggests that in practically all cities that experienced riots between 1964- 1967 there existed hostility and bitterness between police and blacks which eventually resulted in violence. Because of the abuse that black residents received from police officers, the riots of the 1960's were as predictable in American society as Sunday's chicken dinner.

Civil disorders and violence are age-old problems that have plagued American society for generations. Support for this position is provided by historical documentation of the following requests by states to the Federal Government for assistance in dealing with civil disorders and violence during the period 1838 to 1967. During this period federal assistance was requested because of the:

- Buckshot war of 1838
- Dorr Rebellion of 1842
- San Francisco vigilance committee insurgence of 1856
- New Orleans unrest of 1873
- South Carolina riots of 1876
- Railroad strike riots of 1877
- Coeur D'Alene, Idaho mining disturbances of 1892
- Coxey army of unemployed disturbance of 1894
- Colorado mining strike disturbance of 1903
- Nevada mining disturbance of 1907
- Colorado Coal strike of 1914
- Washington D.C. race riot of 1919
- Omaha race riot of 1919
- Gary Indiana steel strike of 1919
- West Virginia coal mine warfare of 1921
- Bonus Army disturbance of 1932
- Detroit race riots of 1967

SOURCE: Report of the National Advisory Commission on Civil Disorders, 1968. pp.531-533

Findings of a study of twenty-eight police departments by the United States Civil Rights Commission (1962) indicate that the percentage of black officers ranged from as low as one (1) percent to a high of twenty-one (21) percent. The percentage of black supervisory personnel employed by these departments was even lower. Findings derived from a study of the 1943 Detroit Race Riot indicate that the Detroit police force which was virtually all white, arrested hundreds of blacks but few whites. Moreover, the officers killed seventeen blacks, but no whites.

The Kerner Commission found that police brutality and white racism were major factors that caused all of the riots in the United States subsequent to 1964. Some observers propose that police brutality and white racism have been major factors in the abuse of black residents because until recently, black officers have held few positions of power. For instance, the Kerner Commission (1968) found that:

1. Only one in every 26 black police officers is a sergeant.
2. One in every twelve white police officers is a sergeant.
3. Only one in every 114 black police officers is a lieutenant.
4. One in every 26 white police officers is a lieutenant.
5. Only one in every 235 black police officers is a captain.
6. One in every 53 white officers is a captain.

The ratio of black police officers to their white counterparts in positions of power has changed since the report of the United States Civil Rights and Kerner commissions were tabled, but blacks still occupy fewer positions of power in police services in the United States and Canada than their white colleagues.

In a recent study of Systemic Racism in the Criminal Justice System in Ontario, Canada (December, 1995), researchers found that during the period of 1978 to 1994 sixteen blacks in the province were shot by on duty officers; of these, 10 were killed. In 1988 police officers in Ontario shot 3 black men in a four month period. Also, within a fifty day period in 1991, 4 more blacks were shot by police officers in Ontario, Canada, a country that many foreigners consider to be peace-loving and fair, where all people are provided equality and justice. In Table 8:1 we list the names of the black victims who were shot by Ontario police officers.

TABLE 8:1: BLACK RESIDENTS SHOT BY POLICE IN ONTARIO, CANADA			
NAME	DATE OF SHOOTING	OUTCOME	POLICE FORCE
Andrew "Buddy" Evans	Aug. 9, 1978	killed	Metro Toronto
Albert Johnson	Aug. 26, 1979	killed	Metro Toronto
Michael Sargeant	Nov. 20, 1979	killed	Metro Toronto
Leander Savoury	Jan. 30, 1985	killed	Metro Toronto
Lester Donaldson	Aug. 9, 1988	killed	Metro Toronto
Earl Edwards	Nov. 7, 1988	injured	Ottawa
Michael Wade Lawson	Dec.8, 1988	killed	Peel Region
Sophia Cook	Oct. 27, 1989	injured	Metro Toronto
Marlon Neil	May 4, 1990	injured	Metro Toronto
T.T. (a young offender)	Sept. 20, 1991	injured	Metro Toronto
Vincent Gardner	Sept 26, 1991	killed	Nepean
Royan Bagnaut	Nov 3, 1991	injured	Metro Toronto
Jonathan Howell	Nov 9, 1991	injured	Metro Toronto
Raymond Lawrence	May 2, 1992	killed	Metro Toronto
Ian Coley	April 20, 1993	killed	Metro Toronto
Albert Moses	Sept. 29, 1994	killed	Metro Toronto

SOURCE: Commission on Systemic Racism in the Ontario Criminal Justice System. December, 1995.

Toronto police officers have killed eight blacks since 1992. The victims are:

1. Raymond Lawrence
   - age 22
   - killed in May of 1992
   - alleged that the victim ignored police orders to put down knife

2. Ian Coley
- age 21
- killed in April of 1993
- alleged that the victim was running away from police

3. Albert Moses
- age 41
- killed in October of 1994
- victim killed by police in a Toronto rooming house
- two police officers were cleared of wrong doing

4. Tommy Barnett
- age 25
- killed in January of 1996
- alleged that the victim lunged at an officer with a sword

5. Andrew Branwell
- age 24
- killed in March of 1996
- alleged that the victim pointed what appeared to be a handgun in the direction of the police officer

6. Wayne Williams
- age 24
- killed in June of 1996
- alleged that the victim was using a crow bar to smash car windows

7. Faraz Suleman
- age 16
- killed in June of 1996
- alleged that the victim tried to run an officer over with a stolen car

8. Hugh Dawson
- age 31
- killed in April of 1997
- alleged the victim was shot in his car during a drug bust

SOURCE: Edmonton Journal, April 5, 1997, A4, p.4.

The Ontario Civil Commission on Police Services have the power to conduct investigations of police conduct. However at the time of this writing, the Commission (OCCPS) comprised of civilians has never exercised its broad powers to address the issue of police conduct. The following findings of the study of systemic racism in the Ontario Justice system provide additional strong support for the position which purports that blacks are victims of racist acts directed towards them by police officers. Findings of the study indicate that:

1. Whites who were accused and charged by police for the same offense as blacks were more likely to be released by officers and less likely to be detained after a bail hearing.

2. Whites were treated more favorably by police officers although they were more likely than their black counterparts to have a criminal record and one that is more serious.

3. The pre-trial rate for blacks charged with drug possession was 15 times higher than that of their white counterparts charged with the same offense.

4. The pre-trial rate for blacks charged with obstructing justice was 13 times higher than that of their white counterparts who were charged with the same offense.

5. Accused blacks were more likely to be detained by police although they were less likely to have criminal records than their white counterparts.

6. Accused blacks were more likely to be denied release by police than their white counterparts

7. 74 percent of black respondents, 54 percent of Chinese and 47 percent of whites who participated in the study reported that they felt that police officers do not treat black people the same as they do white people.

   • Of those who perceive that there is differential treatment of black and white people, 93 percent of black, 91 percent of Chinese and 87 percent of whites reported that they felt that Toronto police officers treated black people worse than white people

   • Of those who perceive that there is differential treatment of Chinese and white people, 82 percent of black, 79 percent of Chinese and 79 percent of whites reported that they felt that Metropolitan Toronto police officers treat Chinese people worse than white people.

- Of those who perceive that there is differential treatment of black and Chinese people, 90 percent of black, 74 percent of Chinese and 87 percent of whites reported that they felt that Metropolitan Toronto police officers treat black people worse than Chinese people.

8. Blacks residing in Metropolitan Toronto reported that they were stopped more frequently by police officers than their white and Chinese counterparts.

The following four incidents are presented to illustrate the problem of "police stops." A civilian police employee describes a "ride-along" with uniformed officers:

> ...This white police officer was giving me a lot of information. We stopped four cars, and three out of the four cars had black guys in them. Every time he saw a black guy with a nice car, he said, 'That looks like trouble.' They weren't speeding, they weren't breaking any noise barrier with their radios; he still said this. I asked him why he says that, and he goes, 'Just the way they're dressed, and the way they're driving their cars' I [ask if they're speeding], and he said no....

A researcher records a black university student's experience when he tried to be a good citizen:

> ...A black university student waiting for a bus decided to do a good deed and moved three turned-over traffic cones left in the road which were causing traffic to swerve. As he put them on the sidewalk, a police car pulled up and two white male officers jumped out and asked him why he was moving the "fucking'"cones. He explained calmly, but was told in an aggressive manner to return them to the road. He refused, saying he didn't want to be responsible if someone was hurt. One officer kept swearing at him, calling him a "fucking smart ass" and started advancing towards him. At this time an elderly white woman came up and told the police she had seen him moving the cones and thought it was a good thing because there could have been an accident. The officers told her quite politely that they would handle the situation, and she shouldn't be so quick to defend 'these people' because they were proven troublemakers. The officers then asked the student for [identification]. He refused, saying he had done nothing wrong. There were six other people at the bus stop (five of them white) and they all tried to explain to the officers that the student had done the right thing. When they heard this, the police officers stopped being so loud and threatening, but they

were still angry. They went away, leaving the cones on the sidewalk, but none of them apologized for their insulting behavior....

A Chinese man describes stops in Metro Toronto:

...I've had three run-ins with the police in the last two years, all of which occurred when I was driving alone. I drive a 1991 BMW 385. One officer told me he pulled me over because I looked too young to be driving. I showed him my driver's license and he was shocked to learn that I was 23 years old. Two more times almost exactly the same thing happened. All the officers were white, between 25 and 35. I can understand being stopped once even twice, but three times in two years makes me believe those cops were racist. The stops happened twice in the Scarborough area and once in Chinatown....

A lawyer describes her black client's experiences over 18 months in a complaint to the Metro Toronto Police Chief:

...My client is a young man, without a criminal record, who owns and operates his own business...He tells me that since June of last year he has been pulled over 11 times by the police. This has happened in the Jane/Finch area, in Scarborough , out by the airport and in the downtown core. My client tells me that the police will see him drive by, they will then follow the car for a while, and eventually he is asked to pull over and produce identification. [He] has not been charged with any driving offenses or criminal offenses as a result of these incidents. The police officers who have pulled him over have been polite to him, and have indicated to him that 'they are only doing their job.' Nevertheless, my client does have a right not to be continually harassed in this fashion, and believes (I suspect, quite rightly), that the reason he is always being stopped is because he is a young black man driving a very nice car....

Paul Butler (1995, p.691), in his controversial paper entitled "Racially Based Jury Nullification: Black Power in the Criminal Justice System" summarizes the following three experiences in his efforts to show how some police officers treat black people:

...Erroll McDonald (executive editor of Pantheon Magazine) tells of renting a Jaguar in New Orleans and being stopped by the police simply "to show cause why I shouldn't be deemed a problematic Negro in a possibly stolen car"....

...Jazz trumpeter Wynton Marsalis said "Shit, the police slapped me up side the head when I was in high school. I wasn't Wynton Marsalis then. I was just another nigger standing out somewhere on the street whose head could be slapped"....

...Novelist Walter Mosley recalls, "When I was a kid in Los Angeles, the police used to stop me all the time, beat on me, follow me around, tell me I was stealing things"...

In the following report sociologist William Julius Wilson provides some insights regarding his concerns when he said:

...I wonder why I was stopped near a small New England town by a policeman who wanted to know what I was doing in those parts....

Some black Americans propose that there exists a moving violation in the United States called D.W.B. (Driving While Black) which refers specially to Afro-Americans.

The following four additional incidents are provided to illustrate the problem of racism in police services:

...A small group of 16 and 17 year old boys were waiting in a liquor store in a medium sized community in Northwestern Canada for two of their friends who were using the bathroom. Shortly after they entered the store two white officers "stormed" the store, searched all of the black kids and handcuffed the biggest one. These police officers however, did not search the white boy who was standing beside the big kid who was handcuffed. The police officer who handcuffed the black kid charged him with 'Theft by Conversion.' When the father of the boy who was charged spoke with a veteran black police officer who served on the force for more than 15 years, he said he had never heard of the charge. When a white friend of the boy's father spoke with a veteran white officer, he made the same response that the black officer made....

...A parent of a 16 year old black boy reports, "My son never has any problems when he goes out with his white friends; however, when he goes out on the weekends with his black friends he and his peers are routinely stopped by police, handcuffed and harassed." This parent said that she dreads weekends because on Friday and Saturday nights she cannot sleep. During this period she anxiously sits beside the telephone anticipating the worst and fearing that the police squad car will arrive at her home with her son in it....

...During conversation with a Canadian judge in a social setting, he said that when he had the responsibility of assisting American black athletes in acquiring immigrant status in Canada, he discovered that a large proportion of them had criminal records. I responded by assuring him that his observation of young black American males with criminal records are in concert with statistical data which confirms that police officers tend to lay more charges against black males and that more of these individuals have to endure court trials, are found guilty of charges and are awarded more severe sentences by judges that their white counterparts....

...I recall hearing a senior level police officer in Canada boasting about the fun he has raiding Chinese gambling parties. When good friends of this officer came to visit him, he would take them with him to raid Chinese gambling parties just for the 'fun' of it....

Data derived from my personal observations of youths aged 13 to 17 years for whom I provide psychological treatment clearly indicate that the black and aboriginal young people I serve are charged with crimes by police, arrested, handcuffed, fingerprinted, photographed and taken to trial for offenses at rates that are much higher than those of their white counterparts.

The incidents listed in this section are revealing. However, the highly publicized case of Rodney King, a black American who was brutally beaten by white Los Angeles police officers whose actions were captured on video is probably the most vivid illustration of a racist act of aggression and violence by members of a police service.

Because of the important role that police officers play in the community, I am of the opinion that they should be administered tests and racial attitude inventories prior to being hired and required to attend instructional sessions that have demonstrated effectiveness in assisting participants in acquiring the ability and desire to interact in an "appropriate" fashion determined by democratic principles with individuals of all ethnic and racial groups.

JAILS AND PRISONS

When compared to whites, a greater percentage of blacks per capita are incarcerated in the jails and prisons of the United States and Canada. Support for this position is provided by a vast amount of findings derived from research studies. Also my own personal observations support this position. For instance:

...While on sabbatical in 1993, a very good friend of mine with whom I attended university invited me to come to Chicago and address the social workers he supervised at the Cook County Jail. While working with this group, I was told that there were more than 9,000 inmates (approximately 85 percent blacks) in the facility and that the authorities were adding additions to the institution because there was a great need for extra space to the incarcerate their mostly black population of prisoners....

In jails and prisons in both the United States and Canada white inmates who commit the same offenses while incarcerated tend to receive less severe penalties than their black counterparts. For instance, in prisons in the province of Ontario, Canada, black inmates are most often found guilty of offenses and punished by being sent to segregation. Also, in Ontario prisons, both black and white inmates report that they feel correctional officers punish black prisoners more frequently, more severely and for less reason than white prisoners. In addition, both black and white correctional officers expressed similar concerns when they said:

1. *Black inmates are more severely punished for insignificant incidents such as answering back to a CO (correctional officer)*

2. *Twice as many blacks are put in segregation, not because they have done anything wrong, but because they are black.*

3. *Black inmates receive far harsher misconducts than white inmates due to the perception that black inmates are more violent or are instigators in most incidents.*

4. *A white inmate may use 'profane' language towards a white officer and nothing happens. A few moments after, a black inmate may just suck his teeth towards the same officer and [he] receives a misconduct. (p.304).*

Data derived from research studies provide strong evidence which indicates that individuals who function as guards and corrections persons in jails and prisons display racism and brutality towards inmates. What is not as clear is whether this behavior is due to pathological conditions within individuals who work in jails and prisons or if their actions are due basically to the institution (e.g. jail, prison) in which they work. In an attempt to identify factors that may be responsible for guards and correction officers displaying racist, cruel and brutal behavior towards inmates, Philip Zimbardo created a simulated prison in the basement of the psychology department at Stanford University. In his experiment, Zimbardo flipped a coin to designate one-half of the young men who participated in the study to function as guards and the other half to serve as prisoners. Zimbardo summarized his observations in the following fashion:

> *...At the end of only six days we had to close down our mock prison because what we saw was frightening. It was no longer apparent to us or most of the subjects where they ended and their roles began. The majority had indeed become "prisoners" or "guards," no longer able to clearly differentiate between role-playing and self. There were dramatic changes in virtually every aspect of their behavior, thinking and feeling. In less than a week, the experience of imprisonment undid (temporarily) a lifetime of learning; human values were suspended, self-concepts were challenged, and the ugliest, most base, pathological side of human nature surfaced. We were horrified because we saw some boys ("guards") treat other boys as if they were despicable animals, taking pleasure in cruelty, while other boys ("prisoners") became servile, dehumanized robots who thought only of escape, of their own individual survival, and of their mounting hatred of the guards....(Aronson, 1972. p.6)*

I suspect that both personal qualities and institutional factors compel guards and correction officers to respond with cruelty and brutality towards inmates they are mandated to monitor.

I am of the opinion that guards and correction officers should be administered psychological tests and racial attitude inventories prior to being hired, and be required to attend instructional sessions that have demonstrated effectiveness in preparing participants to interact in a mutually respectful fashion with individuals who comprise all ethnic and racial groups.

CRIMINAL COURTS AND RACISM

As mentioned earlier in this section, beliefs are very powerful dispositions that generally exert a strong effect on the behavior one emits. For instance, if a criminal court judge has incorporated in his psyche system, the belief that blacks are more predisposed to committing criminal acts than whites, he will find more blacks guilty of charges laid against them per capita than whites. In addition, chances are, if a judge possesses this belief about blacks, he or she will award them more severe penalties than their white counterparts for the same offense. Support for this position is provided by findings of a recent study (December , 1995) entitled "Report of the Commission on Systemic Racism in the Ontario Criminal Justice System." Findings of this major study indicate that::

- 58 percent of black participants reported that they felt that judges do not treat blacks the same way that they treat whites.
- 31 percent of Chinese participants reported that they felt judges do not treat blacks the same way that they treat whites.
- 36 percent of white participants reported that they felt judges do not treat blacks the same way they treat whites.
- 80 percent of those blacks, Chinese and whites who reported that they felt there was differential treatment of blacks and whites by judges said that they were of the opinion that judges treated black defendants worse than white defendants.
- The majority of defense counselors (40 percent) who are mostly white, reported that they felt that blacks are not treated fairly in the Ontario Justice System.
- 33 percent of provincial division judges appointed since 1989 reported that they felt that whites were treated better than blacks in the Ontario Criminal Justice System.
- A larger percent of blacks who are convicted are given prison sentences than their white counterparts who are convicted for the same offenses.
- Black convicted men were less likely than their white counterparts to have a criminal record or a lengthy record.
- Black convicted men were more likely than their white counterparts to have contested the charge, been detained before trial and been prosecuted by indictment.
- During the period 1986-1993, black women were placed in Ontario prisons at a rate per capita that was 7 times greater than that of their white counterparts.
- During the period 1986-1993, black men were placed in Ontario prisons at a rate per capita that was 5 times greater than that of their white counterparts.
- During the period 1992-1993 pre-trial imprisonment of blacks for discretionary charges was 27 percent greater than that of whites.

- During the period 1986-1993 the number of black prisoners admitted to Ontario prisons increased by 204 percent, while during the same period the number of white prisoners increased only 23 percent.

The following remarks provide support for the position which assumes that crown prosecutors and judges display racist behavior while working in the Ontario Criminal Justice System:

...THE COURT: *It is on behalf of one of the accused that there are no aggravating factors to be considered. I respectfully disagree. A sexual assault itself, the sexual nature of it, is a very aggravating factor. Three male persons overpowered the victim. They did so at night.* **They did it to a stranger and not one of their own, and when I say one of their own, somebody they knew or a member of the - or a person who was a person of the group of the ethic origin of both the accused....**

...THE COURT: *In Toronto, in these courtrooms, sometimes I send young men from Vietnam to jail rather severely for offenses. They've been in Canada a short time; they've been in Canada a year or two or three, and I have to work out a kind of sentence that appears to have no bias. We're supposed to treat everyone in front of us the same way. Again and again I have to lay out - thankfully not again and again - but often I have to lay out sentences trying to make it clear in the circumstances of recent immigrants' arrival into Canada, on a charge of threatening or extortion, that's sometimes connected with Vietnamese gangs and sometimes with not too much evidence in front of me on a sentencing hearing. I lay out some severe sentences that perhaps wouldn't apply in the same set of facts with someone who'd been in Canada 20 of 30 years....*

...THE COURT: *The most recent report I had [about criminal proceedings in China] was of a gentleman convicted in Beijing for putting white wine in the mai tai bottles and selling it. You know what the penalty he received was. Prostitution among other crimes have been similarly punished. So perhaps Mr. Ho's at the stage where he'll have to learn that even our society is not quite as weak as he thinks it is....*

...*He's from China, I understand that, but it is still Canada...People have to obey the law....*

...*[To* THE DEFENDANT]: *You come from Canton, you were born there and you've lived long enough to know what the law is like there. [In] the most recent reported case that I've found...a gentleman put white wine in the mai tai bottles and sold it as mai tai . The penalty that he received was that of execution by a bullet in the back of the neck. So, you know what the rules are there, and I'm sure that you're thinking that you've come to a very soft society and will just get a slap on the wrist. Now, we don't deal with criminals in the same way, but you've still got to be dealt with as a criminal because that's what you are... .*

...You've brought dishonor on your father's name and you know the cruelest form of oath in China...You have got to learn, sir, that this is a country where the laws must be obeyed. You will be given credit for the time you spent in pre-trial custody, namely six days...You will be sentenced to a period of incarceration of nine days....

SOURCE: Racism In the Ontario Criminal Justice System. December, 1995. pp. 227-229.

Further support for the assumption that racism occurs in the criminal justice system of Ontario is provided by the following statements offered by duty and defense counsels respectively:

...DUTY COUNSEL: I've had problems with one particular judge on a number of occasions. For example, I had a young Vietnamese client who was charged with theft. The judge proceeded to comment that he had read in a New York paper how Vietnamese gangs were taking over the streets. There wasn't a suggestion that this young person was in a gang, or that he was a member of a Vietnamese gang, or that he came from New York...This judge makes comments like that quite frequently....

...DEFENSE COUNSEL: Most criminal defense lawyers know of judges who have a reputation for holding racist views, and being biased against certain groups (Jews, blacks, etc)...If you have a non-white accused, you may do everything to avoid a particular judge, or to work out a joint submission with a crown on a plea or be careful to preserve avenues of appeal on a trial....

SOURCE: Racism In The Ontario Criminal Justice System. December, 1995, pp. 227-229.

The data listed above regarding racism in the justice system in Ontario, Canada listed in this segment of the chapter are similar to those reported in the discriminatory administration of Justice section of the American document entitled "Report of the National Advisory Commission on Civil Disorders" which indicate that:

- blacks received discriminatory treatment in the courts
- lower courts act as an arm of the police departments rather than as an objective arbiter in truly adversary proceedings
- presumption of guilt is the norm when police officers testify against blacks (1968, p. 14)

The following report is offered to provide an additional illustration of operations that occur in Criminal Justice Systems.

...During October, 1996, the same group of crown prosecutors in Edmonton, Alberta Canada who spent a day in court trying a youth for "Theft by Conversion" of a bottle beer that was never found (see pp.135-136), failed to submit documents within the required time period for application to have a youth who viciously assaulted and shot a black youth tried in adult court. Because of this the presiding judge ruled that the perpetrator who shot and fired upon the black youth five (5) times would be tried in youth court....

Unfair treatment of blacks by criminal court judges is not a recent occurrence. For example Wolfgang (1952), in his study of criminal homicide in the city of Philadelphia, Pennsylvania, between the years of 1948 and 1952 found that:

- 81 percent of blacks were found guilty, whereas the value for whites was 62 percent
- regardless of the degree or level of the charge, blacks received more severe sentences
- blacks received more severe sentences than whites although they were more often provoked by their victims
- blacks received more severe sentences although fewer blacks than whites possessed a previous police record. (pp. 299-309)

Additional support for the position which holds that blacks are treated unfairly by criminal court judges is provided by findings which indicate that:

1. In 1930 in the same Texas community
   - a black man was fined $12.50 for raping a black woman
   - a black man was given the death penalty for raping a white woman

2. During the period 1930 through 1971, 3859 individuals were executed in the United States; 53 percent were black, although blacks made up less than 10 percent of the American population.

SOURCE: Battle, J. An Anatomy of An American Blackman: A Comprehensive Text of Black-White Relations. 1973.

Wynton Marsalis expressed concern held by many black Americans when he said:

> ...*My worse fear is to have to go before the criminal justice system....*

SOURCE: Butler, 1995. pp. 691.

Historical facts and contemporary observations have led Paul Butler (1995, pp.706) to assert that black jurors have a moral right to use jury nullification in the cases of some blacks. He offers two reasons to support his position. These are because:

1. The idea of "the rule of law" is more mythological than real
2. "Democracy", as practiced in the United States, has betrayed African- Americans far more than they could betray it.

Butler cites the following cases as evidence to support his point-of-view.

- Plessy versus Ferguson, 163 U.S. 537 (1896): Holding that racial segregation in public transportation, mandated by legislation, does not violate the equal protection clause of the Fourteenth Amendment, and rejecting argument that such racial separation treats African- Americans as inferior
- Dred Scott versus Sandford, 60 U.S. (19 How.) 393, 404-07 (1857): Declaring that slaves were not "citizens" within meaning of constitution because at time of framing of constitution they had been "considered...a subordinate and inferior class of beings, who had been subjugated by the dominant race, and, whether emancipated or not, yet remained subject to their authority" and were "so far inferior, that they had no rights which the white man was bound to respect." (pp.707)

A number of writers have proposed that the actions of some judges who possess the belief that blacks are more violent than whites may have been influenced by authors such as William Sweet, Frank Erwin and Vernon Mark who said, in their paper entitled "Role of Brain Disease In Riots and Urban Violence":

> ...If slum conditions alone determine and initiated riots, why are the vast majority of slum dwellers able to resist the temptation of unrestrained violence? Is there something peculiar about the violent slum dweller that differentiates him from his peaceful neighbor? It would be more than passing interest to find what percentage of the attempted and completed murders committed during the recent wave of riots were done without motive. We need intensive research and clinical studies of the individuals committing the violence. The goal of such studies would be to pinpoint, diagnose and treat these people with low violence thresholds before they contribute to further tragedies....

B.J. Mason, in Ebony, February 1973, states that Drs. Sweet, Mark and Erwin's letter presents racial overtones and at the same time advocates a national screening program designed to identify blacks who may commit violent crimes.

The senate appropriations committee in response to Dr. Sweet's proposal instructed the National Institution of Mental Health to award a $500, 000 grant to Dr. William Sweet, chief of neurosurgery at the Massachusetts General Hospital, to determine if there is any connection between violent behavior and brain disease. Dr. Sweet was especially requested to develop a technique of identifying and controlling individuals who commit senseless violence. Dr. Sweet furthermore was commissioned to develop means of identifying and controlling those individuals who constantly experience difficulties with legal officials for minor crimes, assaults and as a result vacillate between incarceration and parole.

The Justice Department Law Enforcement Assistance Administration, closely following the example set by the Senate Appropriations Committee, appropriated $108,930 to two of Dr. Sweet's colleagues, Dr. Frank Erwin, a psychiatrist, and Dr. Vernon Mark, chief of neurosurgery at Boston City Hospital, to support brain or behavioral control research. The Justice Department's Law Enforcement Assistance Administration requested Drs. Erwin and Mark to develop means of determining the incidence of brain disorders in a state penitentiary for men, to establish their presence in a civilian population and to improve, develop and test the usefulness of electrodes and brain surgery (Ebony, February 1973).

Another proponent of psychosurgery, Dr. V.J. Andy, neurosurgeon at the University of Mississippi medical center states: "I think that those who are involved in any uprising such as those in Watts or Detroit could have abnormal brains. Those people should undergo tests with whatever capacity we now have. People who are unstable and explosive should then be operated on because society demands correction or appropriate control." (Ebony Feb. 1973, pp.65)

Dr. Alvin Poussaint, Associate professor of Psychiatry at Harvard University Medical School, commenting on the Justice Department's sponsoring of the brain alteration study states: "The study is racist." It assumes that black people are genetically damaged, and that they are so animal and savage that whites have to carve on their brains to make them human beings. (Ebony Feb. 1973, pp.64) Dr. Poussaint, reacting to Dr. Sweet's statement that many senseless incidences of violence occur in the urban ghettos, states that whites consider black violence to be senseless, because it is their way of not looking at the system and seeing how it produces criminals. Instead of saying that blacks commit crimes because they're out of work or out of a thousand other things, they say it is because of brain damage. Dr. Poussaint further states that it is because of a spinoff of the old genetic theory which holds that blacks commit crimes because of inferior intelligence which goes one step further by insisting that not only are blacks retarded and dumb, but they also have some brain activity out of whack. (Ebony, Feb. 1973)

Another writer, Thomas William (1901) made one of the most demeaning statements regarding blacks and violence when he said:

> ...*the most heinous crimes are by those who read and write and are members of black churches; by black culprits who are sinners fallen from grace....He further states that, if blacks were convincingly assured of personal security, all the maldignity of his slumbering savagery would immediately find expression in the most revolting acts of physical lawlessness....*

Historical accounts of violent acts perpetuated by whites and directed toward blacks (e.g. Lynching) make it clear that violence in the United States of America is not limited to any racial group. The following statement regarding violence and brutality offered by President Woodrow Wilson provides support for this position:

...The drive to revenge is connected with the drive to win the battle, and "to be victorious you must be brutal and ruthless"....

SOURCE: Towards Social Change. pp.184.

Many blacks feel that white police officers tell lies during court proceedings in their efforts to convict blacks and that judges who are usually white, generally support the officer's testimonies. In the following we provide an example from an actual court trial to illustrate this tendency:

...One white police officer testified under oath that he searched only the defendant; another white police officer testified that he did not search anyone during the incidence in which two black youths were arrested. Four young men who were present at the location where the incidence occurred, and the defendant who was being tried testified that three of the black males were searched during the incident. Also, a witness for the prosecutor testified that the officers searched the men. Inspite of this, the judge found the defendant guilty....

In the following letter entitled "Father-To-Son," a father encourages his child to use the experience of being exploited to motivate himself to achieve success:

FATHER-TO-SON

DEAR SON:

PLEASE THINK POSITIVE AND USE THE RULING OF "THEFT BY CONVERSION OF A BOTTLE OF BEER" TO:

1. SHOW OTHERS THAT YOU WERE RULED GUILTY OF A FALSE CHARGE OF TAKING A BOTTLE OF BEER FOR APPROXIMATELY FIVE SECONDS AND RETURNING IT TO A SHELF.

2 SHOW OTHERS THAT YOU WERE CHARGED BY A POLICE CONSTABLE OF AN ACT THAT YOU DIDN'T COMMIT.

3. SHOW OTHERS THAT YOU WERE RULED GUILTY OF "THEFT BY CONVERSION" ALTHOUGH THE POLICE OFFICER WHO LAID THE CHARGE REPORTED ONLY THE FOLLOWING IN HIS GENERAL OCCURRENCE REPORT NARRATIVE:

   A. PROPERTY
      (1 BOTTLE OF BIG ROCK TRADITIONAL ALE
      $2.95 + TAX = $3.25)

B. Exhibits (none)

4. Show others that you were given a conditional discharge of charges rather than an unconditional one because you refused to go along with the prosecutor's offer and say that you took a bottle of beer while waiting for your friends to come out of the bathroom when you didn't take anything.

5. Show that you were ruled guilty of a charge by Your Honor, who is white, based on the testimony of an all white group, which included the Crown Prosecutor, the two Constables and the two store employees.

6. Motivate you to utilize your potential fully in both academics and sports.

7. Motivate you to achieve success in academics, sports and relationships.

8. Commit yourself to helping others and doing the best that you can to ensure that everyone is treated fairly.

9. Live an exemplary life in which you do God's will and do the very best that you can to help others who are less fortunate than you are.

With Unconditional Love, Always, Your Dad.

Because of the important role that judges play in society, I am of the opinion that they should be administered psychological tests and racial attitude inventories prior to receiving assignments, and encouraged to attend instructional sessions that have demonstrated effectiveness in assisting participants in acquiring the ability and desire to provide individuals who comprise all ethnic and racial groups fair treatment and respect based on our democratic principles of equality of rights and opportunities for all residents.

RACISM IN THE MILITARY

Although racism has always been a factor in the military, the American black man has through the years, established a reputation as being a rugged courageous fighting man. He has fought effectively for his country during all its confrontations, from the War of Independence to Desert Storm. The first man, black or white, to give his life for American freedom was a black man, Crispus Attucks. Attucks was not a soldier but a runaway slave from Frammingham, Mass. who was killed during the Boston massacre. During the War for Independence there was an average of thirty-five blacks in each regiment of the continental army. Approximately three thousand blacks fought during the War of Independence for the liberation of the United States of America. Seven hundred- seventy five of these men served under General George Washington. (Woodson, 1966)

When the Civil War came along a major decision was to decide whether or not to arm blacks and permit them to fight against white Americans. This question seems to be present to some degree even today. Some contemporary whites, as in the past fear that if blacks are armed they will revolt against the white community. This fear of black revolt was in this writer's opinion the reason for the hesitation as to whether blacks should be able to fight with union forces during the civil war. On the issue of whether blacks should be permitted to fight, Fredrick Douglas wrote:

> *...Colored men were good enough to fight under Washington. They were not good enough to fight under Andrew Jackson. They are not good enough to fight under General Halleck. They were good enough to help win American Independence, but they are not good enough to help preserve that independence against treason and rebellion....*

Continuing with the question of whether blacks should be permitted to fight and kill American white men during the Civil War, James Madison Bell who served with John Brown wrote:

Shall we arm them? yes, arm them: Give to each man
* a rifle, a musket, a cutlass or sword;*
Then on to charge: Let them war in vain
Where each may confront with this merciless Lord,
And pruge from their race, in the eyes of the brave,
The sting and scorn now attending the slave:
I would not have the wrath of the rebel to cease,
Their hope to grow weak nor their courage to wane,

Till the contrabands join the securing peace,
Whose glory shall vanish the last galling chain,
And win for their race an undying respect
In the land of their prayers, their tears and neglect.
Is war won for freedom? then why, tell me why
Should the wronged and oppressed be debarred from fight?
Does not reason suggest it were noble to die
In the act of supplanting a wrong for the right?
Then lead to charge: for the end is not far,
When the contraband host are enrolled in the war

Finally, after considerable discussion and controversy, blacks were employed by the union forces to assist in fighting the rebel confederate states. Blacks again proved to be highly courageous and effective fighters. Roscoe Jamison's poem about blacks during the Civil War exemplifies this point. He wrote:

These truly are the brave
These men who cast aside
Old memories, to walk the
Blood-stained pave
of sacrifice, joining the solemn tide
That moves away, to suffer and to die.
For freedom, when their own
Is yet denied:
O pride: O prejudice. When they pass you by
Hail them the brave, for you
now crucified. (DuBois 1970)

It is felt by many and rightly so, that the black soldier was probably the determining variable which enabled the union forces to defeat the confederate separatists. It is quite conceivable that, had it not been for the black Americans involvement during the Civil War, the United States of America as it is today may not be a reality. Historians suggest that blacks proved to be the determining factor in the Civil War. For instance in 1864, when Grant attacked Richmond his first decision was to bring in six thousand black soldiers. Their part in the siege and fall of Richmond was such that a black regiment was given the honor of being among the first who marched into the capital.

Blacks represented their country well in combat and in numbers as well. For example on July 15, 1865 there were a total of one hundred twenty-three thousand black soldiers in the union army; there were one hundred twenty infantry regiments, twelve heavy artillery regiments, ten batteries of light artillery and seven calvary regiments. Blacks comprised approximately twelve percent of the union total military force. (Sable Arm, 1965)

Following the Civil War there were black soldiers fighting in the west assisting in the country's confrontation with the Indians. The ninth and tenth cavalries were the most famous black regiments during the campaign. These rugged, expert horsemen who were organized in 1866, fought the Apache, Comanche, Kiova and Sioux. (Gilligan, 1969)

Further evidence concerning black soldiers' courage and commitment is presented by Norwood P. Hallowell, Colonel, 55 Massachusetts Infantry in 1892 when he wrote:

We called upon them in the day of our trial when volunteering had ceased, when the draft was a partial failure and the country system a senseless extravagance. They were ineligible for promotion, they were not to be treated as prisoners of war. Nothing was definite except that they could be shot and hanged as soldiers. Fortunate indeed it is for us, as well as them, that they were equal to the crisis; that the grand historic moment which comes to a race only once in many centuries came to them and that they be recognized. (Sable Arm, 1956)

Blacks represented their country well again during World War I. For example, the 369th, the first black regiment to fight in World War I, was under fire for one hundred ninety-one days without relief, the longest ordeal of any United States unit. During World War I, two million two hundred ninety thousand, five hundred twenty-seven blacks registered for service; of these four hundred fifty eight thousand, eight hundred thirty-eight were accepted and two hundred thousand of these were shipped to Europe. (Sable Arm, 1956)

Approximately nine hundred thousand black men and women served their country during World War II. Blacks continued their meritorious service to their country during the Korean conflict, in the Vietnam conflict and most recently, in the Desert Storm initiative. History has proved that the black soldier has been equal to the challenge of the crisis.

Recently in the highly publicized Somalia affair, Canadian paratroops conducting peace-keeping functions in this African country (Somalia), made racist statements, displayed racist actions, tortured, and killed a black Somali teenager named Shidane Arone during March of 1993. Shidane was killed while in custody of members of the Canadian Airbourne Regiment. Prior to the killing, one soldier, Clayton Matchee allegedly held a weapon to Arone's head posing for pictures taken by Kyle Brown, another member of the unit. (Edmonton Journal, Thursday April 4, 1996. p.A3)

In the United States military, accusations of racist actions by white personnel continue to be made. These allegations of racism toward black military personnel are not new and have persisted since the first black troops took arms to fight for the United States of America to ensure that liberty and freedom be provided for all Americans.

SUMMARY

- historically blacks have been victims of racists acts and police brutality

- blacks in every major city in the United States have reported incidences of police brutality

- police maltreatment of blacks was identified as being a major factor in black riots

- the Kerner Commission found that police brutality and white racism were major factors that caused all of the riots in the United States subsequent to 1964

- ten black residents in the province of Ontario were killed by on-duty police officers during the period 1978 to 1994

- eight black males were killed by police officers in Toronto, Ontario during the period 1992 to April, 1997

- a greater percentage of blacks per capita are incarcerated in the jails and prisons of the United States and Canada

- in jails in the United States and Canada white inmates who commit the same offenses while incarcerated generally receive less severe penalties than their black counterparts

- guards and correction officers in jails and prisons display racism and brutality towards inmates

- Zimbardo found that the roles individuals played in prison settings influenced their behavior

- findings from a study of the Ontario Criminal Justice System indicate that blacks, Chinese and whites felt that judges treated black defendants worse than white defendants

- 33 percent of provincial division judges reported that they felt whites were treated better than blacks in the Ontario Criminal Justice System

- during the period 1986 - 1993, black men were placed in Ontario's prisons at a rate per capita that was 5 times greater than that of their white counterparts

- during the period 1986 - 1993, black women were placed in Ontario's prisons at a rate per capita that was 7 times greater than that of their white counterparts

- unfair treatment of blacks by criminal court judges is not a recent occurrence
- during the period 1930 - 1971, 53 percent of the individuals who were ordered executed by judges were black, although blacks made up less than 10 percent of the American population
- some practitioners and researchers have reported that they are of the opinion that individuals who participate in civil unrest could have abnormal brains
- Poussaint asserts that the brain alteration studies funded by the American Justice Department Law Enforcement Administration were racist studies
- blacks comprised approximately twelve percent of the union military forces during the Civil War in the United States
- after considerable controversy, blacks were employed by the union forces to fight the rebel confederate states
- blacks proved to be highly courageous and effective fighters
- blacks proved to be the determining factor in the Civil War
- Canadian peace-keeping military personnel tortured and killed a black Somali youth

CHAPTER 9
SCHOOLS AND RACISM

IN THIS CHAPTER we delineate the role that teacher expectations play in racism, show how racism is practiced in schools and provide an overview of black education and black history.

TEACHER EXPECTATIONS AND RACISM

Teachers who perceive that black students are not as capable of performing academics as their white counterparts typically set lower expectations for their black pupils. Also, when teachers establish these expectations the result is usually a self- fulfilling prophecy, characterized by a tendency to behave in a fashion that is in concert with previously established expectations. This occurs because once expectations are set, both the child and teacher tend to behave in a fashion to ensure that prophecies are fulfilled. Research findings support this position and indicate that teachers who set high expectations for their students obtain higher levels of academic performance from them than teachers who set low expectations. The expectations that teachers possess regarding what they feel students can and cannot learn, often become self-fulfilling prophecies. Because of this, students tend to learn as little, or as much as their teachers expect. Also, when teachers expect less from students, they tend to treat them differently and usually:

- give them less direct instruction
- have them sit farther away from the teacher's desk
- ask them to do less work
- provide them fewer opportunities to learn new material
- call on them less frequently and when they do, the questions they ask are generally simple, basic non-complex ones
- provide them less time to respond to questions and give them less help when their answers are incorrect.

In the case of black-white relationships the black student may tend to emit behavior that is in concert with his or her white teacher's expectation. Hence, the self-fulfilling prophecy. For instance, if a teacher possesses the expectation that a black student is a poor reader, the student will tend to behave in a fashion to ensure that this prophecy is fulfilled. For example, a colleague asked me to recommend a school for his son that was near the university where he taught. Shortly after he enrolled his son in the school I recommended, the boy's teacher, who was white, asked my friend to come to the school for a parent-teacher interview to discuss his son's reading difficulties. During the interview the teacher told my friend that his son had a reading problem and recommended that he be placed in a resource room (a small group classroom for students experiencing learning problems). During the interview a teacher on the staff of the school who was taking a course from my friend at the university came in the staff room where they were meeting, recognized him and said "Hi Dr. ——, how are you?" After this, the interviewing teacher made a dramatic change in her statements regarding his son's ability. She had incorporated the expectation that his son was not a capable student and would not do well in reading. His son, however, was reading at a grade three level when he was in grade one and his grade one teacher had recommended that he be accelerated.

Earlier in the section, we stated that the beliefs, perceptions and expectations that teachers who work with school-age children possess can become self-fulfilling prophecies and exert strong effects on, pupils' progress. Thus, if teachers are convinced that black and aboriginal students are not as good as white students they will communicate this disposition to their students either consciously or unconsciously, and the result would probably be that the proportion of these students (e.g. black, aboriginal) will tend to decrease as they move from elementary to high school. Statistics indicate that black and aboriginal students in the United States and Canada tend to "drop out" of school at a higher rate per capita than their white counterparts. Also, if teachers are convinced that black and aboriginal students are not as good academically as whites, they (teachers) will tend to recommend a greater percentage of them for special needs programs (e.g. educably mentally retarded level programs). Again, statistics in the United States and Canada indicate that black and Aboriginal students are over-represented in special needs programs designed for pupils who achieve academically at lower levels than their chronological age mates.

Also the policies of local school boards regarding the hiring and promotion of staff can influence the progress of pupils. For instance, if local school boards hire few colored teachers and place only a small percentage of those in positions of power (e.g. principals; associate superintendents) these decisions will tend to impede the development of colored students because it limits the number of available models to serve as mentors for these students. Support for this position is provided by my personal experiences while teaching in the department of psychology at a mid-sized university in the United States, when a number of my black students said to me, "I am so very happy that you are our instructor. You are the first black instructor that I have ever had". Additional support for this position is derived from research findings which indicate that my black students rated me more positively on each item of an evaluation scale than my white pupils (see chapter one).

The problem of few black educators in positions of power is one that has persisted. For instance, in 1967, 13.7 percent of Michigan's total student population was black, but only 8 percent of the teachers hired by school boards to instruct students were black. Also, during this period, there were 3,374 building principals in the state of Michigan; of these 97.3 percent were white, whereas only 2.7 percent were black.

Additional support for the position that blacks occupy few positions of power in school systems is provided from my personal observations of the district in which I serve. At the time of this writing, I was not aware of any Afro-Canadian principals in any regular elementary, junior high or senior high schools. However, recently a black female was appointed by this public district that employs approximately 200 principals to serve as principal of a school for unwed pregnant teenagers for the 1996-1997 school year. Also, at the time of this writing I was not aware of any black principals for the Catholic district in this city of approximately 450,000. In addition, I am not aware of any aboriginal principals in either the Public or Catholic Districts.

The following personal experience is provided to illustrate how the practice of racism in schools can exert a negative effect on the lives of colored staff and their families:

...In May of 1972, I completed my Ph.D degree. Shortly afterwards, I accepted a position as an assistant professor in the Department of Psychology at Eastern Michigan University. Prior to accepting

the position at Eastern Michigan, I requested permission to take a two-year leave of absence from my job with a local school board in the city where I resided. My request was denied. However, whites who finished their Ph.D. degrees during the same period and accepted jobs at universities were granted approval of their requests for leaves of absence. After two years at Eastern Michigan University I returned to the same school district but lost two years of pensionable service because my request for a leave of absence was denied....

Some research findings (e.g. Racial Census, 1967) indicate that teachers tend to possess more negative attitudes towards their black pupils and tend to rate them lower on scales that measure academic ability and motivation. Support for this position is provided from findings of a recent study (December, 1995) which addressed systemic racism in the province of Ontario, Canada. In this study 569 staff (e.g. principals, vice principals, classroom teachers, educational assistants, guidance counselors) participated; of these, 84 percent were white, 51 percent were male and 49 percent were female. Findings derived from responses provided by staff on the research questionnaire indicate that:

- 35 percent of the staff members reported that they felt that black students are more involved than white students in incidents that require police intervention
- only 1 percent of staff members reported that they think black students are less involved in incidents that require police intervention

One white teacher provided the following comments regarding blacks:
... Everyone wants to avoid the truth that certain black cultures are criminal and in conflict with most other cultures morally...

Also, in this study 2,172 students participated; of these, 47 percent were white, 14 percent were black, 14 percent were East Indian, 10 percent were South Asian, whereas students who identified themselves as other made up the remaining 15 percent; 56 percent of participants were male, whereas 44 percent were female. Findings derived from responses provided by students on the research questionnaire indicate that:

- 50 percent of black students reported that they feel that their school is "more likely" to call the police over incidents involving black students than whites and students of other racial groups

- 53 percent of black students reported that they feel the police treat black students worse than they do whites and students of other racial groups
- black students reported that they feel that school authorities treat them less fairly than whites and students of other racial groups

Some teachers who participated in the study reported that they felt that the following may lead teachers to make faulty judgements regarding black student's behavior:

STEREOTYPING - "By default, the search for 'troublemakers' more often than not rests on the so-called 'Jamaican' black kid - usually male, but sometimes female. It is as if we look for 'trouble' there first. I believe this is a 'perception' or stereotype that has emerged." (white male staff member)

RACIST PROVOCATION OF STUDENTS- "Often black or other racial minority students seem to be more involved in incidents that require suspension because they are targeted by white students or pushed to physical responses by verbal barbs." (white female staff member)

TEACHER'S MISINTERPRETATIONS OF UNFAMILIAR CULTURAL NORMS- "Fear is also a factor as to why teachers do not approach black students. If they understood some cultural points, such as [that] the loudness of black youth is not something to fear, etc., then they would be a little less afraid to approach these young black students." (black female staff member) (pp. 362-63).

A black student shared his perceptions regarding how he feels white teachers tend to interact with black students in the following fashion:

...As a black person I've noticed teachers taking two steps backward in dealing with me...[I]f teachers automatically put their guard up every time a minority student walks into a classroom, then nothing will ever get done. The minute the teacher's guard goes up, so does the student's. Some black people might deem a teacher racist because the teacher deals with the student in such an apprehensive, 'I'm not even going to try to reach out to you,' kind of manner.... (pp. 363)

SOURCE: Systemic Racism in the Ontario Justice System.

The following experience reported to me by a social worker employed by the public school district in a community in Canada where I reside provides a vivid illustration of the process of racism in schools:

...During the spring of 1992, a 14 year old junior high school white girl was referred to me by her school. Shortly after receiving the referral, I phoned the principal of the school to discuss the student. During my telephone conversation with the principal he told me that the girl was dating a black guy and stated "you know all of those black guys are pimps." When I visited the school to discuss the student, the principal appeared to be "shocked" when he discovered that I was black....

A very good colored friend of mine from the Caribbean told me that a "distinguished" dean of the University of Alberta which we both attended, sent him a letter when he was an undergraduate in which he said:

...You are not university material and you should return to your country and marry one of your own kind....

Fortunately, my friend did not take the dean's advice. Rather he "showed" him, and at this point has provided a wide array of exemplary services and, for his efforts is the recipient of more than thirty awards including:

- Edmonton Alberta's Citizen of the Year Award on two occasions·
- Fellow of the Canadian College of Teachers
- Order of Canada
- Alberta Achievement Award for Excellence
- The Premier's award for Excellence in Education
- The Sir Frederick Haultain Award for Excellence in Education
- An Honorary Doctor of Law Degree from the University of Alberta
- The Immigrant Achievement Award
- The Great Canadian Award

The following two reports are presented to provide additional illustrations of the problem of racism in schools:

...During a conversation, two white friends of mine told me that they met with a white assistant principal of a large high school in the community in which I reside to discuss their daughter's behavior at school.

They said that the assistant principal assured them that their daughter's behavior was not that bad, and that they should see how some of the nigger kids in this school behave. This popular assistant principal made this statement to my friends without realizing that they were the parents of two black children....

...A black youth was suspended by the principal from his high school two days after his seventeenth birthday for refusing to use a knife and fight another student. Some of the supporters of the boy who challenged the black youth told teachers that the black youth was given a knife during the ordeal, but promptly gave it back to the person who passed it to him. Supporters of the black youth insisted that there was no knife in the ordeal that involved only an exchange of words. The principal apparently believed the account of the supporters of the boy who challenged the black youth and discounted the comments made by the supporters of the black youth. The principal summoned the school's liaison police officer to the office who searched the black youth and found no knife on his person. In spite of this, the principal suspended the black youth for a five day period and recommended that he be expelled from the school....

The following excerpt is taken from a letter written by the black youth's father which was sent to each school board trustee:

...At this point, I am sad because of the way some individuals treated our minor son. On this date I am also sad for my son and family and find it difficult to understand why some individuals interacted with our son the way they did and apparently assumed that a child who has been in your district for thirteen years and never displayed significant behavioral problems, who refused to fight, would be guilty of an offense that he and other students said he did not commit....

At this point, no trustee has replied to the father's letter.

Teachers can exert both positive and negative effects on their students that can have long lasting influences. Because of the important role that teachers play in the lives of their pupils, I am of the opinion that they should be administered psychological tests and racial attitude inventories prior to being hired. They should be required to attend instructional sessions that have demonstrated effectiveness in assisting participants in acquiring the ability and desire to interact in an appropriate fashion determined by our democratic principles of equality of rights and opportunities for individuals who comprise all ethnic and racial groups.

BLACK EDUCATION AND HISTORY

Historically in the United States politicians and educators have, in my view, deliberately established obstacles intended to deny American blacks the opportunity to acquire effective literacy skills. Support for this position is provided by documented evidence which indicates that some American states passed laws which denied its black residents the right to receive education or attend school. For example, the state of Georgia passed a law which stated:

> *...If any slave, black or free person of color, or any person shall teach any other slave, black or free person of color, to read or write, either written or printed characters, the same person of color or slave shall be punished by fine and whipping, or fine or whipping at the discretion of the court; and if a white person so offend, he, she or they shall be punished with a fine not exceeding $500,000.00 and imprisoned in a common jail at the discretion of the court.... (Dubois, 1968).*

Over the years, educators at all levels have omitted exposing students to valid information regarding the historical contributions that blacks made in the development of the United States of America. My personal observations provide support for this position. For instance:

> *...I attended university for 13 years during the period 1959 through 1972. During this period the only information I recall learning about black history in the United States and Canada were that blacks were slaves and that president Abraham Lincoln freed them. I did not receive any information from my instructors regarding the contributions that blacks made in the development of the United States and the world community. In 1971 during the final stages of studies for my Ph.D. degree and, because of the lack of information that my professors (who numbered over 150) offered regarding blacks, I decided to research the topic and attempt to discover relevant information regarding the challenges that blacks in the United States had to endure and the contributions that they made in spite of obstacles that often seemed to be insurmountable....*

My research revealed that in spite of the many hardships and challenges that blacks had to endure as a race of people, many reached major heights and contributed greatly to the United States and the world as well. In the next few pages, we briefly summarize the contributions that a few blacks made to humankind.

BENJAMIN BENNEKER

Benjamin Benneker was born November 9, 1731 in Maryland. His father was a slave and his mother was free. As a result he was free because offspring took the status of the mother. Although he only completed eighth grade, he showed unusual aptitude in the field of mathematics and possessed a similarly unusual knowledge of the heavens. A white neighbor who was a surveyor gave him a book on logarithms and went over a couple of weeks later to explain them to him. To the man's surprise Benneker had mastered them himself. Benneker, while studying stars and the universe, wrote an almanac which won him much praise. In 1789, he predicted an eclipse of the sun. Benneker also had the honor of making the first clock which was produced in America. He was the first black to receive a presidential appointment. In 1791, George Washington named him as one of the six men chosen to lay out the City of Washington, D.C.. Benneker was an astronomer, mathematician, inventor, surveyor, philosopher and abolitionist. In addition, he was a proponent for black rights who outlined a plan for the establishment of a Secretary of Peace, and recommended that the government provide an opportunity for everyone to be taught the "three r's." Many historians suggest that his plan outdated that of Woodrow Wilson s League of Nations by one hundred twenty-five years.

JOSEPH BLAIR

Joseph Blair was born in Augusta, Georgia in 1904. Blair completed two years of college before he became interested in aerodynamics at the age of 24. A few years later, in 1928, he developed plans for two stage rockets. His plans at this time however, were felt to be fantastic and impossible. Nevertheless thirty years later he was called to Washington to tell the officials why it was not impossible for them to get rockets off the ground successfully. After three days of consultation with Washington officials, rocketry was accepted by the United States government and three of his rocket designs were accepted by the Navy. In addition to developing rockets, Blair developed dishwashing machines, mouse traps, a submersible submarine that was capable of making eighty miles an hour beneath the water. He also developed the propeller for the P-47, the American government's long distance fighter bomber. In addition, Blair made superchargers for high powered racing boats.

DR. CHARLES DREW

Dr. Charles Drew was born in Washington, D.C.. Dr. Drew attended Amherst College where he was an outstanding athlete, captain of the track team and a halfback on the football team. After graduation he accepted a coaching position at Morgan College in Baltimore. After functioning as a successful coach, he decided to enroll at McGill University where he completed his degree in medicine. Dr. Drew's major interest at McGill was in the conservation of blood plasma. In 1940 he journeyed to England where he developed the first blood bank. In 1942 Dr. Drew returned to the United States and guided the development of blood banks throughout the country. Dr. Drew received many honors for his outstanding work and was honored by being made a member of the College of Surgeons. (Lillian Anthony 1971).

W.E.B. DUBOIS

Dr. DuBois was born in 1868 in Great Barrington, Mass. Dr. DuBois studied at Fisk University, Harvard College and the University of Berlin. He was an intellectual giant who fought vigorously for black rights and for improved living conditions for America's poor. Dr. DuBois wrote many papers and books and developed three classics, "Suppression of the African Slave Trade," written in 1896 and, "The Philadelphia Negro" and "The Souls of Black Folks". Dr. Dubois later became very critical of white historians whom he felt had grossly distorted the blackman's role during reconstruction. As a result in retaliation, he wrote "Black Reconstruction". Dr. Dubois, a relentless militant black genius, possessed a tremendous love and dedication for his people. He was a scholar, writer, sociologist and philosopher who helped organize the National Association for the Advancement of Colored People (NAACP) in 1909. He was editor of NAACP's "Crisis" magazine and the author of more than twenty books. Dr. DuBois was exiled from the United States and spent his final years in Ghana, West Africa among his cherished ancestors where he died on August 27, 1963, the day when thousands of people were planning to march on Washington, D.C.

PAUL JOHNSON

Although Paul Johnson was born in Georgia, he spent most of his life in Chicago. Johnson, while living in Chicago acquired a job with a physician who specialized in X-ray treatments. He became extremely interested in x-ray technology and began to study procedures for the treatment, manufacture and production of x-ray tubes. As a result of his acquired competency in this area, he set up his own organization which developed and supervised the treatment of x-ray equipment for hospitals throughout the United States.

DR. EARNEST EVERETT JUST

Earnest Just attended Dartmouth College in New Hampshire, and later taught at Howard University in Washington, D.C.. At the age of thirty-one Just received the SPINGARN MEDAL for his accomplishments in the field of science. A year later Just received his doctor's degree from the University of Chicago and shortly afterwards won world wide recognition for his contributions to the scientific community. Contemporaries in his field estimated that he was approximately thirty years ahead of his time. Just also did outstanding work for the government in Marine biology at the famous Woods Hole Institute in Massachusetts and published over fifty dissertations in the field of biology.

DR. MARTIN LUTHER KING

Dr. Martin Luther King, who was born in 1929 in Atlanta, Georgia was a strong advocate for civil and human rights for all peoples. He graduated from Morehouse College at the age of nineteen, three years later he received a bachelor of divinity degree from Crozer Theological Seminary and two years afterwards received his doctorate degree. Dr. King was a strong advocate for non-violence and justice and equality for all. Because of his love for all people and belief in non-violence he employed peaceful methods of protest such as sit-ins, marches and boycotts in his fight for equal rights and equal opportunities for all Americans. In 1963, Dr. King led the historic march on Washington, D.C. where he delivered his famous speech entitled "I Have a Dream". In 1964 Dr. King was awarded the Nobel Peace Prize and four years later, at the age of 39, he was assassinated in Memphis, Tennessee. Dr. King is the second American to be honored with a holiday on his birthday. George Washington, the father of the country was the first.

LEWIS LATIMER

Lewis Latimer was an associate of Thomas Edison who did experimentation work in the field of electricity. Latimer solved the problem of transforming electrical current when he invented the incandescent light. Because of his accomplishments in the field of electricity he was appointed to supervise the installation of electric lights in New York City, Philadelphia, London and other cities. Latimer also served as chief draftsperson for General Electric and Westinghouse companies. He developed plans for Alexander Graham Bell which led to the development of the first telephone.

JAN MATZELIGER

Jan Matzeliger, whose father was a Dutch businessman and mother a black African, was born in Dutch Guiana in 1852. Matzeliger as a youth observed that most people were barefooted because they couldn't afford shoes. At the age of eighteen, Matzeliger left Guiana and went to Philadelphia where he acquired a job in a shoe factory. After a few years in Philadelphia Matzeliger moved to Lynn, Mass. where he continued his work in the shoe industry. While working in Lynn, Mass. Matzeliger developed the first machine made for lacing shoes. His machine adjusted the shoe, arranged the leather over the shoe and drove in the nails. As a result of his successful achievements, he was able to organize and develop his own company which specialized in making shoes. Matzeliger however, as a result of complications, died at the age of thirty-seven, never realizing the benefits of his invention. His patents were purchased by Sidney Winslow who, in turn, bought forty companies and organized them into the United Shoe Machine Company.

ELIJAH MCCOY

Elijah McCoy was born in Canada in 1844 to escaped slaves who made it to Canada by way of the underground railroad. After slavery was declared illegal in the United States, McCoy moved to Detroit, Michigan where he applied for his first patent in 1872. McCoy's major invention was the drip cup lubrication system for heavy machinery; a container with a little stop cock on the bottom which allowed the flow of oil on bearings to be regulated. The McCoy drip cup system was incorporated on most heavy equipment. Following his drip cup invention which had international significance on railroads and sea going vessels, McCoy patented over fifty other devices for the lubrication of machinery. McCoy is rightly referred to as the "father of lubrication.

GARNET A. MORGAN

Garnet A. Morgan who was born in Paris, Kentucky on March 4, 1877, moved at an early age to Cleveland, Ohio where he died on August 27, 1963. Morgan was an inventor who sold his first invention (an adjunct to the sewing machine), for one hundred fifty dollars. His inventions included the gas mask which was used during World War I and the electric stop light signal which he developed in 1924 and sold for forty thousand dollars.

NORBERT RILLIEUX

Norbert Rillieux, the son of a wealthy Frenchman and a black woman, was born in New Orleans, Louisiana. While attending school in Paris, Rillieux became interested in the manufacturing of sugar products. Some years later he invented the vacuum evaporating pan which revolutionized the production of sugar. Rillieux, who was born in 1806, died at the age of 98.

DR. DANIEL HALE WILLIAMS

Daniel Williams was born in Hollidaysburg, Pennsylvania in 1858. He migrated from Pennsylvania to Wisconsin where he studied barbering full time and medicine in his spare time. Williams received his degree in medicine from Northwestern Medical School at the age of twenty-five. His accomplishments include the founding of the Provident Hospital, and the organizing and development of the Freemans Hospital in Washington, D.C.. Williams later returned to Chicago and performed the first successful operation on the human heart. William's patient (Cornish) lived many years after the operation. Williams who functioned as an instructor at Meharry Medical College, later became a Fellow of the American College of Surgeons. He died in 1931 at the age of 73.

GRANVILLE T. WOODS

Woods (an inventor) filed his first application for a patent on a steam boiler in 1889. Woods contributions included the invention of fifteen electric railway appliances control systems. Woods who later organized the Woods Electric Company, also invented the first electric incubator for hatching eggs.

In addition to those listed in this chapter there are thousands of other blacks who have made exemplary contributions to the American and world communities including:

- **MARY MCLEOD BETHUNE** (1875-1955) who helped make education available to thousands of black Americans. She fought for the equal rights of black people and founded the National Council of Negro women in 1935. Also, she was an advisor to four presidents of the United States.

- **FREDERICK DOUGLAS** (1817-1895) was the greatest anti-slavery speaker of his time who helped convince President Abraham Lincoln to accept black soldiers into the Union Army. Douglas, who was a United States Marshall in Washington, D.C. established the North Star newspaper in 1847 and was appointed minister to Haiti in 1889.

- **JEAN BAPTISTE DUSABLE** (1745-1818) discovered a place he called Eschikaqov, where he built a cabin for his family in 1774, which was later named Chicago.

- **HENSON MATTHEW** (1866-1955) an explorer, placed the American flag on the North Pole for the first time. Matthew was an assistant to Admiral Robert E. Peary. When they were a few miles away from the North Pole Admiral Peary became ill and Henson continued and placed the American flag on the North Pole.

- **ALAINE LOCKE** (1886-1954) was the first black person selected as a Rhodes Scholar. He received this scholarship in 1907 which is awarded to only a few outstanding students each year.

- **THURGOOD MARSHALL** (1908-1993) was the first black justice of the United States Supreme Court. In 1940, after graduating from Howard University Law School, Marshall was named chief counsel for the National Association for the Advancement of Colored People (NAACP). While serving in this position, he and his staff won 29 out of 32 Supreme Court cases. In 1954 he won the historic decision of Brown versus the Board of Education of Topeka, Kansas which eliminated the separate but equal doctrine that had justified segregation in schools since 1896.

- **HARRIET TUBMAN** (1820-1913) ran the Underground Railroad which enabled more than 300 black slaves to escape to the north and obtain their freedom. Tubman never lost a passenger as the conductor of the underground railroad and was given the name Black Moses because of her heroic contributions.

- **BOOKER T. WASHINGTON** (1856-1915) an educator, was chosen to head the Tuskegee Normal and Industrial Institute for black students in 1881. Washington was a great educator and powerful leader who felt that education and economic security should be top priorities for American blacks.
- **IDA B. WELLS** (1869-1931) a superb writer who published the Red Record in 1894, the first book to document the lynching of black Americans. She was a powerful, relentless fighter for justice who founded the *National Association for the Advancement of Colored People.*

Although white racists typically insist that blacks have made few worthwhile contributions, J.A. Rogers in his classic book entitled "The World's Great Men of Color" identified more than 200 blacks who made significant contributions to the world community. His list included Aesop, the writer of proverbs; Imhotep, an Egyptian colored man who was the father of medicine; Hannibal, a gifted soldier and leader who was the father of military strategy; Eugene Chen, China's noted Trinidad-born statesman; Alek Sander Pushin, the father of Russian literature; St. Benedict, the Moor, the Christian Church's early leader and Alessandro De Medici, Duke of Florence. (Lu's note book no.844). In addition, Rogers mentioned a number of individuals with varying degrees of black blood, who made major contributions to the world. This list included Robert Browning (Britain's famed poet); Germany's Ludwig Van Beethoven and Mohammed, the founder of Islam, the world's second largest religious group.

Halford H. Fairchild (1988) stated that the reclamation of black history involves the re-writing of white history. He takes this stance because of his position which assumes that history has been used as the knowledge base which gave strength to ideologies that justified racial exploitation, slavery, imperialism, colonialism and the subordination of women (p.3).

Although American blacks came to America as slaves, they came from a proud African tradition from which the first civilization sprang. For instance, the Greek and Roman cultures were borrowed from Africa. Therefore, black Americans were not merely descendants of slaves, they simply encountered slavery along the course of a long proud journey (Ebony, 1990). Black Americans who came from Africa to the United States survived and made great progress in spite of seemingly impossible odds. Black Americans have made great progress during the brief period that they have been in America and continue to strive to higher levels. For instance, in 1991 blacks were mayors of some of the largest cities in the United States and the Governor of the State of West Virginia was black.

SUMMARY

- teachers who perceive that their black students are less capable than their white counterparts tend to set lower expectations for their black pupils

- when teachers expect less from their students they tend to give them less instruction

- when teachers expect less from their students they tend to ask them to do less work

- black educators hold very few positions of power

- in a recent Canadian study, black students reported that they felt that school authorities treated them less fairly than white students and students of other racial groups

- historically, American blacks have been denied the opportunity to acquire effective literacy skills

- historically, some states passed laws that denied its black residents the right to receive education or attend school

- educators over the years at all levels have omitted exposing students to valid information regarding the historical contributors of American blacks

- Benjamin Benneker made the first clock that was produced in America

- Joseph Blair developed dishwashing machines, mouse traps and a submersible submarine

- Dr. Charles Drew developed the first blood bank

- Dr. W.E.B. DuBois fought for rights for blacks and was critical of white historians whom he felt grossly distorted the black man's role during reconstruction

- Dr. Ernest Just published over fifty dissertations in the field of biology

- Lewis Latimer was an associate of Thomas Edison

- Lewis Latimer invented the incandescent light

- Lewis Latimer developed plans for Alexander Graham Bell which led to the development of the first telephone

- Jan Matzeliger made the first machine for lacing shoes
- Garnet Morgan invented the gas mask and the electric stop light
- Dr. Hale Williams found the Provident Hospital, and organized and developed the Freemans Hospital
- Dr. Hale Williams performed the first successful operation on the human heart
- Elijah McCoy invented the "drip cup" lubrication system for heavy equipment
- Elijah McCoy patented over fifty devices for the lubrication of machinery
- Norbert Rillieux invented the vacuum evaporating pan which revolutionized the production of sugar
- Granville Woods invented the first incubator for hatching eggs
- Granville Woods invented fifteen electric railway appliance control systems
- Dr. Martin Luther King was a strong advocate of civil and human rights for all peoples
- Dr. King is the second American who is honored with a holiday on his birthday
- J.A. Rogers identified more than 200 blacks who made significant contributions to the world community
- Great men of color identified by Rogers included Aesop (the writer of proverbs), Imhotep (the father of Medicine), Hannibal (a gifted soldier), Eugene Chen (statesman), Alex Sander Pushin (the father of Russian literature), St. Benedict the Moor (Christian church leader) and Alessandro de Medici (Duke of Florence)
- Individuals of mixed blood identified by Rogers who made major contributions to the world community included Robert Browning (Britain's famed poet), Ludwig Van Beethoven (gifted musical artist) and Mohammed (founder of Islam)

- Halford proposed that history has been used as the knowledge base which gave strength to ideologies that justified racial exploitation, slavery, imperialism, colonialism and the subordination of women
- The first civilization sprang from Africa
- Black Americans who came from Africa to the United States made great progress in spite of seemingly impossible odds
- In 1991 blacks were mayors of some of the largest cities in the United States and the Governor of the State of West Virginia was black
- Benjamin Benneker was the first black to receive a presidential appointment
- Dr. Martin Luther King Jr. fought for justice and equality for all Americans
- Dr. Martin Luther King Jr. was awarded the Nobel Peace Prize in 1964
- Mary McLeod Bethune founded the   National Council of Negro Women
- Fredrick Douglas helped convince President Lincoln to accept black soldiers into the Union Army
- Jean Baptiste Dusable discovered Chicago
- Henson Matthew placed the American flag on the North Pole for the first time
- Alaine Locke was the first black person selected as a Rhodes Scholar
- Thurgood Marshall was the first black justice of the United States Supreme Court
- Harriet Tubman operated the "Underground Railroad" which took black slaves to freedom in the north
- Booker T. Washington was the first person to head the Tuskegee Normal and Industrial Institute for black students
- IDA B. Wells founded the National Association for the Advancement of Colored People.

Chapter 10
Racism in Sports

In this chapter we provide an overview of the challenges and accomplishments blacks have made in sports. Black Americans have excelled in sports in spite of the many obstacles and hardships they had to endure. Some of the early American blacks who succeeded in major league sports included:

1. Jack Johnson who became the first black heavyweight champion of the world although people said blacks could not box because they had glass jaws.

2. Jackie Robinson who became the first black to play major league baseball although people said blacks didn't have the fortitude to play big league baseball.

However, racism in sports at all levels is a problem that has persisted over the years. For instance, on a hot day a husky football player was overcome from exhaustion and passed out while he was running through the ropes. The coach walked over to the player and kicked him in his ribs and said "Get that nigger off the field."

The above mentioned statement illustrates how some white coaches reacted to black athletes in the 1960's. During this period the typical black athlete was usually confronted with daily incidences of biases. For instance, he was usually expected to work harder than his white counterpart and because of the quota restrictions that most clubs employed, he found it considerably more difficult to make the ball club. Racial prejudice in sports was not limited to the United States. For example O'Malley (1970) said that the predominant difference between Canada and the United States vis-a-vis the blackman is not that Canada is less prejudiced but rather it has fewer blacks. From their findings on racism in sports in Canada, Smith and Grindstaff (1970) concluded the following:

1. Opportunities for black athletes in the Canadian Football League are restricted to some extent. Seldom are there more than six black players on any given team and they are usually not placed in positions of authority.

2. Black athletes tend to be prominent at certain positions, particularly offensive halfback. Few blacks are employed in so called intelligent positions (quarterback, center, offensive guard).

3. The form of discrimination known in the United States as stacking does not seem to be prevalent in the Canadian Football League, but the offensive positions do appear to be "stacked" to an extent greater than chance would indicate.

4. Black athletes have been denied access to the power structure of the Canadian Football League. The meagre total of two assistant coaches (only one currently active) is the extent of their representation. Exclusion on the basis of lack of qualification does not appear to be justified.

5. Black athletes must adhere to more rigid standards of social behavior than white players, especially in regard to dating.

6. The black athlete faces prejudice and discrimination in Canada from his white teammates, his coaches and from the community.

7. Other than rooming black and white players together the C.F.L. teams do little to integrate their black players.

However, in spite of the problems listed above, a review of athletic statistics reveal that sports have assisted black athletes both economically and academically. For instance athletic scholarships have enabled many blacks to complete university degrees. However, athletics nevertheless have been of little assistance in the attainment of full social equality and status for the black athlete. Commenting on this point Olsen (1968) concludes that the white American is able to modify his views about the blackman and admire his exploits on the field but nevertheless insists that he sits at the back of the bus on the way home. He must perform on the field and afterwards know his place. Further elaboration of this point was made by Don L. Lee when he wrote:

America calling
Negroes.
Can you dance?
Play football/baseball?
Nanny?
Cook?
Need now Negroes
Who can entertain
Only. (in Rap Brown 1969)

Sports with its many advantages for black athletes also has its adverse counterparts. Edwards (1969) writes:

...The black professional is slurred by his teammates, discriminated against by the public, humiliated and harassed by the fans and emasculated by his coaches, and if he isn't smart, he winds up broke to boot. In this last instance the black professional boxer comes readily to mind....

Black athletes also appear to be limited in opportunities to obtain positions of power. This point is illustrated by Ernie McMillan (1970), a former teammate of mine who states: "If you have the desire to go into coaching or administration you are limited. You just don't think in terms of it. People never consider a black individual or black player as being coaching material."

Further pursuing the matter (lack of employment after playing careers are completed) Koppett (1970) writes:

...It is inconceivable that of hundreds of black major leaguers over a twenty year span, practically none has ever been qualified to manage, coach, or umpire while dozens of white former athletes have been filling such positions....

Commenting on the American black athlete Edwards (1969) states:

...After their playing days are over, few black athletes become managers or coaches in the major leagues. Blacks virtually never receive offers to coach at any of the many colleges which yearly employ professional athletes. By and large these are rewards for meritorious service given and for expertise acquired, but rather reserved for whites only....

The most naive observer will probably agree that sports have not benefited blacks as much as it has whites, and like most segments of the American population, has its vivid prejudices that exploit and limit its black participants. However, I am of the opinion that sports probably have done more to assist blacks than most other American institutions. Further support for this position is provided by Boyle (1967) when he writes:

> ...Sports has often served minority groups as the first rung on the social ladder. As such, it has helped further assimilation of the minority member into American life. It would not be too far-fetched to say that it has done more in this regard than any other agency, including the church and school....

Additional support for this position is expressed by Goodhart and Chataway (1968) who wrote:

> ...The integration of Negro athletes into the mainstream of American sporting life was the most important psychological advance in the field of civil rights between the ending of segregation in the armed forces after the Second World War and the supreme court decision integrating schools in 1954. Profit-seeking baseball clubs did more for the position of the Negro in America than the churches or the main political parties....

Most studies concerned with explaining the enormous success of the American black athlete have used a physiological model; that is, they have suggested that blacks possess physiological characteristics that are different from whites which facilitate their success in major American sports. For instance, researchers have concluded that the black American, on average, tends to have a shorter trunk, more slender pelvis, longer arms (especially forearms) and longer legs (especially from the knees down) than his white counterpart. (Sports Illustrated, Jan. 18, 1991 p. 74)

Dr. J. Tanner (1958) measured, photographed and x-rayed 137 track and field athletes and a number of weight lifters and wrestlers. He concluded as a result of his research, that amongst competitors in both track and field events there were significant racial differences in leg length, arm length and hip width. Tanner stated that black sprinters averaged 86.2 centimeters in leg length, while whites averaged 83. The sitting heights of blacks averaged 92.5 compared with the whites 93.5. Blacks' hip width averaged 26.8 centimeters and whites 28.6. The ratio of leg length at sitting height for sprinters, 400 meter runners and high jumpers averaged 0.88, 0.92 and 0.93 in whites and 0.93, 0.97, and 1.01 for blacks. Tanner further suggests that blacks have wider and narrower muscles.

Dr. Edward E. Hunt Jr., Professor of Anthropology at Pennsylvania State University, suggests that the black athlete has hyperextensibility (i.e. he is considered to be double jointed). He states that the black athlete has more tendon and less muscle than the white, and that black athlete's heels do not protrude as much as his leg and foot which gives him tremendous leverage for jumping. Dr. Hunt further suggests that the black athlete has less body fat than the white athlete. He also observed that the black athlete's muscles tend to get chilled sooner in cold climates and that this might effect his performance in such sports as ice hockey or football when played in extremely northern areas. Lloyd Winter, former San Jose State track coach, states that black athletes have a distinctive ability under pressure. Winter further states that their antagonistic muscles stay loose. Winter however, concludes and reasonably so, that black athletes differ from each other physically as much as whites. (Sports Illustrated Jan. 18, 1971, p.72-83)

I am of the opinion that physiological models cannot adequately explain black athletes' success in American sports for a number of reasons. First, black athletes vary between individuals as much as white athletes. Second, when you study black athletes you are studying a very highly elite and more specific segment of the American black sub-culture. For example the black athlete who makes a professional sports team varies more (from a physiological point of view) from the mass of the black population than do the white athlete from the mass of the white population. Third, only the very exceptional black athlete make the professional team because he generally has to be considerably better than the white athlete with whom he is competing for the same position. Fourth, the black athlete has to be more exceptional than the white athlete in order to acquire a professional contract in the first place. For example many average white athletes obtain professional contracts, but typically only the exceptional black athlete receives the opportunity to even try out for a position on a professional team's roster. Finally concerning stature and physique it seems reasonable to assume that the world champion sprinter probably would possess physiological features regardless of how small, that are somewhat different from the masses of all races, including his own. Furthermore, if he is the best he may have physical characteristics which differ from good sprinters in his own race as well as from other races.

Because of the reasons mentioned, I find it difficult to accept any physiological model alone for explaining the reasons for the black athlete's enormous success in major American sports. Physique of course, is an important factor, however variables such as motivation and perseverance are probably as important, and in some cases more important. One may argue that Jackie Robinson was successful because physiologically he varied somewhat from his white counterparts. However I would repudiate this explanation and suggest that he probably was successful because he possessed the motivation, determination and commitment to play professional baseball.

Although racial prejudice continues to prevail, black athletes have made major strives in professional sports. For example; Sports Illustrated (Jan. 1971 p.p. 73-83), reported that three of the five basketball players named on the NBA's all-rookie team were black and that black athletes have won the National Basketball Association's Most Valuable Player Award twelve times in the past thirteen seasons. In professional football all of the four 1969 Rookies of the Year Awards for offense and defense were won by blacks. In baseball, blacks have won the National League's Most Valuable Player Awards sixteen times in the past twenty-two seasons.

Black accomplishments in major American sports in such a short period of time has been remarkable. For instance, in 1942 there were no blacks on any big league basketball, football or baseball professional teams. In 1968 there were one hundred fifty blacks out of a total of six hundred major league baseball players; there were three hundred thirty blacks out of a total of one thousand forty professional football players; and there were one hundred fifty-three black players out of a total of two hundred eighty players in the professional basketball leagues. Blacks furthermore accounted for all eight U.S. Olympic records at Mexico City in 1968. In a very short time then, black athletes had reached a point in which eight of the ten starters in the 1968 National Basketball League all-star game were black.

In 1990, 60 percent of the players in the National Football League were black and a greater percentage of players in the National Basketball League were black; also, black athletes were well represented in Major League Baseball. In 1990 the National Football

League hired Art Shell as head Coach; there were two black managers in the American Baseball League and several blacks were head coaches in the National Basketball League.

In 1990, blacks won the National Football League Alumni Players of the Year Award in all positions except kicker, offensive lineman and punter. The winners of these awards are presented in Table 10.1:

TABLE 10:1 NFL ALUMNI PLAYERS OF THE YEAR

PLAYER	POSITION	TEAM
Warren Moon	Quarterback	Houston Oilers
Bruce Smith	Defensive Lineman	Buffalo Bills
Keith Jackson	Tight End	Philadelphia Eagles
Anthony Munoz	Offensive Lineman	Cincinnati Bengals
Rohn Stark	Punter	Indianapolis Colts
Nick Lowery	Kicker	Kansas City Chiefs
Jerry Rice	Wide Receiver	San Francisco 49ers
Derrick Thomas	Linebacker	Kansas City Chiefs
Dave Meggett	Return Specialist	New York Giants
Barry Sanders	Running Back	Detroit Lions
Rod Woodson	Defensive Back	Pittsburgh Steelers

Sports have provided a significant proportion of professional black athletes with economic prosperity. For instance, in 1994 Michael Jordan's estimated earnings of approximately 30 million dollars was the highest of all athletes; 1994 was the third consecutive year that Jordan topped the list of earnings of professional athletes. Also, during 1994, Shaquille O'Neal was second on the list of the highest paid professional athletes with estimated earnings of approximately 16 and a half million dollars.

In spite of the challenges that black athletes have had to endure over the years, they have persevered and experienced considerable success in sports. Sports, in my view, has served as the vehicle which has assisted American blacks in their quest for equality more than any other institution.

SUMMARY

- Black Americans have excelled in sports in spite of the many obstacles and hardships they had to endure

- Racism in sports at all levels is a problem that has persisted over the years

- Smith and Grindstaff, in their research study reported that few blacks were employed in so-called intelligent positions

- Smith and Grindstaff, in their research study reported that black athletes were denied access to the power structure of the Canadian Football League

- Smith and Grindstaff, in their research study reported that the black athlete faces prejudice and discrimination in Canada from his white teammates, his coaches and from the community

- Athletics have assisted black athletes both economically and educationally

- Black athletes have traditionally had few opportunities to acquire positions of power

- Sports probably has done more to assist blacks than most other American institutions

- Black athletes physically differ from each other as much as whites

- Hunt proposed that the black athlete has less body fat than the white athlete

- Battle states that physiological models cannot adequately explain black athletes' success in American sports

- Battle proposes that physique is an important factor but, variables such as motivation and perseverance are probably as important

- In 1942 there were no blacks on any big league basketball, football or baseball professional teams

- In 1968 there were 330 blacks out of a total of 1,040 professional football players

- In 1990, 60 percent of the players in the National Football League were black

PART V

STRATEGIES FOR ACHIEVING SUCCESS

CHAPTER 11
SUCCESS STRATEGIES

IF YOU ACQUIRE an adequate base of information which incorporates effective strategies, you can use this knowledge to help you overcome the negative effects of racism and assist you in your efforts to achieve success. One aspect of knowledge that can be beneficial to you is to realize that although it is popular to refer to colored people as being minorities (Canadians use the term visible minorities), people of color comprise the majority of individuals occupying planet earth. Actually whites are a minority because they (whites) comprise only about one-eighth of the earth's population. The remaining seven-eights of the world human population are comprised of colored people. There are as many Africans on earth as there are whites; the value for both is one eighth of the world human population. Although the information presented above is accurate, most individuals possess misconceptions regarding these facts. For instance, during psychotherapy sessions with colored children and youth, I ask them the question "What is the largest race of people in the world?" my young clients almost always answer "white".

In this chapter of the book we describe strategies that you can use to assist you in overcoming the negative effects of racism and achieving success. Also, we describe a program that has demonstrated effectiveness in helping black children and their families achieve success in mainstream society. While reading the sections incorporated in this chapter, I encourage you to make concerted efforts to determine how you can use the information presented to assist you in overcoming racism and achieving success in the areas that are important to you. Two areas which most individuals consider to be important for them to achieve success in are a) work and b) relationships.

Overcoming Racism and
Achieving Success in Work

Achieving success in work is important for most individuals in our contemporary society because it (work) affects one's:

- productivity
- personal control
- flexibility
- status
- self-esteem

Those who desire work and are unable to obtain it generally experience deficits in their self-esteem. Support for this position is provided by the following statement:

> ...Unemployment drastically undermines self-esteem. Women and men who have been unemployed recently for at least six months have the lowest self-esteem. Because nearly one third of young Americans between 18 and 24 have been unemployed, the generation of young people coming of age in a recession may be especially vulnerable to low self-esteem. Unemployment seems equally damaging to men and to women. In the case of men, the low self-esteem may be connected to loss of income. Among women, low self regard may be due to their tendency to blame themselves when they lose their jobs....

To achieve success in employment it is important that you display intelligent behavior. I am also of the opinion that it is important for you to adopt a definition of intelligence that enhances rather than impedes your ability to utilize your potential effectively. To me, intelligence is the "ability to adapt and adjust to environmental demands." This definition in my view does not entertain the prospect of limitations and makes it easier for one to succeed. (Battle, 1995)

When racists and others who consider themselves to be better than you attempt to impede your efforts to succeed, use the following statement entitled "They Said" to help you focus on your strengths.

THEY SAID

Many things that people say cannot be done can be, for instance:

1. They said, that humans couldn't run a four- minute mile, then along came a person named Roger Bannister.

2. They said, that Afro-Americans couldn't box, then along came a person named Jack Johnson.

3. They said, that Afro-Americans couldn't play major league baseball, then along came a person named Jackie Robinson.

4. They said, that Afro-Americans couldn't succeed in professional golf, then along came a person named Eldrick (Tiger) Woods.

SOURCE: Battle (1997)

Use the message incorporated in the following poem entitled "Show Them" to assist you in achieving success in work.

SHOW THEM

When they say that
You cannot succeed.
Show them that you
Are the crop; not the weed.

Stand straight
And tall.
Show them you
Are strong and will not fall.

Don't let them push
You around.
Show them that you
Can stand your own ground.

When they treat you with
Little respect.
Show them that you
Can be firm, steady and erect.

When they try to put
You down.
Show them that you
Are worthy, capable and sound.

Learn how to work
And plan.
Show them that you
Are as good as your fellow man.

James Battle (1995)

It is important for you to realize that the best way to "show" those who attempt to deny you your basic rights and impede your ability to utilize your potential effectively is to achieve success. When striving to succeed, don't say "If I succeed", rather say "When I succeed."

Employ the following success formula in your efforts to overcome the negative effects of racism and achieve success at work. I recommend this formula because the strategies incorporated in it are important ones that I have found to be beneficial.

SUCCESS FORMULA

Although there are a variety of strategies that one can use to obtain success (e.g. Battle, 1992, 1993, 1994) the following are important ones that I have found to be beneficial:

1. **S** = **SELF-ESTEEM**
   - develop and maintain positive perceptions of self-worth

2. **U** = **UNCONDITIONAL POSITIVE REGARD**
   - provide unconditional positive regard for self and others

3. **C** = **CREDIBILITY**
   - do what you promise to do

4. **C** = **CREATIVITY**
   - develop and put into action innovative creative proposals and techniques

5. **E** = **ENCOURAGEMENT**
   - emphasize positives rather than the negative aspects of your behavior and the action of significant others.

6. **S** = **SUPPORT**
   - Support and help others and they will return the same to you.

7. **S** = **STRIVE**
   - to be the very best you can be

Complete the following inventory to determine your success potential.

SUCCESS POTENTIAL INVENTORY
James Battle, Ph.D.

1. Do you provide respect for colleagues, clients and others?
   Always ☐ Usually ☐ Sometimes ☐ Seldom ☐ Never ☐

2. How are your decision making skills?
   Very Good ☐ Good ☐ Average ☐ Poor ☐ Very Poor ☐

3. Do you continue to upgrade your skills, knowledge and informational base?
   Always ☐ Usually ☐ Sometimes ☐ Seldom ☐ Never ☐

4. Do you provide encouragement for your colleagues and clients?
   Always ☐ Usually ☐ Sometimes ☐ Seldom ☐ Never ☐

5. How are your study skills?
   Very Good ☐ Good ☐ Average ☐ Poor ☐ Very Poor ☐

6. How are your listening skills?
   Very Good ☐ Good ☐ Average ☐ Poor ☐ Very Poor ☐

7. How do you rate yourself as being conscientious?
   Very High ☐ Above Average ☐ Average ☐ Below Average ☐ Very Low ☐

8. How do you rate yourself as being reliable?
   Very High ☐ Above Average ☐ Average ☐ Below Average ☐ Very Low ☐

9. How is your attendance at work?
   Very Good ☐ Good ☐ Average ☐ Poor ☐ Very Poor ☐

10. Do you commence work on tasks shortly after you receive assignments?
    Always ☐ Usually ☐ Sometimes ☐ Seldom ☐ Never ☐

11. How is your motivation for success
    Very High ☐ Above Average ☐ Average ☐ Below Average ☐ Very Poor ☐

12. How is your ability to focus and sustain attention?
    Very Good ☐ Good ☐ Average ☐ Poor ☐ Very Poor ☐

13. How do you rate your ability to persevere (stick to tasks until completion?)
    Very High ☐ Above Average ☐ Average ☐ Below Average ☐ Very Poor ☐

14. How are your problem solving skills?
    Very Good ☐ Good ☐ Average ☐ Poor ☐ Very Poor ☐

15. How are your thinking skills?
    Very Good ☐ Good ☐ Average ☐ Poor ☐ Very Poor ☐

16. How are your academic (e.g. writing, arithmetic) skills?
    Very Good ☐ Good ☐ Average ☐ Poor ☐ Very Poor ☐

17. How are your technical (e.g. computer, typing) skills?
    Very Good ☐ Good ☐ Average ☐ Poor ☐ Very Poor ☐

18. How is your self-esteem   (how you feel about yourself)?
    Very High ☐ Above Average ☐ Average ☐ Below Average ☐ Very Low ☐

19. How is your motivation for work?
    Very High ☐ High ☐ Average ☐ Poor ☐ Very Poor ☐

20. How do you get along with employers (bosses)?
    Very Good ☐ Good ☐ Average ☐ Poor ☐ Very Poor ☐

Score the Success Potential Inventory in the following fashion: *Always*, *Very Good*, and *Very High* yield a score of 5 for each of the twenty items; the value for *Usually*, *Good*, and *Above Average* is 4; whereas *Sometimes* and *Average* earn a score of 3; *Seldom*, *Poor*, and *Below Average* yield a score of 2; while *Never*, *Very Poor* and *Very Low* yield a score of 1. The highest possible score you can earn on the Success Potential Inventory is 100, whereas the lowest possible score is 20. Use the classification of scores listed in Table 11:1 to rate your success potential.

TABLE 11:1	CLASSIFICATION OF SCORES FOR THE SUCCESS POTENTIAL INVENTORY
SCORE	**CLASSIFICATION**
90+	Very High
85-89	High
70-84	Intermediate
63-69	Low
62-	Very Low

If you earned a score of 90 or above, your success potential is very high; a score ranging between 85 and 89 indicates that your success potential is high; whereas those between 70 and 84 indicates that your success potential is intermediate or average, while scores of 69 and below indicate low to very low levels of success potential.

ENCOURAGEMENT

In your efforts to overcome racism and achieve success, provide those with whom you select to interact as colleagues and friends with encouragement. Encouragement is a cognitive technique in which a significant other emphasizes the positive aspects of an individual's behavior rather than the negative aspects. That is, the person providing the encouragement minimizes the importance of an individual's mistakes while recognizing his or her assets and strengths.

Encouragement is important because if you encourage others they will return the same and assist you in your efforts to overcome the negative effects of racism and achieve success at work. Complete the following inventory to determine your level of encouragement.

THE ENCOURAGEMENT INVENTORY
James Battle, Ph.D.

DIRECTIONS: Please mark each question in the following way. For each of the questions there are five options for response: "always", "usually", "sometimes", "seldom" and "never". Put a check mark (✓) on the option that most closely describes what you do. Please check only one option for each of the 10 questions. This is not a test, and there are no "right" or "wrong" answers.

1. Do you encourage others to strive to succeed?
   Always ☐ Usually ☐ Sometimes ☐ Seldom ☐ Never ☐

2. Do you provide others mutual respect while interacting with them?
   Always ☐ Usually ☐ Sometimes ☐ Seldom ☐ Never ☐

3. Do you consider the effects that your actions can have on the self-esteem of others when interacting with them?
   Always ☐ Usually ☐ Sometimes ☐ Seldom ☐ Never ☐

4. Do you provide others recognition for their effort and achievement?
Always ☐ Usually ☐ Sometimes ☐ Seldom ☐ Never ☐

5. Do you emphasize the positive aspects of the behavior of others?
Always ☐ Usually ☐ Sometimes ☐ Seldom ☐ Never ☐

6. Do you minimize the importance of the mistakes that others make?
Always ☐ Usually ☐ Sometimes ☐ Seldom ☐ Never ☐

7. Do you tell others that you appreciate their contributions?
Always ☐ Usually ☐ Sometimes ☐ Seldom ☐ Never ☐

8. Do you cooperate with others and provide them support when they desire it?
Always ☐ Usually ☐ Sometimes ☐ Seldom ☐ Never ☐

9. Do you interact with others in a non-judgmental fashion?
Always ☐ Usually ☐ Sometimes ☐ Seldom ☐ Never ☐

10. Do you communicate to others that your caring for them is unconditional?
Always ☐ Usually ☐ Sometimes ☐ Seldom ☐ Never ☐

Score The Encouragement Inventory in the following fashion. *Always* yields a score of 5 for each of the ten items; the value for *Usually* is 4; whereas *Sometimes* earns a score of 3; *Seldom* yields a score of 2; while *Never* yields a score of 1. The highest possible score you can earn on The Encouragement Inventory is 50, whereas the lowest possible score is 10. Use the Classification of scores listed in Table 11:2 to rate your level of Encouragement.

TABLE 11:2	CLASSIFICATION OF SCORES FOR THE ENCOURAGEMENT INVENTORY
SCORE	**CLASSIFICATION**
45+	Very High
40 - 44	High
28 - 39	Intermediate
23 - 27	Low
22-	Very Low

SOURCE: Battle, J. 1995. The Encouragement Inventory. Edmonton, James Battle and Associates, Ltd.

If you earned a score of 45 or above, your level of Encouragement is very high; a score ranging between 40 and 44 indicate that your value is high; whereas those between 28 and 39 indicate that you tend to offer an intermediate or average level of encouragement to others, while a score of 27 or below indicate that you tend to provide others with low to very low levels of encouragement when interacting with them.

Overcoming Racism and Achieving Success in Relationships

The A-B-C Paradigm

The A-B-C Paradigm is a strategy you can use in your efforts to overcome racism and achieve success in relationships. If you employ this cognitive strategy it can assist you in controlling your feelings, solving problems, and emitting or displaying behavior that is self-enhancing rather than self-defeating. This strategy is effective because thought or cognition, and emotion or feelings are closely interrelated. Therefore, as a consequence, how you feel and subsequently behave is basically determined by how you think. When using the A-B-C Paradigm it is important for you to realize that:

1. **A** is:
   - what others say or do
   - what happens in the external environment

2. **B** is:
   - how you feel, which is determined by how you think and what you tell yourself about what others say or do at point A

3. **C** is:
   - what you do or say.

It is important for you to realize that what others say or do at point A does not determine how you feel. Rather, it is what you tell yourself (internalized self-verbalizations or thoughts that typically operate at an unconscious level) that determines how you feel. Therefore, if a racist call you a "bad" name and you become angry, it is not the name calling that makes you angry. Rather, it is what you tell yourself at point B about the name calling that makes you angry; chances are if a very young child called you the same name that the racist youth or adult called you, you wouldn't become angry.

Practice using the A-B-C Paradigm on a regular basis in your efforts to overcome racism and achieve success. Also remember that the A-B-C Paradigm is an effective strategy for all people, those who are racist and those who are not.

THE TEN-STEP COUNTDOWN TECHNIQUE

The Ten-Step Countdown is a cognitive technique that you can use to control impulsivity while interacting with others, which will in turn, assist you in dealing effectively with the negative behavior of racists and increase the probability of you achieving success in spite of racism.

When using the Ten-Step Countdown Technique, count down from ten to one (e.g. 10, 9, 8, 7, 6, 5, 4, 3, 2, 1) at a rate of about one digit per second before responding overtly to an environmental stimulus. For example, when responding to "name calling" or attempts at "put-downs", count backwards slowly from ten to one before reacting overtly to the "name calling" or attempts at "put-downs." By doing this, it increases the probability that you will emit behavior that results in positive consequences. Similarly, if a child or adult is called a "bad" name, his initial impulse may be to respond in a similar fashion and call the initiator a bad name or fight. However, if the child or adult who is the victim of "name-calling" employs the Ten-Step Countdown Technique immediately prior to responding, the employment of this strategy will increase the probability of him or her emitting behavior that is self-enhancing rather than self-defeating.

The Ten-Step Countdown Technique can be used effectively in conjunction with the A-B-C Paradigm described earlier in this section. For instance, you may use the A-B-C Paradigm initially in your attempts to control arousal and immediately afterwards, follow up with the Ten-Step Countdown Technique in your attempts to control impulsivity and emit behavior that is self-enhancing. Like the A-B-C Paradigm, the Ten-Step Countdown Technique is an effective strategy for you to use in your interpersonal interactions with all individuals including those who are not racist.

THOUGHT-PERCEPTION-BEHAVIOR PROCEDURE

You can use the Thought-Perception-Behavior Procedure to assist you in your efforts to overcome racism and achieve success. This is a procedure which illustrates how thought (at an unconscious level) and perception (at a conscious level) compel behavior.

When using the Thought-Perception-Behavior Procedure it is important to realize that it is not beneficial for you to be overly concerned about what racists and others think. To be overly concerned with how others think about things is self-defeating because a) you can never know exactly how another person thinks, and b) how another person thinks cannot exert an effect on you. For example, if a person thinks nice things about you, but exploits you and treats you horribly, his nice thinking does not benefit or help you. Also, if a person thinks badly about you but nevertheless, treats you kindly with respect, and provides you desirable rewards her negative thinking does not effect you.

For each of us personally, thought which generally occurs at an unconscious level, determines our conscious perception which in turn, compels our behavior. Because of this, it is beneficial to think and perceive in a positive fashion, because once we establish our perceptions, we tend to behave in a fashion that is in concert with our perceptions, a process commonly referred to as the self-fulfilling prophecy. Thus, if we think and perceive positively, it will increase the probability of us obtaining desired results or goals. Simply put, if you assume, expect or perceive that you cannot accomplish a task, you generally will not; however, on the other hand, if you maintain the assumption, expectation and perception that you will accomplish success, you increase the probability that you will succeed.

Use the Thought-Perception-Behavior Procedure to diminish your concerns regarding what you think racists and others think of you. By doing this, you increase the probability that you will experience success when interacting with those individuals who are racist and also those who are not.

EFFECTIVE RESPONSES TO "PUT DOWNS"

If you realize that the statements the racist individual directs towards you in attempts to "put" you down at best represents his perception of you and not how you really are, his behavior will have little effect on how you feel and behave. Also use the A-B-C Paradigm and the Ten Step Countdown Technique described earlier in this section to assist you in dealing with "put downs" directed towards you by racists. In addition, when racist individuals attempt to "put" you down, use responses such as the following:

- I realize that you feel this way but most people do not.
- Actually most of the people I know, consider me to be a good person.
- I am sure that's how you feel, but your perceptions don't represent reality to me.
- I'm sure you feel that way, but I don't.
- Why do you have a need to view me as being a bad person?
- Why do you have a need to see yourself as being a person who is better than I am?
- You may think that you are perfect; I know that I am not.
- I realize that I am worthy whether you recognize this fact or not.
- I realize that your views regarding me, at best represent your perceptions.
- It appears to me that you are projecting your characteristics on to me.
- Why do you have a need to use me as a scapegoat?
- How does attacking me benefit you?

SOURCE:Battle, 1995

POSITIVE ACTION STRATEGIES

Use the following Positive Action Strategies in your efforts to overcome the negative effects of racism and achieve success in relationships. When using these positive action strategies:

- Don't utilize your energy complaining about negative actions directed towards you by others; instead use your energy to determine what you will do about what others did to you and DO IT.
- View setbacks as learning experiences and use the knowledge derived from them to assist you in obtaining success.
- Write specific goals and put into action strategies that will enable you to achieve them.
- Realize that you are worthy whether others recognize this basic fact or not and use your talents effectively.
- Realize that you don't have to be perfect to be worthwhile; that perfection in personality does not exist; recognize your strengths and limitations and strive to be the best that you can be.

- Realize that your future is not necessarily dependent on your past; the experiences of your past do not necessarily dictate what will happen to you in the present or future.
- Do not utilize a significant amount of your energy worrying about things you cannot control.

It is important for your to realize that victims often feel that they are in some way responsible for the negative actions directed towards them by perpetrators. These victims often feel that they deserve what they receive from those who exploit them and blame themselves. This type of thinking, in my view, occurs too frequently and generally results in the emission of behavior that is self-defeating for the victim.

Use the information incorporated below regarding self-defeating behavior to assist you in your efforts to overcome the negative effects of racism and achieve success.

Overcoming Self-Defeating Behavior

Some people to whom others do "bad" things blame themselves and display self-defeating behaviors such as:

- underachieving
- dropping out of school
- stealing
- abusing alcohol
- abusing illegal drugs

When others treat you unfairly, use these experiences to motivate you to achieve success. I am of the opinion that the best way to "get back" at those who exploit you is to acquire success, because success typically provides empowerment and with this empowerment, the ability to exert a meaningful effect on one's environment.

Maintain a high level of perseverance in your efforts to overcome the negative effects of racism and achieve success. Use the information incorporated in the following statement entitled "Positive Thinking and Perseverance Promotes Success" to assist you in maintaining the energy and effort required to achieve success.

Positive Thinking and Perseverance Promotes Success

1. Einstein flunked grade school mathematics.
2. Edison tried 9000 kinds of light filaments before he found one that worked.
3. Walt Disney went bankrupt 5 times before he built Disneyland. He was also fired from his first job because the newspaper editor didn't feel he was creative enough.
4. Maxi Taylor of California, took the California Bar Examination forty-eight times before he passed. In 1946 when he wrote his first examination, his two sons who are now lawyers were in elementary school.
5. Michael Jordan was cut from his high school varsity team and had to play junior varsity.

Source: Battle, 1994

In your efforts to overcome racism and achieve success, look for positive examples in both local and world communities and use their accomplishments to motivate you to commit yourself to achieving your goals, and the results you desire. Some positive examples that may be beneficial to you in your efforts to succeed are presented in Table 11:3. The Afro-American graduates of Southern Illinois University during the period 1956 through 1962 listed in Table 11:3 were able to achieve success in spite of the negative effects of racism.

Table 11:3 Successful Graduates of SIU	
Graduate	Position
1. William Norwood	Airline Pilot, Captain, Chancellor of SIU
2. Dr. William Butts	University President, Special Assistant U.S. Department of Education
3. Dr. Dick Gregory	Comedian, Activist, Humanitarian

TABLE 11:3	SUCCESSFUL GRADUATES OF SIU (CONTINUED)
GRADUATE	POSITION
4. Richard Roundtree	Actor
5. Dr. Jim Rosser	University President
6. Rolland Burris	Lawyer, Attorney General, State of Illinois
7. Dr. Seymour Bryson	University Chairman, SIU Sports Hall of Fame
8. Dr. Harold Bardo	University Chairman
9. Jim Thompson	Director of Personnel, Fermie Laboratory
10. Dr. William Pointer	University Professor
11. Amos Bullocks	Professional Football Player, Supervisor of Social Workers, Cook County Jail, SIU Sports Hall of Fame
12. Dr. Sam Silas	Professional Football Player, University Professor, SIU Sports Hall of Fame
13. Dr. Johnny Flamer	University Professor
14. Carver Shannon	Professional Football Player, NFL Official, SIU Sports Hall of Fame
15. Frank Hawkins	M.Ed. School Principal
16. Huston Antwine	Professional Football Player, Sports Commentator, SIU Sports Hall of Fame
17. Dr. James Battle	Publisher, Author, Professional Football Player, SIU Sports Hall of Fame

SOURCE: Battle, 1993, p. 128

STRENGTHENING BLACK FAMILIES: OVERCOMING RACISM AND ACHIEVING SUCCESS IN MAINSTREAM SOCIETY

In 1996, we implemented a program intended to provide black parents and their children the tools they need to achieve success in mainstream society. Parents and their children aged 6 through 16 years who participated in the program, were provided forty-two hours of instruction simultaneously, in twenty-one class periods at the same location.

During the first 90 minutes of each 120 minute session, parents were taught strategies that they could use to enhance their children's self-esteem, achievement and well-being and assist their offspring in adjusting to environmental demands. Also during these periods parents were taught strategies they could use to enhance their own self-esteem, success experiences and well-being. During this same period, participating children were taught strategies intended to assist them in developing their full potential and adjusting more effectively to environmental demands. In addition, during this period, the children were provided remedial instruction in reading, spelling and arithmetic intended to enhance their academic achievement levels.

During the last 30 minute period of each session, parents and their children met together as one combined group for black history instruction. The goals of the program for parents and their children were to:

- provide participating parents and children effective tools to increase the probability of them acquiring self-sufficiency and benefitting from every aspect of society
- provide black parents and their children strategies that will enable them to interact effectively in all sectors of their community
- provide parents and their children personal assessments intended to enable them to gain insights regarding racial relations
- provide black parents and their children the tools they need to overcome racism and achieve success
- provide black families with effective strategies that promote cooperation and racial harmony among all groups
- provide children and youth aged 6 to 16 years experiences to assist them in achieving success at school and in the community

RESULTS

All individuals were administered a battery of instruments during pre and post tests to determine the effects that the program had on participants. Boys and girls were administered *The Culture-Free Self-Esteem Inventory for Children, Form A;* the spelling and arithmetic portions of *The Wide Range Achievement Test-Revised, 3,* and the vocabulary portion of *The Gates MacGinitie Reading Test* during pre-tests that occurred shortly after the program commenced during November, 1996 and on a second occasion when the program ended during April, 1997. Participating parents were administered *The Culture-Free Self-Esteem Inventory for Adults, Form AD, and The Race Relations Inventory* during the same periods.

Results derived from the analysis of pre and post-test scores indicate that participating children and their parents acquired the empowerment needed to assist them in achieving success inspite of the negative effects of racism. The children experienced positive shifts in their self-esteem, reading, spelling, and arithmetic scores. Their parents experienced positive gains in their self-esteem and race relations scores.

Summary

- People of color comprise the majority of individuals on earth.

- Whites are a minority because they comprise only about one-eighth of the earth's population.

- Africans comprise approximately one-eighth of the earth's population.

- Achieving success in work is important for most individuals because it (work) affects one's personal control, status and self-esteem.

- Employing a definition of intelligence that does not entertain the prospect of limitations makes it easier to achieve success in work.

- Many things that people say cannot be done, can be done.

- The best way to overcome the negative effects of racism is to achieve success.

- Self-esteem is an important variable influencing success.

- Encouragement is an important strategy to use in efforts to overcome racism and achieve success because when we encourage others, they generally return the same to us.

- The A-B-C Paradigm is a strategy that can be used to overcome racism and achieve success in relationships.

- The Ten-Step Countdown Technique is an effective strategy that can be used to increase the probability of achieving success in spite of racism.

- The Thought-Perception-Behavior procedure is a strategy that you can use in efforts to overcome the negative effects of racism and achieve success.

- There are effective responses that can be used to deal with "Put-downs."

- The statements that racists make in their attempts to "put" others down, at best represent their perceptions of these persons and not how they truly are.

- Positive action strategies can be used to overcome the negative effects of racism and achieve success.

- Victims often feel that they are responsible for the negative actions directed towards them by perpetrators.

- The best way to "get back" at those who exploit is to achieve success.

- Success typically provides empowerment and the ability to exert a meaningful effect on one's environment.

- Positive thinking and perseverance promotes success.

- Battle and his colleagues developed and implemented programming strategies that have proven to be effective in assisting black children and their parents in overcoming racism and achieving success in mainstream society.

PART VI

GLOSSARY OF TERMS, REFERENCES AND INDICES

GLOSSARY OF TERMS

A

ABHOR: To dislike very strongly

ABOLITIONIST: Person who work to do away with an evil such as slavery

ABORIGINALS: Original inhabitants of a country

ABSTRACT REASONING: Ability to see relationships among things, objects, patterns, diagrams or designs

ABUSE: To humiliate

ACADEMIC SELF-ESTEEM: An individual's perceptions of his or her ability to succeed academically

ACCOMMODATE: To fit or harmonize with

ACHIEVEMENT: Level of information acquired in a given area of knowledge

ACHIEVEMENT TEST: A measure of what has been acquired in a given area of knowledge

ADJUSTMENT: A satisfactory state of functioning

ADVOCATE: One who supports another

AFFECT: Emotion or mood

AGGRESSION: An unprovoked attack

ALTRUISM: The principle of living and doing good for others

AMBIGUOUS: Meaning is not clear

AMBIVALENCE: Opposite feelings, views or emotion to the same thing

AMELIORATE: To make better

ANACHRONISM: Some thing out of keeping with the time

ANARCHY: Lawlessness

ANGLO-SAXON: Whites of English descent

ANNIHILATE: To destroy or reduce to nothing

ANTI-INTRACEPTION: Impatience with subjective or "tender mindedness"

ANTI-SEMITISM: Hostility or negative prejudice against individuals of Jewish ancestry

ANXIETY: Irrational apprehension

AFRO-AMERICAN: A black American of African ancestry

ANGLOCENTRIC: Favoring individuals of Anglo Saxon ancestry

ANXIETY DISORDER: A condition characterized by irrational apprehension

APARTHEID: Segregation of races

APTITUDE: Ability or capacity to learn certain tasks

ASSIMILATE: To make similar

AUTHENTIC: Real, genuine

AUTHORITARIAN PERSONALITY: Disposition characterized by rigidity and intolerance

AVERAGE: Measure of central tendency

B

BELIEF: Opinion

BIAS: A one sided inclination

BIGOT: One who is obstinately in support of a group, party or creed

BIOGENIC: Due to biological factors

BIOPHYSICAL DETERMINANTS: Anatomy and biochemistry determinants

BLACK: A person of a black skinned race

BOYCOTT: Concerted refusal to deal with

C

CHRISTIAN: A follower of Christ

CHRONOLOGICAL AGE: Actual age

COLOR: Hue

CONSANQUINTY: Method of studying abnormalities that occur more frequently in individuals in a given family than they do in members of the general population

CORRELATION: The tendency of certain arrays of frequency distributions to be positively, negatively, or not at all associated

COGNITION: The process of thinking and perceiving

COGNITIVE: The mental process or faculty of knowing

COGNITIVE DISSONANCE: The tendency to maintain psychological consistency and stability in spite of information which is contrary to, or disapproves our assumptions or beliefs

COPING STRATEGIES: Strategies used to promote adjustment and reduce stress

CULTURALLY SPECIFIC TESTS: Tests that incorporate tasks that favor a given culture

D

DNA (DEOXYRIBONUCLEIC ACID): Protein in molecule which determines genetic composition

DEFENSE MECHANISM: Mechanism employed by the ego as a defense against anxiety and threat

DENIAL: Defense mechanism in which the individual refuses to admit that something real exists

DEPERSONALIZATION: Feelings of estrangement from the self and the environment

DEPRESSION: An emotional disorder characterized by difficulties concentrating or despondent mood

DEVIATION: The amount by which a score deviates from the measure of central tendency

DISPLACEMENT: Defense mechanism in which psychic energy is rechannelled or redirected from one object, person or situation to another

DISSONANCE: Incompatible attitudes or emotions

DYSFUNCTION: Deviant or abnormal functioning

E

EGO: Term employed by intrapsychic or Freudian theorists to refer to the dimension of the personality that mediates between the id and superego

EGO STRENGTH: The ability of the individual to cope with the demands of his or her environment

EMOTION: A neurophysiological reaction to impending stimuli

ENCOURAGEMENT: To inspire, spur and support another

ENDOGENOUS: Originating within the individual

EQUAL OPPORTUNITY: Position which supports the practice of unbiased employment opportunity

EROTIC: Pertaining to sexual impulses and sensations

ETHNIC STEREOTYPE: A generalization made about an ethnic group concerning a trait attribution that is not substantiated by factual evidence.

EXPERIMENT: A controlled application of the empirical method of inquiry in which the investigator varies one factor at a time for the purposes of testing an hypothesis

EUGENICS: Practice of creating conditions intended to result in the production of fine offspring

F

FAMILIAL: Pertaining to characteristics that appear to occur more frequently among particular families

G

GENE: Unit of inheritance housed in chromosomes

GENERAL SELF-ESTEEM: An individual's general perception of his or her worth

GENERALIZATION: The process of transferring the learning acquired in a given situation to another situation

GENETIC INFERIORITY: Inadequacy due to genetic factors

GENETICS: Science of heredity transmission of traits

H

HEREDITY: Genetic transmission of characteristics or traits from one generation to another

HOMEOSTASIS: Maintaining optimal constancy or equilibrium in psychological processes

HYPOTHESIS: A proposition which is empirically tested to determine whether or not it is valid

I

ID: The dimension of personality, according to intrapsychic or Freudian theorists, which is the source of primitive instinctual impulses

IQ: See Intelligence Quotient

INNATE: Inborn

INDIGENOUS: Born in a country

INDIVIDUAL RACISM: The person possesses racist beliefs and displays racist acts

INSIGHT: Increasing awareness and understanding of meaningful relationships

INSTRUCTOR EVALUATION INVENTORY: A rating scale that measures students' perceptions of instructor competence

INTELLIGENCE: The ability to adapt or adjust to environmental demands

INTELLIGENCE QUOTIENT: A score derived from performance on standardized tests of intelligence - commonly referred to as IQ

INTERNMENT: To quarter in someplace

L

LATENT: A disposition that is dormant or inactive

LIBIDO: The energy of the id which is associated with the sexual drive

M

MATURATION: Sequence of development in which bodily organs progressively unfold into specific functional units

MEAN: The arithmetical average; $m = \dfrac{(x)}{n}$

MELANIN: A biochemical substance that produces skin color

MELANOCYTES: Cells that produce skin color

MENTAL AGE (MA): Level of one's intellectual functioning

MENTAL ILLNESS: General term used to refer to psychological disorders

MISCEGENATION: Marriage or sexual relationships between different races

MODELLING: A form of learning which involves imitation

MOOD: Characteristic emotional state

MOTIVATION: Drive

MUTUAL RESPECT: Mutuality and respect for others

N

NEGRO: Term used to refer to blacks of African ancestry

NORMAL: The value representing the average

NUMERICAL ABILITY: Ability to reason with numbers; to deal intelligently with quantitative materials and ideas

NUMERICAL INFERIORITY: Inferior feelings experienced by members of a group that is smaller than others

NURTURE: Environmental influence on behavior

O

OBTAINED SCORE: The value before statistical treatment is given

P

PARENT SELF-ESTEEM: An individual's perception of his status at home with his parents

PERCENTILE RANK: The relative position of each score in the distribution as arranged on a scale of one hundred

PERCEPTION: Faculty of experiencing; a subjective personal view

PERSONA: The mask we present to others; a protective device which conceals one's true or inner self

PERSONAL: Subjective

PERSONALITY: Characteristics that distinguish one individual from others

PERSONAL SELF-ESTEEM: An individual's most intimate perception of self-worth

PHENOMENOLOGICAL ABSOLUTISM: A disposition in which in-group members perceive that an out-group member is as the in-group member perceives him

PHENOTYPE: Observable components of an individual's genetic endowment

PRECONSCIOUS: Areas of the mind that are not conscious, but are capable of becoming conscious

PREJUDICE: A judgement or bias that is likely to cause harm to a person or his or her rights because of the actions of others

PROGNOSIS: Prediction of future outcomes

PROFILE: A graphic representation of an individual's test scores

PROJECTION: Defense mechanism in which the individual rids him or herself of threatening drives, impulses and needs by attributing them to others

PSEUDO: Not real, non genuine

PSEUDO SELF-ESTEEM: Not real; nonauthentic perceptions of self-worth

PSYCHOGENIC: Traceable to psychological or environmental experiences

PSYCHOTHERAPY: A general term for psychological treatment procedures

Q

QUOTIENT: The number obtained by dividing one number by another number

R

RACE: Descendants of a common ancestry

RACE RELATIONS INVENTORY: A self-report inventory that measures racial acceptance and caring

RACISM: The belief that one's own race is superior which often results in antagonism towards members of a different race because of this belief

RACIST: A person who emits racist behavior

RANGE: Difference between the largest and smallest value in a distribution

RATING: Estimating on some systematic basis, the presence or absence or the magnitude of some trait, characteristic or quality of a person, thing, or process

RATIONALIZATION: Defense mechanism in which the individual provides a socially acceptable reason for his undesirable behavior

REACTION FORMATION: Defense mechanism in which the individual feels compelled to react in a fashion that is exactly opposite to how he or she feels

REALITY PRINCIPLE: A principle which holds that the individual must respond to the demands of his environment

RELIABILITY: The extent to which a measurement device measures whatever it purports to measure

REPRESSION: Defense mechanism in which one removes from conscious awareness those events that are threatening or anxiety inducing

RESULTS: The outcome of an empirical investigation upon which the conclusion is based

RIOT: Unrestrained disorder

S

SAMPLE: A group of subjects participating in a research study

SCAPEGOATING: A form of displacement which is characterized by the tendency to transfer or displace feeling towards a powerful person to someone or something else which is considered to be less threatening

SELECTIVE ATTENTION: The tendency to attend to only those aspects of an individual's behavior that is in agreement with one's point-of-view

SELF-CONCEPT: The totality of perceptions an individual has and customarily maintains regarding himself or herself

SELF-ESTEEM: An individual's perception of his or her own self-worth

SELF-IMAGE: An individual's perception of his or her own traits

SELF-REPORT INVENTORY: An objective check list or inventory

SOCIAL SELF-ESTEEM: An individual's perception of interpersonal interactions

SOCIAL INTEREST: A desire to assist others

SOCIOCULTURAL FACTORS: Societal factors which impringe upon and shape an individual's life

STANDARD DEVIATION: The square root of the deviations squared from the mean distribution (in a normal frequency distribution, the middle 68.34 percent of the scores)

STANDARDIZATION: The creation of uniform conditions

STANFORD-BINET INTELLIGENCE TEST: Commonly used standardized individual intelligence test

STANINES: Units dividing the population into nine groups ranging from 1 to 9 with a mean of 5

STATISTICS: The application of techniques of mathematics to the treatment of data

STEREOTYPE: A belief about another group that is a rigidly established conception of the traits of others that is difficult to change

STRESS: Force applied to a system that taxes the coping strategy of the individual

SUB-TEST: A logical division of a test

SUBJECTIVE: Not directly observable by another person but accessible through the individual's own verbal report or introspection

SUCCESS: Achieving desired goals

SUPEREGO: According to intrapsychic or Freudian theorists, the moral aspect of the personality

SURROGATE PARENT: Substitute parent

SYSTEMIC RACISM: Structures of society that promote and perpetuate racism

T

T-SCORE: A score on a 100-unit scale with a mean of 50 and a standard deviation of 10

TEMPERAMENT: A constitutional disposition

TEST: Any technique for validating or invalidating any hypothesis

TEST BATTERY: A group of tests

TESTEE: Examinee or person being tested

TEST ITEMS: Items that comprise a test

TEST PROFILE: A graphic display of test findings

THEORY: An empirically derived framework of concepts and hypothesized propositions

TOTAL SELF-ESTEEM: A composite score; for children, derived from general, social, academic and parent facets; for adults, derived from general, social and personal facets

TRAIT: An enduring characteristic of an individual

U

UNCONDITIONAL POSITIVE REGARD: Caring that is not contingent on behavior

UNCONSCIOUS: Below the threshold of consciousness

V

VALIDITY: The extent to which an instrument measures what it purports to measure

VARIABLE: A trait on which events or people differ

VERBAL REASONING: Ability to reason with words, to understand and use concepts expressed in words

VIOLENCE: The act of injuring or directing hostility towards self, objects or others

W

WECHSLER ADULT INTELLIGENCE SCALE (WAIS-REVISED): Comprehensive test of intelligence for males and females 16 years and older

WECHSLER INTELLIGENCE SCALE FOR CHILDREN: REVISED (WISC-R): Comprehensive test of intelligence for boys and girls aged 6 through 16

WHITE: Pale, light in color

Z

ZERO CORRELATION: A lack of any association between two distributions of scores

REFERENCES

ABRAMSON, J. *We the Jury: The Jury System and the Ideal of Democracy.* 1994

ADLER, A. *The Practice and Therapy of Individual Psychology.* New York: Harcourt. 1927

ADORNO, T., FRENKEL-BRUNSWIK, E., LEVINSON, D., and SANFORD, R.N *The Authoritarian Personality.* New York: Harper. 1950

ALLPORT, G.*The Nature of Prejudice.* Reading, MA: Addison-Wesley Co. 1979

ALLPORT, G.W. *Personality: A Psychological Interpretation.* London Constable. 1937

ALLPORT, G.W. *Personality.* New York: Holt. 1937

ALLPORT, G.W. *Pattern and Growth in Personality.* New York: Holt. 1961

ALLPORT, G.W. *The Nature of Prejudice.* Cambridge, Mass: Addison-Wesley. 1954

ALLPORT, G.W. and KRANAR, B.M. *Some Roots of Prejudice.* Journal of Psychology. 22, 9-39. 1946

ANTHONY, Lillian. *Sensitivity in Human Relations.* Minneapolis, Minnesota. 1971

ARISTOTLE. *The Politics.* New York: Penguin Books. 1981

ARONSON, E. *The Social Animal.* San Francisco. Freeman. 1972

ARONSON, E. *The Social Animal.* San Francisco. Witt, Freeman and Company. 1976

ARONSON, E., BLANEY, N., SIKES, J., STEPHANS, C. and SNAPP, M. *Busing and Racial Tension: The Jigsaw Route to Learning and Liking.* Psychology Today (February) pp. 43-50. 1975

ASANTE, M. *Afrocentricity: Theory of Social Change.* New York: Amulefi. 1980.

ASCH, S. *Studies of Independence and Conformity: A Minority of One Against a Unanimous Majority.* Psychological Monographs, 70,: no. 9, Whole No. 416. 1956

ASCH, S. *Effects of Group Pressure Upon the Modification and Distortion of Judgement in Groups, Leadership and Men*, ed. M.H. Guetzkow, Pittsburgh: Carnegie. pp 117-190. 1951

ASCH, S. *Social Psychology.* Englewood Cliffs, N.J. Prentice Hall, 1952

BALDWIN, J. *The Fire Next Time.* New York: Dial Press. 1963

BALDWIN, J. *African (Black) Psychology: Issues and Synthesis.* Journal of Black Studies. Vol. 16, pp. 235 - 249. 1986

BARNICOT, N.A. *Taxonomy and Variation in Modern Man.* In M. F. A. Montagu (ed.) The Concept of Race. New York: Collier. pp. 180-227. 1969

BATTLE, J. *The Relationship Between Intelligence and Self-Esteem.* Edmonton, Alberta: Edmonton Public Schools. 1972

BATTLE, J. *An Analogy of An American Blackman.* Ypsilanti, Eastern Michigan University. 1974

BATTLE, J. *Lectures on Prejudice and Discrimination.* Ypsilanti, Eastern Michigan University. 1974

BATTLE, J. *Relationship Between Self-Esteem and Depression.* Psychological Reports, 42: 745-746. 1978

BATTLE, J. *Culture-Free Self-Esteem Inventories for Children and Adults.* Seattle: Special Child Publications. 1981

BATTLE, J. *Enhancing Self-Esteem: A New Challenge to Teachers.* Academic Therapy (May), 16:5, pp. 541-550. 1981

BATTLE, J. *The Teacher's Role in the Enhancement of Self-Esteem and Achievement.* Prime Areas (Winter), 24:2. 1983

BATTLE, J. *Relationship Between Self-Esteem and Depression Among Children.* Edmonton: Edmonton Public Schools. 1984

BATTLE, J. *Effective Parenting Tips That Build Self-Esteem.* Seattle: Special Child Publications. 1985

BATTLE, J. *The Effects That Systematic Intervention Have on the Self-Esteem of Little Sisters.* Paper prepared for the Big Sisters Society of Edmonton. Edmonton, Alberta, Canada. 1985

BATTLE, J. *Enhancing the Self-Esteem of Students.* Presentation at the Fourth Annual Self-Esteem Conference of the Self-Esteem Institute. Santa Clara, CA. 1987

BATTLE, J. *Test-Retest Reliability of Battle's Depression Inventory for Children.* Psychological Reports, 61: 71-74. 1987

BATTLE, J. *The Effects That Junior Leadership Programs Have on Self-Esteem, Depression and Behavior of Adolescents.* Paper prepared for the Boys' and Girls' Clubs of Edmonton. Edmonton, Alberta, Canada. 1988.

BATTLE, J. *Test-Retest Reliability of Battle's Anxiety Scale for Children.* Psychological Reports, 63: 127-130. 1988

BATTLE, J. *Enhancing Self-Esteem and Achievement.* Edmonton, Alberta: James Battle and Associates, Ltd. 1990

BATTLE, J. *9 to 19: Crucial Years for Self-Esteem in Children and Youth.* Edmonton, Alberta: James Battle and Associates, Ltd. 1990

BATTLE, J. *Self-Esteem: The New Revolution.* Edmonton, Alberta: James Battle and Associates, Ltd. 1990

BATTLE, J. *Culture-Free Self-Esteem Inventories for Children and Adults.* Austin: Pro Ed. 1992

BATTLE, J. *Enhancing Self-Esteem: A Comprehensive Program of Strategies.* Edmonton, Alberta: James Battle and Associates, Ltd. 1992

BATTLE, J. *The North American Depression Inventories for Children and Adults.* Edmonton: James Battle and Associates, Ltd. 1992

BATTLE, J. *Self-Esteem, Personality and Adjustment.* Edmonton, Alberta: James Battle and Associates, Ltd. 1992

BATTLE, J. *Self-Esteem Poems.* Edmonton, Alberta: James Battle and Associates, Ltd. 1992

BATTLE, J. *The Anxiety Scales for Children and Adults.* Austin: Pro Ed. 1993

BATTLE, J. *Misconceptions Regarding Self-Esteem.* Edmonton, AB: James Battle and Associates Ltd. 1993

BATTLE, J. *Promoting Self-Esteem, Achievement and Well Being: An Effective Curriculum for All Levels.* Edmonton, AB: James Battle and Associates Ltd. 1994

BATTLE, J. *Strategies You Can Use to Enhance Your Own Self-Esteem and Well Being.* Edmonton, AB: James Battle and Associates. 1994

BATTLE, J. *For Teachers, Parents and Kids: Strategies That Promote Self-esteem, Achievement and Behavioral Self-control.* Edmonton, AB: James Battle and Associates Ltd. 1994

BATTLE, J., JARRATT, L., SINHA, S. and PRECHT, D. *The Relations Among Self-Esteem, Depression and Anxiety of Children.* Psychological Reports. 62, 999-1005. 1988

BELL, D. *Faces at the Bottom of the Well: The Permanence of Racism.* New York: Basic Books. 1992

BELL, D. *Racism and American Law.* Regin Austin.3rd. ed. 1992

BELL, D. *The Racism is Permanent Thesis: Courageous Revelation or Unconscious Denial of Racial Genocide.* V.L. Rev. 571. 1993

BELLAH, R. *The Broken Covenant.* New York: Seabury Press. 1975

BENEDICT, R. *Patterns of Culture.* New York: Penguin Books. 1934

BERKHOFER, R. *The White Man's Indian: Images of the American Indian From Columbus to the Present.* New York. 1981

BERLIN, I.. *Slaves Without Masters: The Free Negro in the Antebellum South.* New York. 1974

BETTELHEIM, B., and JANOWITZ, M. *Dynamics of Prejudice.* New York: Harper and Row. 1950

BETTELHEIM, B., and JANOWITZ, M. *Social Change and Prejudice.* New York: Free Press, 1964

BETTELHEIM, B., and JANOWITZ, M. *Social Change and Prejudice Including Dynamics of Prejudice.* New York: Free Press. 1964

BILLINGSLEY, A. *Black Families in White America* Englewood Cliffs, N.J: Prentice Hall. 1968

BILLINGSLEY, A. *Climbing Jacob's Ladder.* New York: Simon and Schuster. 1992

BLAUNER, R. *White Racism, Black Culture.* Boston: Little Brown. 1970

BLAUNER, R. *Talking Past Each Other: Black and White Languages of Race.* The American Prospect. p. 63. Summer, 1992

BLUNER, H. *United States of America Research on Racial Relationships.* International Social Science Bulletin. 10, pp. 403 - 447. 1958

BOYD, R. *Proving Race is Only Skin Deep.* Washington: Knight-Ridder Newspapers. Washington, D.C. October 20, 1996

BOYD, R. *Genes and Race.* Washington, D.C. Knight-Ridder, 1996

BRACE, C.L. *A Non-Racial Approach Towards the Understanding of Human Diversity.* In M.F.A. Montagu (ed.) The Concept of Race. New York: Collier, pp. 103-152. 1969

BRADLEY, M.*Chosen People From the Caucasus*. Chicago: Third World Press. 1992

BRANDEN, N. *The Psychology of Self-Esteem*. New York: Bantam Books. 1971

BRIGGS, D.C. *Your Child's Self-Esteem*. Garden City, New York: Doubleday. 1970

BRIGHAM, C.C. *A Study of American Intelligence*. Princeton: Princeton University Press. 1923

BRIGHAM, J.C. *Ethnic Stereotypes, Attitudes and Treatment of Ethnic Groups*. PhD. Dissertation, University of Colorado. 1969

BRIGHAM, J.C. *Ethnic Stereotypes*. Psychological Bulletin. 76, 15-38. 1971

BRIGHAM, J., and WEISSBACH, T. *Racial Attitudes in America: Analyses and Findings of Social Psychology*. New York: Harper and Row Publishers. 1972

BUCKHOUT, R. et. al. *Toward Social Change*. New York: Harper and Row. 1971

BULLOCK, A. *A History of Negro Education in the South From 1619 to the Present*, Cambridge, Massachusetts: Harvard University Press. 1967

BURFOOT, A. *White men can't run*. Runner's World. August 1992

BURKEY, R.M. *Racial Discrimination and Public Policy in the United States*. 1971

BUTLER, P. *Racially Based Jury Nullification: Black Power in the Criminal Justice System*. The Yale Law Journal, 105 Yale, L.J. 677... 1995

CALABRESI, M. *Skin Deep 101*. Time. p. 16. February 14, 1994

CAPLAN, N.S., and PAGE, J.M. In O. Kerner et. al. *Report of the National Advisory Commission on Civil Disorders*. New York: Bantam Press. 127-137. 1968

CARMICHAEL, S.F., and HAMILTON, C.V. *Black Power: Politics of Liberation in America*. New York: Random House. 1967

CLARK, K.B. *Prejudice and Your Child*. Boston: Beacon, 1955

CLARK, K.B. *Youth in the Ghetto*. New York: Harper and Row Associates. 1964

CLARK, K.B. *Dark Ghetto*. New York: Harper and Row. 1965

CLARK, C. and CLARK, M. *Racial Identification and Preference in Negro Children.* In Reading in Social Psychology, ed. T.M. Newcomb and E.L. Hartley, New York: Holt. pp. 169-178. 1942

CLARK, K. *The Pathos of Power: A Psychological Perspective.* American Psychologist, 26. pp. 1047-1057. 1971

COHEN, B.W. *The French Encounter with Africans: White Response to Blacks, 1530-1880.* Bloomington: Indiana University Press. 1980

COLE, B.J. *Conversations: Straight Talk with America's Sister President.* New York: Anchor Books. 1993

COLEMAN, J. S. , et al. *Equality of Educational Opportunity.* Washington, D.C: U.S. Office of Education. 1966

COMER, J. P., and POUSSAINT, A.F. *Raising Black Children.* New York: Penguin. 1992

COON, C.S. *The Origin of Races.* New York: Knopf. 1962

CORBETT, C. *The Hidden Unemployables.* Winnipeg, Manitoba. 1985

COSE, E.*The Rage of A Privileged Class.* New York: Harper Collins, p. 38. 1993

COWLEY, G. *Can Melantonin Stop the Clock.* Newsweek, 1995, pp. 46 - 49.

COWLEY, G. *Melantonin.* Newsweek, 1995, pp. 60 - 63.

COX, T. *Cultural Diversity in Organizations.* San Francisco: Berrett-Koehler Publishers. 1993.

CRYDERMAN, B.K and O'TOOLE, C.N. *Police, Race and Ethnicity: A Guide For Law Enforcement Officers.* Toronto. 1986

DARWIN, C. *The Descent of Man and Selection in Relation to Sex.* Chicago: Rand McNally. 1874

DAVIDSON, B. *The African Slave Trade.* Boston: Little Brown Press. 1989

DEPAUW, J. *Keeping Children in School: Springfield's District Wide Prevention and Intervention Program for All at Risk Students.* Assoc. Bulletin, April. 1987

Diagnostic and Statistical Manual of Mental Disorders. Washington, D.C: American Psychiatric Assocation. (3rd ED.) 1994

DILLARD, J. L. *Black English.* New York: Vintage. 1972

DILLARD, J. L. *Black History: Its History and Usage in the United States.* New York: Vintage Books. 1972

DOLLARD, J. *Caste and Class in a Southern Town.* Madison: University of Wisconsin Press. 1937

DOUGLASS, F. *The Life and Times of Fredrick Douglass.* New York: Collier Books. 1962

D'SOUZA, D. *The End of Racism.* The Free Press. 1995

DUBOIS, W.E.B. *Souls of Black Folk.* New York: Fawcett. 1961

DUBOIS, W.E.B. *The World and Africa.* New York: International. 1965

DUBOIS, W.E.B. *Autobiography: A Soliloquy on Viewing My Life from the Last Decade of Its First Century.* New York: International. 1968

DUBOIS, W.E.B.*Dust to Dawn.* New York, Schoker Books. 1968

DUBOIS, W.E.B. *Darkwater.* New York: Schoken. 1969

DUBOIS, W.E.B. *The Gift of Black Folk.* Millwood, New York: Kraus-Thomson. 1975

DUBOIS, W.E.B. *The Souls of Black Folk.* New York: American Library. 1982

DYSON, M.E. *Melanin Madness.* Emerge p. 33.February 1992.

EDWARDS, A., AND POLITE, C.K. *Children of the Dream.* New York: Double Day. 1992

EDMONTON JOURNAL. *Proving Race is Only Skin Deep.* Edmonton. p. E8. October 20, 1996

EDMONTON JOURNAL, *Canadian Born Minorities Earn Less Than Whites.* Edmonton, p. A3. January 19, 1997

EDMONTON JOURNAL, *Police under fire after shooting.* Edmonton, A4, p.4, April 5, 1997

EDWARDS. H. *The Forces of the Black Athlete Superiority.* The Black Scholar. November 1971

EDWARDS, H. *20th Century Gladiators for White America.* Psychology Today. November 1973

EDWARDS, H. *On the Issue of Race in Contemporary American Sports.* Western Journal of Black Studies. 6, No. 3. 1982

ELKINS, S. *Slavery: A Problem in American Institutional and Intellectual Life.* Chicago: University of Chicago Press. 1976

EYBERTH, K. *Leistungen Verschiedener Gruppen von Besatzungskindern in Hamburg-Wechsler Intelligenz test für Kinder (HAWIK),* Archiv für die gesamte Psychologie. pp. 113, 222-241. 1961

EYSENCK, H.J. *The IQ Argument: Race, Intelligence and Education.* New York: Library Press. 1971

FAIRCHILD, H.H. *Black History, Black Psychology and the Future of the World.* Washington D.C: Psych. Discourse. Vol. 27, no. 2., p. 3. February, 1996

FANON, F. *Black Skin, White Faces.* New York: Grove Press. 1967

FARMER, J. *Freedom: When?* New York: Random House. 1965

FEAGIN, J. *Racial and Ethnic Relations.* Englewood Cliffs, New Jersey. 1984

FEAGIN, J., and SIKES, M.P. *Living with Racism: The Black Middle Class Experience.* Boston: Beacon Press. 1994

FELK, L.A. *A Comparative Study of Transracial and Inracial Adoptions.* Child Welfare, 49, 82-88. 1970

FESTINGER, L. *A Theory of Social Comparison Processes.* Human Relations, 7. pp. 117-140. 1954

FESTINGER, L. *A Theory of Cognitive Dissonance.* Stanford: Stanford University Press, 1957

FESTINGER, L. *A Theory of Cognitive Dissonance.* New York: Harper and Row. 1957

FESTINGER, L. *A Theory of Cognitive Dissonance.* Evanston, Ill: Row, Peterson. 1957

FOLKMAR, D. And FOLKMAR, E.C. *Dictionary of Races and Peoples.* Reports of the Immigration Commission, vol. 43. Washington, D.C: U.S. Government Printing Office. 1911

FRANCIS, S. *Prospects for Racial and Cultural Survival.* American Renaissance. March 1995

FRANKLIN, B. *The Papers of Benjamin Franklin.* New Haven: Yale University Press. pp. 118-119. 1961

FREDRICKSON, G. *White Supremacy: A Comparative Study in American and South American History.* New York: Oxford University Press. 1981

FREUD, S. *The Ego and The Id.* London: Hogarth. 1927

FREUD, S. *The Standard Edition of the Complete Psychological Works of Sigmund Freud.* Strachey, J. (ed.) London: Hogarth. 1953

FRYE, C. *Towards a Philosophy of Black Studies.* San Francisco: R and E. Research Associates, Inc.

GAINES, P. *Laughing in the Dark.* New York: Doubleday. 1994

GALTON, F. *Heredity Genius: An Inquiry into the Laws of Consequences.* New York: World Publishing. 1962

GARBER, H. *The Milwaukee Project: Preventing Mental Retardation in Children At Risk.* Washington, D.C: American Association of Mental Retardation. 1988

GARN, S.M. *Human Races.* (3rd ed.) Springfield, Ill: Thomas. 1971

GATES, H. L. *Race, Writing and Difference.* Chicago: University of Chicago Press. 1986

GATES, H. L. *The Signifying Monkey: A Theory of African-American Literary Criticism.* New York: Oxford University Press. 1988

GATES, H. L. *Loose Cannons: Notes on the Culture Wars.* New York: Oxford University Press. 1992

GATES, H.L. *Colored People.* New York: Vintage Books, A Division of Random House, Inc. 1994

GATES, H.L. *The Future of Race.* New York: Alfred, A. Knopf. 1996

GILLINGTON, F. *The Morality of the Color Line.* New York: Negro University Press. 1969

GIOVANNI, N. *Racism 101.* New York: William Morrow. 1994

GLAZER, N. *Ethnic Dilemmas 1964 - 1982.* Cambridge: Harvard University Press. 1983

GOLDBERG, D. *The Anatomy of Racism.* Minneapolis: University of Minnesota Press. 1990

GOLDBERG, S. *When Wish Replaces Thought. Black Athletic Superiority: Why Are Blacks Better Athletes?* Buffalo: Prometheus Books. 1990

GOODHART and CHATAWAY., Sports Illustrated, p. 74. Also, pages 72 through 83. January 18, 1971

GORDON. *Assimilation in American Life.* pp. 126-27.

GOSSETT, T.F. *Race: the History of An Idea in America.* Dallas: Southern Methodist University Press

GOTTESMAN, I.I. *Biogenetics and Races and Class.* In M. Deutsch, I. Katz, and A.R. Jensen (eds.), Social Class, Race, and Psychological Development. New York: Holt, Rinehart and Winston. pp. 11-51. 1968

GOULD, S.J. *The Mismeasure of Men.* New York: W.W. Norton. 1981

GOULD, S.J. *Curveball.* New York: The New Yorker. November 28, 1994

GREEN, T.A. *Verdict According to Conscience: Perspectives on the English Criminal Trial Jury.* 1985

GRENSHAW, K. *Race, Reform and Retrenchment: Transformation and Legitimation in Antidiscrimination Law.* Harvard Law Review 101. p 1131. 1988

GRIER, W.H. and COBBS, P.M. *Black Rage.* New York: Basic Books, 1968

GUNNAR, M. *An American Dilemma.* New York: Harper and Row. 1944

HACKNER, A. *Two Nations: Black and White, Separate, Hostile, Unequal.* New York: Ballantine Books. 1992

HARRIS, M. *Patterns of Race in the Americas.* Westport, CN: Greenwood Press. 1964

HEBER, R., and GARBER, H. *An Experiment in the Prevention of Cultural-Familial Mental Retardation.* Paper presented at the Second Congress of the International Association for the Scientific Study of Mental Deficiency, Warsaw, Poland, August 25 - September 2, 1970

HEBER, R., GARBER, H., HARRINGTON, S., HOFFMAN, C., and FULENDER, C. *Rehabilitation of Families at Risk For Mental Retardation.* Progress Report, Rehabilitation, Research and Training Center in Mental Retardation. 1970

HEBERT, B.. *Throwing A Curve.* New York: New York Times. October 26, 1994

HERNTON, C. *Sex and Racism in America.* New York: Grove Press. 1965

HERRNSTEIN, R. *I.Q.* The Atlantic, 228 (3), 43-64. 1971

HERRNSTEIN, R., AND MURRAY, C. *The Bell Curve: Intelligence and Class Structure in America Life.* New York: Free Press. 1994

HERSKOVITS, M.J. *The Myth of the Negro Past.* New York. 1941

HIGGINBOTHAM, A.L. *In the Matter of Color: Race and the American Legal Process.* 1978

HUNG, J. *Adjustment and Assimilation of Vietnamese Amerasians to the United States Based on Assessments of Their Self-esteem and Depression.* New York: College Park. 1993

HUXLEY, T. H. *Emancipation: Black and White: Science and Education.* New York: Collier Books. 1901

Impact of Head Start: An Evaluation of the Effects of Head Start on Children's Cognitive and Affective Development. Westinghouse Learning Corporation. Ohio University, Vols. I, II, Appendices A-J. June 12, 1969

Independent Commission on the Los Angeles Police Department. Los Angeles. 1991

JACKSON, J. *Bell Curve Exemplifies the Retreat on Race.* Los Angeles: Los Angeles Times. October 23, 1994

JACKSON, J. *A Challenge to the New Generation.* Ebony, August 1990

JAMES, W. *The Principle of Psychology.* Vol. 1, New York: Dover Publications. 1890

JAMES, W. *Principles of Psychology.* New York: Smith. 1891

JAYNES, G.D. AND WILLIAMS, R.M. (Eds). *A Common Destiny: Blacks and American Society.* Washington, D.C: National Academy Press. 1989

JENSEN, A.R. *How Much Can We Boost I.Q. and Scholastic Achievement?* Harvard Educational Review.39, 1-123. (a) 1969

JENSEN, A.R. *Reducing the Heredity-Environment Uncertainty.* Harvard Educational Review. 39, 209-243 (b) 1969

JENSEN, A.R. *The Race X Sex X Ability Interaction.* In R. Cancro (ed.), Intelligence: Genetic and Environmental Influences. New York: Grune and Stratton. pp. 107-161. 1971

JENSEN, A.R. *Kinship Correlations* Reported by Sir Cyril Burt. Behavior Genetics. 1-28(a). 1974

JONES, J. *Prejudice and Racism.* Reading, Mass: Addison-Wesley. 1972

KAGAN, J.S. *Inadequate Evidence and Illogical Conclusions.* Harvard Educational Review. 39, 126-129. 1969

KATZ, D. and BRALY, K. *Racial Stereotypes of One Hundred College Students.* Journal of Abnormal and Social Psychology. 28, 280-290. 1933

KAMIN, D.J. *Heredity, Intelligence, Politics and Psychology.* Paper presented at the Annual meeting of the Eastern Psychological Association. Washington, D.C. 1973

KAMIN, L. *The Science and Politics of I.Q.* New York: John Wiley. 1974

KAMIN, L. *Some Historical Facts About I.Q. Testing.* In Eysenck and Kamin. The Intelligence Controversy. p. 91. 1989

KAMIN, L. *Behind the Curve.* Scientific America. February 1995

KANT, I. *Observations on the Feelings of the Beautiful and Sublime.* Translated by John Goldthwait. Berkeley: University of California Press. 1960

KENT. *Cloth in the Dock.* Washington Times. June 13, 1992

KENISTON, K. *The Uncommitted: Alienated Youth in American Society.* New York: Harcourt, Brace and World. 1965

KERNER, O. et. al. *Report of the National Advisory Commission on Civil Disorders.* New York: Bantam Books, 1968

KILSON, M. *Realism and the Black Experience.* Dissert. 1990

KILSON, M., AND COTTINGHAN, C. *Thinking About Race Relations.* Dissert. Fall 1991

KING, R. *African Origin of Biological Psychiatry.* Germantown, TN: Seymour-Smith Press. 1990

KING, M.L. *A Testament of Hope: The Essential Writing of Martin Luther King, Jr.* New York: Harper and Row, 1986

KISKER, G.W. *The Disorganized Personality.* New York: McGraw-Hill. 2nd Edition. 1972

KISKER, G.W. *The Disorganized Personality.* New York: McGraw-Hill. 3rd Edition. 1977

KLEINMUNTZ, B. *Essentials of Abnormal Psychology.* New York: Harper and Row. 1974

KLINEBERG, O. *Characteristics of the American Negro.* New York: Harper and Row. 1944

KOCHMAN, T. *Black and White: Styles in Conflict.* Chicago: University of Chicago Press. 1981

KOVEL, J. *White Racism: A Psychohistory.* New York: Columbia University Press. 1984

LABARCE, L. (ed.) *The Papers of Benjamin Franklin.* New Haven: Yale University Press. 1961

LEE, S. *The Playboy Interview.* Playboy. p. 52. July, 1991

LEE, S., and GATES, H.L. *Rap on Race, Politics and Black Cinema.* Transition Issue 52, p. 198. 1991

LEE, S., and GATES, H.L. *Generation X: A Conversation with Spike Lee and Henry Louis.* Gates. Transition, Issue 55. 1992

LERNER, R.M. *Final Solutions: Biology, Prejudice and Genocide.* University Park: Pennsylvania State University Press. 1992

LEVERT, S. *Melantonin: The Anti-Aging Hormone.* New York: Avon Books. 1995

LEVINE, L.W. *Black Culture and Black Consciousness: Afro-American Folk Through From Slavery to Freedom.* New York. 1977

LEWONTIN, R. *Race and Intelligence.* Science and Public Affairs, pp. 2 - 8. March 1970

LEWONTIN, R., ROSE, S., and KAMIN, L. *Not in our Genes: Biology, Ideology and Human Nature.* New York: Pantheon. 1984

LINCOLN, C.E. *The Black Muslims in America.* 3rd edition. Trenton, New Jersey: Erdsmans/Africa World Press. 1994

LINCOLN, C.E. *Race, Religion and the Coming American Dilemma.* New York. 1984

LINDZEY, G., LOEHLIN, J., MANOSEVITZ, M., and THIESSEN, D. *Behavioral Genetics, Manual Review of Psychology,* 22, 39-94. 1971

LOEHLIN, J.C., LINDZEY, G., and SPUHLER, J.N. *Race Differences in Intelligence.* Witt. Freeman and Company: San Francisco. 1975

LOEHLIN, J.C., VANDENBERG, S.G. and OSBORNE, R.T. *Blood Group Genes and Negro-White Ability Difference.* Behavior Genetics 3, 263-270. 1973

LOMAX, L.E. *The Negro Revolt.* New York. 1962

LORENZ, K. *On Aggression.* New York: Harcourt, Brace and World. 1966

MALCOLM, X. *The Autobiography of Malcolm X.* New York: Grove Press. 1964

MARSALIS, W. *Why We Must Preserve our Jazz.* Ebony, p. 131. February, 1986

MARX, G.T. *Protest and Prejudice.* Rev. ed. New York: Harper and Row, 1969

MATSUDA, M.J., LAWRENCE, C.R., DELGADO, R., CVENSHAW-WILLIAMS, K. *Words That Womb: Critical Race Theory, Assaultive Speech and the First Amendment.* Boulder, Colorado: Westview Press. 1993

MCCORD, W.M., and DEMERATH, N.J. III. *Negro Verses White Intelligence: A Continuing Controversy.* Harvard Educational Review. 28, 120-135. 1958

MEAD, Margaret. *Sex and Temperament in Three Primitive Societies.* New York: Williams Morrow. 1963

MERCER, J. R. *Pluralistic Diagnosis in the Evalution of Black and Chicano Children: A Procedure for Taking Socio-Cultural Variables into Account in Clinical Assessment.* Paper Presented at the Annual Meeting of the American Psychological Assocation. Washington, D.C. September, 1971

MERTON, R.K. *Discrimination and the American Creed.* In R.M. MacIver (ed.) Discrimination and National Welfare. New York. Institute of Religious and Social Studies. pp. 99-126. 1949

MILGRAM, S. *Nationality and Conformity.* Scientific American, 205 (5) 45-51. 1961

MILGRAM, S. *Behavioral Study of Obedience.* Journal of Abnormal and Social Psychology, 67. pp. 371-378. 1963

MILGRAM, S. *Some Conditions of Obedience and Disobedience to Authority.* Human Relations, 18. pp. 57-76. 1965

MONTAGU, M.F.A. *Race: Man's Most Dangerous Myth.* New York: World Publishing. 1964

MONTAGU, M.F.A. *The Idea of Race.* Lincoln: University of Nebraska Press, 1965

MONTAGU, M.F.A. *The Concept of Race.* New York: Collier Press. 1969

MOORE, T.O. *The Science of Melanin: Dispelling the Myths.* Maryland: Beckham House Publishers. 1995

MOORE, T. O. *Melantonin Mania.* Washington, D.C: Psych Discourse. Vol. 27, no. 2. February 1996. pp. 4 - 10

MUHAMMAD, E. *Message to the Black Man in America.* Newport News. VA: United Brothers Communications System, pp. 53, 134. 1992

MUSE, B. *The American Negro Revolution: From Non Violence to Black Power, 1963-1967.* Bloomington, Indiana. 1968

MYRDAL, G. *An American Dilemma: The Negro Problem and Modern Democracy.* New York: Harper and Row. 1944, reprint, 1962

NASH, G. B. AND WEISS, R. *The Great Fear: Race in the Mind of America.* New York: Rinehart and Winston. 1970

NATIONAL ADVISORY COMMISSION ON CIVIL DISORDERS REPORT, Washington, D.C. U.S. Government Printing Services. pp. 299-306. 1968

NATIONAL FOOTBALL ALUMNI ASSOCIATION. *Pro Legends.* vol. 8, no. 1. January/February, 1991

New York Times. *Report of the National Advisory Commission on Civil Disorders.* New York: E.P. Dutton and Company Inc. 1968

NOBLES, W. *African Psychology: Toward its Reclamation, Reascension and Revitalization.* Oakland, CA: Black Family Institute. pp. 65, 73, 85-87, 104. 1986

NOEL, D.L. *The Origins of American Slavery and Racism.* Columbus, Ohio: Charles E. Merrill.

NOEL, D.L., and PINKNEY, A. *Correlates of Prejudice: Some Racial Differences and Similarities.* American Journal of Sociology. 69 (6), 609 - 622. 1964

NOTT, J. *Southerner, Physician and Racial Theorist.* Baton Rouge: Louisiana State University Press. 1987

OLSEN, J. *The Black Athlete, A Shameful Story.* New York Times, Life Inc. 1968

ONTARIO JUSTICE SYSTEM. *Report of the Commission on Systemic Racism in the Ontario Criminal Justice System.* December, 1995

PAGE, C. *Showing My Color.* New York: Harper Collins Publishers. 1996

PAGE, E.B. *Miracle in Milwaukee: Raising the IQ.* Educational Researcher, 1 (10) 8-16. 1972

PATTERSON, O. *Toward a Study of Black America.* Dissert., Fall, 1989

PETTIGREW, T.F., FREDRICKSON, G., KNOBEL, D., GLAZER, N., AND VEDA, R. *Prejudice.* Cambridge: Harvard University Press. 1982

PETTIGREW, T.F. *A Profile of the Negro American*. Princeton, New Jersey: Van Nostrand, 1964

PINKNEY, A. *The Myth of Black Progress*. Cambridge: Cambridge University Press. 1984

POUSSAINT, A. *A Negro Psychiatrist Explains the Negro Psyche in Confrontation*. New York: Random House. pp. 183-184. 1971

POUSSAINT, A. *Why Blacks Kill Blacks*. New York: Emerson Hale Publishers. 1972

QUAY, L.C. *Language Dialect Reinforcement, and the Intelligence-test Performance of Negro Children*. Child Development. 42, 5-15. 1971

QUARLES, B. *The Negro in the Civil War*. Boston. 1953

QUARLES, B. *The Negro in the American Revolution*. Chapel Hill, N.C. 1961

QUARLES, B. *Black abolitionists*. New York. 1969

QUARLES, B. *The Negro in the Making of America*. New York: Touchstone. MacMillan Publishing Company, Inc. 1969

QUARLES, B. *The Negro in the Making of America*. New York: Collier. 1987

RAINWATER, L., AND YANCY, W.L. *The Moynihan Reports and the Politics of Controversy*. Cambridge: MIT Press. 1967

READ, A. *Looking Backward*. The Nation. November 28, 1994.

Report of the National Advisory Commission on Civil Disorders. New York: E.P. Dutton and Co. Inc. 1968

RICHARDSON, B. *Great American Negroes*. New York: Thomas Y. Croswell Company, New York. 1954

ROBERTS, D.E. *Punishing Drug Addicts who Have Babies: Women of Color, Equality and The Right of Privacy*. Harvard Law Review. 1419, pp. 435-36. 1996

ROGERS, J.A. *World's Great Men Of Color*. New York: Collier Macmillan. Vol. 1. 1972

ROGERS, C.R. *A Theory of Therapy, Personality and Interpersonal Relationships as Developed in a Client-Centered Framework*. In Psychology: A Study of Science, ed. Koch. New York: McGraw-Hill. 1959

ROKEACH, M. *Political and Religious Dogmatism: An Alternative to Authoritarian Personality*. Psychological Monographs. 1956 - (whole no. 425)

ROKEACH, M. *The Open and Closed Mind.* New York: Basic Books. 1960

ROKEACH, M. *Belief Versus Race as Determinants of Social Distance: Comment on Triandis' paper.* Journal of Abnormal and Social Psychology. 62, 187-188. 1962

ROKEACH, M., and ROTHMAN, G. *The Principle of Belief Congruence and the Congruity Principle as Modes of Cognitive Interaction.* Psychological Review. 72, 128-142. 1965

ROSENBERG, M. *The Association Between Self-Esteem and Anxiety.* Psychological Review. 1: 135-156. 1965

ROSENTHAL, R. AND JACOBSON, L. *Pygmalion in the Classroom: Teacher Expectation and Pupils' Intellectual Development.* New York: Holt, Rinehart and Winston. 1968

ROTHENBERG, P. (Ed.) *Racism and Sexism: An Integrated Study.* New York: St. Martin's Press. 1988

SABLE, Arm. Negro *Troops in the Union Army. 1861-1865.* New York: Longmans, Green and Company. 1956

SARASON, I.G. and SARASON, B.R. *Abnormal Psychology: The Problem of Maladaptive Behavior* (5th Ed.) Englewood Cliffs, N.J: Prentice Hall. 1987

SARASON, S.B. *Jewishness, Blackness, and the Nature-Nurture Controversy.* American Psychologist, 28, 926-971. 1973

SARNOFF, I. *Identification with Aggressor: Some Personality Correlates of Anti-Semitism Among Jews.* Journal of Personality. 20, 199 - 218. 1951

SCARR, S., and WEINBERG, R. I.Q. *Test Performance of Black Children Adopted by White Families.* American Psychologist, pp. 726 - 739. 31, 1976.

SCHNEIDER, F.W. *Conforming Behavior of Black and White Children.* Journal of Personality and Social Psychology, 16. pp. 466-471. 1970

SHANKLIN, E. *Anthropology and Race.* Belmont, CA: Wadsworth Publishing. 1996.

SHAW, L. L. and WICKER, D.G. *Teaching About Racism in the Classroom and the Community.* Radical Teacher. Vol. 21, pp. 9 - 14. 1981

SHERWOOD, J.J., and NATOWPSKY, M. *Predicting the Conclusions of Negro-White Intelligence Research From Biographical Characteristics of the Investigator.* Journal of Personality and Social Psychology. 8, 53-58. 1968

SHOCKLEY, W. *Dysgenics, Geneticity, Raceology: A Challenge to the Intellectual Responsibility of Educators.* Phi Delta Kappa. 53, 297-307. 1972

SHUEY, A.M. *The Testing of Negro Intelligence.* 2nd ed. New York: Social Science Press. 1966.

SKERRY, P. *The Charmed Life of Headstart.* The Public Interest, 73, pp. 18-39. Fall, 1983

SKINNER, B.F. *Science and Human Behavior.* New York: MacMillan. 1953

SMITH, J. and GRINDSTAFF. *Race and Sport in Canada.* University of Western Ontario. Sports Illustrated, pp. 73-83. January 18, 1971

SNYDER, L.L. *The Idea of Racialism.* Princeton, N.J: D. Van Nostrand. 1962

SNYDER, L.L. *The Idea of Racialism: Its Meaning and History.* Princeton: D. Van Nostrand. 1962

SPUHLER, J.N. and LINDZEY, G. *Racial Differences in Behavior.* In J. Hirsch (ed.) Behavior - Genetic Analysis. New York: McGraw-Hill. pp. 366-414. 1967

STECKLER, G. *Authoritarian Idealogy in Negro College Students.* Journal of Abnormal and Social Psychology: 54, 396-399. 1957

STEINBERG, S. *The Ethnic Myth: Race, Ethnicity and Class in America.* Boston: Beacon Press. 1989

STEPHAN, N. *The Idea of Race in Science.* Hamden, CT: Anchor Books. 1982

SWEET, W. , ERWIN, J. and MARKS, V. *Role of Brain Disease in Riots and Urban Violence.* Ebony Magazine. Mason, B.J. 1973

SWOBODA, F. *Glass Ceiling Firmly in Place.* Panel Finds. Washington Post. p. A-18. March 16, 1995.

TAKAKI, R.A. *Tale of Two Decades: Race and Class in the 1880's and 1980's.* In Herbert Hill and James Jones (eds.) Race in America: The Struggle for Equality. Madison: University of Wisconsin Press. 1993

TERMAN, L.M. *The Measurement of Intelligence.* Boston: Houghton-Mifflin, 1916

THOMAS, A. and SILLEN, S. *Racism and Psychiatry.* New York. 1972

THOMAS, B., AND MCGUE, M. *Genetic and Environmental Influences on Adult Personality: An Analysis of Adopted Twins Reared Apart.* Journal of Personality. 58, pp. 263-293. 1990

THOMAS, J.B., TELLEGEN, A., LYKKEN, D.T., WILCOX, K.J., SEGAL, N.L. AND RICH, S. *Personality and Similarity in Twins Reared Together and Apart. Journal of Personality and Social Psychology.* 54, No. 6. 1988

THOMAS, J.B., DAVID, L., MATTHEW, M., SEGAL, N., AND TELLEGEN, A. *Sources of Human Psychological Differences: the Minnesota Study of Twins Reared Apart.* Science. 250, pp. 223-28. 1990

THORNBROUGH, E.L. *Booker T. Washington.* Englewood Cliffs, New Jersey: Prentice Hall. 1967

TIZARD, B. *IQ and Race.* Nature, 247, 316. 1967

TOPPIN, E.A. *A Biographical History of Blacks in America Since 1528.* New York. 1971

TRIANDIS, H.C. *Attitude and Attitude Change.* New York: Wiley. 1971

TUCQUEVILLE, A.D. *Democracy in America.* In J. P. Mayer. New York: Harper and Row. 1988

TUDOROV, T. *On Human Diversity: Nationalism, Racism and Exoticism in French Thought.* Cambridge: Harvard University Press. 1993

TYLER, L.E. *The Psychology of Human Differences.* 3rd ed. New York: Appleton-Century-Crofts. 1965

U.S. BUREAU OF THE CENSUS: *1994 Statistical Abstract of the United States.* Washington, 1994

U.S. COMMISSION ON CIVIL RIGHTS. *Racial Isolation in the Public Schools.* Washington, D.C. U.S. Government Printing Office. 1967

U.S. PRESIDENT'S COMMISSION on Law Enforcement and Administration of Justice: *The Challenge of Crime in a Free Society:* A Report. Washington, D.C: U.S. Government Printing Office. 1967

UNITED STATES. *The Civil Rights Act of 1964.* 42, U.S.C. Section 200e2 (j). 1964

UNITED STATES CIVIL RIGHTS COMMISSION. 1962

UNITED STATES DEPARTMENT OF COMMERCE, ECONOMICS AND STATISTICS ADMINISTRATION: BUREAU OF THE CENSUS. *Statistical Abstract of the United States.* 1994

UNITED STATES DEPARTMENT OF JUSTICE. *Statistics Sourcebook of Criminal Justice Statistics.* 1993

UNIVERSITY RESEARCH CORPORATION of WASHINGTON, D.C. *Prevention and Control of Urban Disorders.* 1980

VANDENBERGE. *Race and Racism.* New York: John Wiley and Sons. 1975

VERON, P.E. *Intelligence and Cultural Environment.* London: Methuen. 1969

WADE, R.C. *Slavery in the Cities: the South, 1820-1869.* New York. 1964

WADE, H., WILSON, W.V. *Book of Black Heroes, A to Z.* New Jersey: Just Us Books. 1988

WASHINGTON, B.T. *The Awakening of the Negro.* The Atlantic Monthly. September, 1896

WECHSLER, D. *The Measurement and Appraisal of Adult Intelligence.* Baltimore: Williams and Wilkins. 1958

WECHSLER, D. *Manual for Wechsler Adults Intelligence Scale-*Revised. San Antonio, TX. The Psychological Corporation. 1981

WECHSLER, D. *Manual for the Wechsler Intelligence Scale for Children,* Third Edition. New York: The Psychological Corp. Harcourt Brace Jovanovich, Inc. 1991

WEISBERG, J. *Who? Me? Prejudiced?* New York. October 17, 1994

WELLMAN, D.T. *Portraits of White Racism.* Cambridge: Cambridge University Press. 1977

WELSING, F.C. *The Isis Papers: The Keys to the Colors.* Chicago: Third World Press. 1989

WELSING, F.C. *Personal Correspondence.* Washington, D.C. 1996

WEST, C. *Keeping Faith: Philosophy and Race in America.* New York: Routledge. 1993

WHITE, J. and PARHAM, T. *The Psychology of Blacks: An African-American Perspective.* Englewood Cliffs, N.J.: Prentice Hall. 1990

WHITTEN, L.A. *Infusing Black Psychology Into the Introductory Psychology Course.* Teaching Psychology. Vol. 20, no. 1. February, 1993.

WHITTEN, N.E., and SZWED, J. eds. *Afro-American Anthropology; Contemporary Perspectives.* New York: Free Press. 1970

WILLIAMS, E. *Capitalism and Slavery.* New York: Capricorn Books. 1966.

WILLIAMS, G. *Growing Black Debate: Racism Or Excuse?* New York: New York Times. p. A-1. April 5, 1992

WILLIAMS, R.L. *Collective Black Mind: An Afrocentric Theory of Black Personality.* St. Louis, MO: Williams and Associates.

WILLIAMS, R.L. *The Bitch-100: A Culture-Specific Test.* Paper presented at the annual convention of the American Psychological Association. Honolulu. 1972

WILLIAMSON, J. *New People: Misconceptions and Mulattoes in the United States.* New York: Free Press. 1980

WILLIAMSON, T.*The Crucible of Race: Black-White Relations in the American South Since Emancipation.* New York: Oxford University Press. p. 109. 1984

WILLS, C. *The Skin We're In.* Discover pp. 77-81. November 1994

WILSON, W. *Reconstruction in the Southern States.* Atlantic Monthly. January 1901

WILSON, W. J. *The Declining Significance of Race.* Chicago: University of Chicago Press. 1980

WINKS, R.W. *The Blacks in Canada.* Montreal, McGill, Queen's University Press

WINTHROP, J. *The White Man's Burden.* New York: Oxford University Press. 1974

WRIGHT, B. *Black Robes, White Justice.* New York: Carol Publishing. 1987

WOODSON, C. G. *Free Negro Owners of Slaves in the United States in 1830.* Journal of Negro History. 9, January, 1924.

WOODSON, C. and WISELY, C. *The Negroes in Our History.* Washington, D.C. The Associated Publishers Inc. 1966

ZACK, N. *Race and Mixed Race.* Philadelphia: Temple University Press. pp. 3-4. 1994

ZIMBARDO, P. T*he Psychological Power and Pathology of Imprisonment.* A paper prepared for the U.S. House Judiciary; Subcommittee No. 3: Hearings on Prison Reform, San Francisco, Calif., p.3, October 25, 1971

Subject Index

ACHIEVEMENT:
race and - 150-161
self-esteem and - 22, 47, 175-179

AFRO-AMERICANS:
racism and - xiii - xv, 8-10,16, 25, 36, 55, 75-77, 108
sports and - 13, 109, 163
education and - 41-43
police services and - 115-125
criminal courts and - 109, 128, 141, 147
schools and - 143-149

ANXIETY:
defenses and - 57, 60

BLACKS:
racism and -xiii, 22, 24, 65,77
challenges of -95, 150-161
relations and - 71, 73-8

BEHAVIOR:
racism and -63, 68, 70, 73, 147
racist and - 85

COLOR:
racism and - xiv, 4 -10, 12, 64-70, 85, 92, 108
peoples of - xiv
melanin and - 4-5, 64
fear of - 73-

DEFENSE MECHANISMS:
operations of -53-61
types of -58-67
racist and - 66-69

EDUCATION:
blacks and - 39-44, 47, 50, 74, 91, 96, 98, 143-158
racism and - 11, 13, 14, 20, 85, 143-149

EXPECTATIONS:
teachers' perceptions and - 2, 21,41, 43, 44, 98, 143-149
self-fulfilling prophecy and - 47, 50, 143-147

FEAR:
racism and -78, 79

GOVERNMENT:
racism and - 115-125, 134

GENOCIDE:
racism and -4, 13, 75, 76, 79, 91, 97
blacks and - 97

SELF-ESTEEM:
defined - 89, 90
assessment of - 92
development of - 92
enhancement of - 181-190
success and - 47- 50
victims of racism and - 89-94
achievement and - 151-159,
169, 173-190

**SELF-FULFILLING
PROPHECY:**
expectations and - 150-159,
163
teacher expectations and -
143-147
success and - 173

STEREOTYPES:
assessment of - 31-35
racism and - 30, 54, 74, 83
personality and - 35, 68
degrees of - 33
beliefs and - 34, 37, 74
defense mechanisms and -
58-61
perceptions and - 143-147
justice system and - 115-125

SUCCESS:
relationships and - 36, 71-81,
181-183
work and - 9, 10, 91, 174-
175
thinking and - 38, 41
perseverance and - 150-161,
186-187
strategies for - 51, 173-191
assessment of - 189
encouragement and -
179-190

TEACHERS:
expectations of - 20, 24, 41,
143-149
racism and - 20, 21, 91
student ratings and - 21
perceptions of - 22
stereotypes of - 147

WORK:
success in - 9-12, 174-175,
188-190
self-esteem and - 22, 47,
175-179, 184-190
goal setting and - 150-161

AUTHOR'S INDEX

Adorno, T.W. - 35, 36, 63, 68
Aesop - 61, 157, 160
Allport, G. - 3, 29, 32, 57, 61, 63
Amby - xiv
American Anthropological
    Association - 42
Anderson - 82
Andy, V.J. - 134
Anthony, L. - 152
Antwine, H. - 187
Archille, L.T. - 79
Armstrong L. - 107
Arone, S. - xiii, 140
Aronson, E. - 33, 127
Artshell - 169
Ashley - 3
Atlantic Monthly - 12
Attucks, C. - 137
Augustine, S.
Baldwin, J. - 103
Bannister, R. - 175
Bardo, H. - 187
Battle, J. - 12, 14-16, 21, 29, 39,
    40, 50, 51, 62, 66, 69, 70,
    81k, 82, 86, 87, 89, 91, 92,
    94, 108 - 110, 132, 170, 174-
    179, 184, 186, 187
Baxter - 82
Beethoven, L.V. - 157 , 160
Bell, A.G. - 154, 159
Bell J.M. - 137
Bellah - 12

Benneker, B - 151, 159, 161
Berkhofer, R. - 6
Bethune, M.M. - 156, 161
Bettelheim, B. - 34
Binet, A. - 43
Blair, J. - 151, 159
Blake - 29
Blauner, R. - 61
Bond, J. - 107, 111
Bowman - 22
Boyd, R. - 4
Boyle - 166
Brace, L. - 3, 44
Branden, N. - 66
Briggs, D. - 89, 94
Brown, J. - 137
Brown, K. - 140
Brown, N - 31, 32
Brown, R. - 165
Browning, R. - 157, 160
Bruce - 3
Brufoot, A. - xiv
Brunswik, S. - 68
Bryson, S. - 187
Bullocks, A. - 187
Burris, R. - 187
Butler, P. - 123, 132
Butts, W. - 186
Byrne, E. - 82
Campbell - 31, 32
Canadian Airborne -xiii, 140

PART VII

BOOKS &
RESOURCE MATERIALS

BOOKS

ARONSON , E. 1976. *The social animal.* San Francisco: W.H. , Freeman And Company.

The text provides an overview of relevant research and shows readers how findings derived from socio-psychological studies can be employed in practical fashions to assist in achieving solutions to many societal problems.

BATTLE, J. 1990. *9 to 19: Crucial years for self-esteem in children and youth.* Edmonton, AB: James Battle and Associates Ltd.

In *9 to 19*, Dr. Battle identifies characteristics of positive and negative self-esteem, and traces the development of both dispositions. The important role that self- esteem plays in contemporary problems such as learning disabilities, conduct problems, anxiety disorders, depression and suicide is described. In *9 to 19*, Dr. Battle offers 110 strategies for remediating these and other problems. The effectiveness of these strategies are documented and actual case reports are provided to illustrate how positive shifts in self-esteem can be induced in students and clients. In the book, Dr. Battle offers concrete ways of identifying problems and acting to correct them, both in the classroom and in the home.

BATTLE, J. 1990. *Self-esteem: The new revolution.* Edmonton, AB: James Battle and Associates Ltd.

In *Self-Esteem: The New Revolution*, Dr. Battle provides a comprehensive text that address the important issue of self-esteem. In the book the author offers 300 strategies that can be used to enhance the self-esteem of individuals at all developmental levels. Empirical data is provided to document the effectiveness of these strategies and actual case reports are presented to illustrate how positive shifts in self-esteem can be induced in individuals of all ages.

BATTLE, J. 1993. *Misconceptions regarding self-esteem.* Edmonton, AB: James Battle and Associates Ltd.

Dr. Battle addresses a comprehensive number of misconceptions associated with the construct of self-esteem, and offers factual information associated with each misconception. In addition, the author delineates specific strategies derived from empirical findings that practitioners can apply in real-life settings to enhance self- esteem, achievement and well-being.

BATTLE, J. 1994. *For teachers, parents and kids: strategies that promote self-esteem,achievement and behavioral self-control.* Edmonton, AB: James Battle and Associates Ltd.

In this practical book, Dr. Battle shows teachers, parents and kids how to employ strategies that promote self-esteem, achievement and behavioral self-control. The important role that self-esteem plays in achievement and behavior is delineated and readers are shown how to employ time-tested strategies to enhance the self-esteem and achievement levels of students and assist them in exhibiting behavior that is self-enhancing rather than self-defeating.

BATTLE, J. 1994: *Strategies that you can use to enhance your own self-esteem and well-being.* Edmonton, AB: James Battle and Associates Ltd.

In this concise book, Dr. Battle describes strategies that individuals at all stages of development can use to enhance their own self-esteem, achievement and well- being. *In Strategies That You Can Use to Enhance Your Own Self-Esteem and Well-Being*, the importance of self-esteem and positive interactions are emphasized and readers are shown how to think and behave in ways that are self-enhancing rather than self-defeating.

BATTLE, J. 1994. *Promoting self-esteem, achievement and well-being: an effective curriculum for all levels.* Edmonton, AB: James Battle and Associates Ltd.

In this timely book, Dr. Battle offers a comprehensive instructional program in which he describes techniques that have proven to be effective and shows instructors how to teach each strategy and activity incorporated in the curriculum. In this concise program, Dr. Battle shows readers how to use the curriculum to teach regular and special students as well as high risk pupils experiencing problems such as conduct disorders and attention deficit hyperactivity disorders. Also in this book, the author describes a life skills instruction program for high school and adult students and offers quantitative data to illustrate the effectiveness of the curriculum in enhancing the self-esteem of students and diminishing symptoms of depression and anxiety of participants.

BLAUNER , R. 1972. *Racial oppression in america* . New York: Harper and Row Publishers.
The book provides an overview of the problem of racism in America and offers theoretical perspectives and case studies of the effects of this persistent problem (racism) that have plagued the United States over the years.

D SOUZA , DINESH. *The end of racism.* 1995. New York: The Free Press.
In the text the author provides a comprehensive, historical overview of the construct of racism and proposes that it (racism) is a distinctly Western phenomenon. In the book D Souza presents and supports the point of view which assumes that the American obsession with race is fuelled by a civil rights establishment that has vested interest in perpetuating black dependence.

HUDSON, W. AND WILSON-WESLEY, V. 1988. *Book of black heroes: From a to z.* Orange, New Jersey: Just Us Books.
In the text, the author recognizes the contributions of forty-nine blacks and provides concise summaries of their achievements.

LOEHLIN , J.C.   LINDZEY , G. AND   SPUHLER , J.N. 1975. *Race differences and intelligence.* San Francisco: Witt , Freeman And Company.
The text provides an objective review of evidence regarding the relative contributions of the genes and the environment to racial and ethnic differences in intelligence test performance.

LOYE , D. 1971. *The healing of a nation.* New York: Dell Publishing Company.
The text applies the knowledge and insights derived from sociopsychological studies to explore the causes of racism that have persistently plagued the United States. Also the text shows how theories and findings derived from empirical research can be used to assist in efforts to solve racial problems. The book offers

specific and practical recommendations for healing racism in the United States.

PETTIGREW , T.F. 1971. *Racially separate or together.* New York: McGraw -Hill BookCompany.
The text focuses on white racism in the United States and supports the thesis which proposes that genuine racial integration is a necessary condition for the eradication of white racism at both individual and institutional levels in America.

PROVINCE OF ONTARIO. 1995. *Commission on systemic racism in the ontario criminal justice system.* Toronto: Queen's Printer for Ontario.
The text focuses on anti-black racism, provides analyses of a comprehensive study of racism in the province of Ontario and offer recommendations regarding the extent to which criminal justice practices, procedures and policies in Ontario reflect systemic racism.

ROGERS, J.A. 1946; 1972. *World's great men of color .* New York: Collier Books:MacMillan Publishing Company.
In this classic text J.A. Rogers rejects the racist myth that blacks played minor roles in world history and documents the contributions of hundreds of individuals of pure or mixed Negro blood who won distinction in every part of the world and in every period of recorded history.

SILBERMAN , C.E. 1964. *Crisis in black and white.* New York: Vintage Books.
The book provides an overview of the relationships between black and white Americans and identifies problems that have persisted over the years at both personal and societal levels.

Resource Materials

ALLPORT, G. 1979. *The nature of prejudice.* Reading, MA: Addison-Wesley Co.

BARNES, C. *Melanin: The chemical key to black greatness.*

BELLAH, R. 1975. *The broken covenant.* New York: Seabury Press.

BERKHOFER, R. 1981. *The white man's indian: Images of the american indian from columbus to the present.* New York.

BERLIN, I. 1974. *Slaves without masters: The free negro in the antebellum south.* New York.

BLAUNER, R. Summer, 1992. *Talking past each other: Black and white languages of race.* The American Prospect. p. 63.

BRADLEY, M. 1992. *Chosen people from the caucasus.* Chicago: Third World Press.

BURFOOT, A. August 1992. *White men can't run.* Runner's World.

CALABRESI, M. February 14, 1994. Skin deep 101. Time. p. 16.

COHEN, B.W. 1980. *The french encounter with africans: White response to blacks, 1530-1880.* Bloomington: Indiana University Press.

COLE, B.J. 1993. *Conversations: Straight talk with america's sister president.* New York: Anchor Books.

COSE, E. 1993. *The rage of a privileged class.* New York: Harper Collins.

COX, T. 1993. *Cultural diversity in organizations.* San Francisco: Berrett-Koehler Publishers.

DAVIDSON, B. 1989. *The African slave trade.* Boston: Little Brown Press.

DYSON, M.E. February 1992. *Melanin madness.* Emerge p. 33.

EDWARDS, A., AND POLITE, C.K. 1992. *Children of the dream.* New York: Double Day.

EDWARDS. H. November 1971. *The forces of the black athete superiority.* The Black Scholar.

EDWARDS, H. November 1973. *20th century gladiators for white america.* Psychology Today.

EDWARDS, H. 1982. *On the issue of race in contemporary american sports.* Western Journal of Black Studies. 6, No. 3.

ELKINS, S. 1976. *Slavery: A problem in american institutional and intellectual life.* Chicago: University of Chicago Press.

FEAGIN, J.B. 1984. *Racial and ethnic relations.* Englewood Cliffs, New Jersey.

FERGIN, J.R. AND SIKES, M. 1994. *Living with racism: The black middle class experience.* Boston: Beacon Press.

FRANCIS, S. March 1995. *Prospects for racial and cultural survival.* American Renaissance.

FRANKLIN, B. 1961. *The papers of Benjamin Franklin.* New Haven: Yale University Press. pp. 118-119.

FREDRICKSON, G. 1981. *White supremacy: A comparative study in american and south american history.* New York: Oxford University Press.

GARBER, H. *The Milwaukee project: Preventing mental retardation in children at risk.* Washington, D.C: American Association of Mental Retardation.

GATES, L.H. 1992. *Loose cannons: Notes on the culture wars.* New York: Oxford University Press.

GOLDBERG, D. 1990. *The anatomy of racism.* Minneapolis: University of Minnesota Press.

GOLDBERG, S. 1991. *When wish replaces thought. Black athletic superiority: Why are blacks better athletes?* Buffalo: Prometheus Books.

GORDON. *Assimilation in american life.* pp. 126-27.

GOSSETT, T.F. *Race: The history of an idea in america.* Dallas: Southern Methodist University Press.

GOULD, S.J. 1981. *The mismeasure of men.* New York: W.W. Norton.

GOULD, S.J. November 28, 1994. *Curveball.* New York: The New Yorker.

GRENSHAW, K. 1988. *Race, reform and retrenchment: Transformation and legitimation in antidiscrimination law.* Haward Law Review 101. p 1131.

HARRIS, M. 1964. *Patterns of race in the americas.* Westport, CN: Greenwood Press.

HEBERT, B. October 26, 1994. *Throwing a curve.* New York: New York Times.

HERRNSTEIN, R., AND MURRAY, C. 1994. *The bell curve: intelligence and class structure in america life.* New York: Free Press.

HERSKOVITS, M.J. 1941. *The myth of the negro past.* New York.

HUNG, J. 1993. *Adjustment and assimilation of vietnamese amerasians to the united states based on assessments of their self-esteem and depression.* New York: College Park.

JACKSON, J. *Bell curve exemplifies the retreat on race.* October 23, 1994. Los Angeles: Los Angeles Times.

JAYNES, G.D. AND WILLIAMS, R.M. (eds). 1989. *A common destiny: Blacks and american society.* Washington, D.C: National Academy Press.

JONES, J. 1972. *Prejudice and racism.* Reading, Mass: Addison-Wesley.

KAMIN, L. 1989. *Some historical facts about I.Q. testing.* in Hans, Eysenck and Kamin. *The IQ controversy.*

KAMIN, L. February 1995. *Behind the curve.* Scientific America.

KAMIN, L. 1989. *Some historical facts about I.Q. testing.* In Eysenck and Kamin. The intelligence controversy.

KANT, I. 1960. *Observations on the feelings of the beautiful and sublime.* Translated by John Goldthwait. Berkeley: University of California Press.

KILSON, M. Fall, 1990. *Realism and the black experience.* Dissert

KILSON, M., AND COTTINGHAN, C. Fall, 1991. *Thinking about race relations.* Dissert.

KING, R. 1990. *African origin of biological psychiatry.* Germantown, TN: Seymour-Smith Press.

KOVEL, J. 1984. *White racism: A psychohistory.* New York: Columbia University Press.

LABARCE, L. (ed.) 1961. *The papers of Benjamin Franklin.* New Haven: Yale University Press.

LEE, S. *The playboy interview.* Playboy. July, 1991. p. 52.

LEE, S., AND GATES, L. 1991. *Rap on race, politics and black cinema.* Transition Issue 52, p. 198.

LEVINE, L.W. 1977. *Black culture and black conciousness: Afro-American folk though from slavery to freedom.* New York.

LINCOLN, C.E. 1984. *Race, religion and the coming american dilemma.* New York.

LOMAX, L.E. 1962. *The negro revolt.* New York.

MATSUDA, M.J., LAWRENCE, C.R., DELGADO, R., CVENSHAW-WILLIAMS, K. 1993. *Words that womb: Critical race theory, assaultive speech and the first amendment.* Boulder, Colorado: Westview Press.

MONTAGU, A. 1964. *Race: Man's most dangerous myth.* New York: World Publishing.

MUHAMMAD, E. 1992. *Message to the black man in america.* Newport News. VA: United Brothers Communications System, pp. 53, 134.

MUSE, B. 1968. *The american negro revolution: From non violence to black power, 1963-1967.* Bloomington, Indiana.

NASH, G. B. AND WEISS, R. 1970. *The great fear: Race in the mind of america.* New York: Rinehart and Winston.

NOBLES, W. 1986. *African psychology:Toward its reclamation, reascension and revitalization.* Oakland, CA: Black Family Institute. pp. 65, 73, 85-87, 104.

NOEL, D. *The origins of american slavery and racism.* Columbus, Ohio: Charles E. Merrill.

NOTT, J. 1987. *Southerner, physician and racial theorist.* Baton Rouge: Louisiana State University Press.

PETTIGREW, T., FREDRICKSON, G., KNOBEL, D., GLAZER, N., AND VEDA, R. 1982. *Prejudice.* Cambridge: Harvard University Press.

QUARLES, B. 1953. *The negro in the civil war.* Boston.

QUARLES, B. 1961. *The negro in the american revolution.* Chapel Hill, N.C.

QUARLES, B. 1969 *The negro in the making of america.* New York: Touchstone. MacMillan Publishing Company, Inc.

QUARLES, B. 1969. *Black abolitionists.* New York.

RAINWATER, L., AND YANCY, W.L. 1967. *The moynihan reports and the politics of controversy.* Cambridge: MIT Press.

READ, A. November 28, 1994. *Looking backward.* The Nation.

ROTHENBERG, P. (ed.) 1988. *Racism and sexism: An integrated study.* New York: St. Martin's Press.

SKERRY, P. Fall, 1983. *The charmed life of headstart.* The Public Interest, 73, pp. 18-39.

SYNDER, L.L. 1962. *The idea of racialism: Its meaning and history.* Princeton: D. Van Nostrand.

SNYDER, L.L. 1962. *The idea of racialism.* Princeton, N.J: D. Van Nostrand.

STEPHAN, N. 1982. *The idea of race in science.* Hamden, CT: Anchor Books.

SWOBODA, F. March 16, 1995. *Glass ceiling firmly in place.* Panel Finds. Washington Post. p. A-18.

TAKAKI, R.A. 1993. *Tale of two decades: race and class in the 1880's and 1980's.* In Herbert Hill and James Jones (eds.) Race in America: The Struggle for Equality. Madison: University of Wisconsin Press.

THOMAS, B., AND MCGUE, M. 1990. *Genetic and environmental influences on adult personality: An analysis of adopted twins reared apart.* Journal of Personality. 58, pp. 263-293.

THOMAS, J.B., DAVID, L., MATTHEW, M., SEGAL, N., AND TELLEGEN, A. 1990. *Sources of human psychological differences: The Minnesota study of twins reared apart.* Science. 250,. pp. 223-28.

THOMAS, J.B., TELLEGEN, A., LYKKEN, D.T., WILCOX, K.J., SEGAL, N.L. AND RICH, S. 1988. *Personality and similarity in twins reared together and apart.* Journal of Personality and Social Psychology. 54, No. 6.

THORNBROUGH, E.L. 1967. *Booker T. Washington.* Englewood Cliffs, New Jersey: Prentice Hall.

TOPPIN, E.A. 1971. *A biographical history of blacks in america since 1528.* New York.

TRIANDIS, H.C. 1971. *Attitude and attitude change.* New York: Wiley.

TUDOROV, T. 1993. *On human diversity: Nationalism, racism and exoticism in French thought.* Cambridge: Harvard University Press.

U.S. Bureau of the Census: 1994 *Statistical abstract of the united states.* Washington, 1994.

United States. 1964. *The civil rights act of 1964.* 42, U.S.C. Section 200e2 (j)

VANDENBERGE. 1975. *Race and racism.* New York: John Wiley and Sons.

WADE, R.C. 1964. *Slavery in the cities: The south, 1820-1869.* New York.

WEISBERG, J. October 17, 1994. *Who? Me? Prejudiced?* New York.

WELLMAN, D.T. 1977. *Portraits of white racism.* Cambridge: Cambridge University Press.

WELSING, F.C. 1989. *The isis papers: The keys to the colors.* Chicago: Third World Press.

WEST, C. 1993. *Keeping faith: Philosophy and race in america.* New York: Routeledge.

WILLIAMS, E. 1966. *Capitalism and slavery.* New York: Capricorn Books.

WILLIAMS, G. April 5, 1992. *Growing black debate: Racism or excuse?* New York: New York Times. p. A-1.

WILLIAMS, R.L. 1972. *The bitch-100: A culture-specific test.* Paper presented at the annual convention of the American Psychological Association. Honolulu.

WILLIAMSON, J.1980. *New people: Misconceptions and mulattoes in the united states.* New York: Free Press.

WILLIAMSON, T. 1984. *The crucible of race: Black-white relations in the american south since emancipation.* New York: Oxford University Press. p. 109.

WILLS, C. November 1994. *The skin we're in.* Discover pp. 77-81.

ZACK, N. 1994. *Race and mixed race.* Philadelphia: Temple University Press. pp. 3-4.